Workbook for
News Reporting and Writing

Workbook for News Reporting and Writing

Ninth Edition

THE MISSOURI GROUP

Brian S. Brooks
George Kennedy
Daryl R. Moen
Don Ranly

School of Journalism
University of Missouri

Bedford/St. Martin's
Boston ▪ New York

For Bedford/St. Martin's

Executive Editor for Communication: Erika Gutierrez
Editor: Lai Moy
Developmental Editor: Linda Stern
Editorial Assistant: Ada Fung
Production Supervisor: Jennifer Peterson
Marketing Manager: Casey Carroll
Marketing Assistant: Zoe Kazmierski
Project Management: Books By Design, Inc.
Cover Design: Billy Boardman
Cover Photo: *U.S. Troops and Iraqi Police Fight Gun Battle in Tal Afar.* Charles Crain (L), a reporter
    working for *Time* magazine, takes notes during a gun battle between insurgents and the 1st
    Battalion, 5th Infantry Stryker Brigade Combat Team of the 25th Infantry Division, January 16,
    2005, in Tal Afar, Iraq. A routine patrol in the insurgent stronghold turned into an hour-long
    running gun battle, with a combined U.S. and Iraqi police force battling insurgents across alleys
    and down boulevards. © Chris Hondros/Getty Images.
Composition: Books By Design, Inc.
Printing and Binding: Victor Graphics

President: Joan E. Feinberg
Editorial Director: Denise B. Wydra
Director of Marketing: Karen Melton Soeltz
Director of Editing, Design, and Production: Marcia Cohen
Manager, Publishing Services: Emily Berleth

Library of Congress Control Number: 2007925327

Manufactured in the United States of America.

2   1   0   9   8   7
f   e   d   c   b   a

For information, write: Bedford/St. Martin's, 75 Arlington Street, Boston, MA 02116
(617-399-4000)

ISBN-10: 0-312-47412-1
ISBN-13: 978-0-312-47412-6

Acknowledgments

Acknowledgments and copyrights appear at the back of the book on page 214, which constitutes an
extension of the copyright page.

Preface

The *Workbook for* NEWS REPORTING AND WRITING, Ninth Edition, like the text, is focused on the challenges journalists face in the converging news rooms of the 21st century.

The strengths of the text and the *Workbook* are similar. In both we provide explanations and exercises to help you understand and develop the attitudes and skills required by the multimedia work environment. We do that while maintaining our emphasis on the basics. You'll find that the exercises in the *Workbook* provide even more opportunities to apply your new skills to both reporting and writing for new as well as traditional media.

You'll also discover that the *Workbook for* NEWS REPORTING AND WRITING is thoroughly practical. Its exercises are tied directly and clearly to the principles explained in the text. The exercises provide more variety and allow for more practice, especially with the computer as a learning tool. Perhaps the most valuable experience these exercises offer is the class discussions that will inevitably follow.

Another feature is the Challenge Exercise, which asks you to test your skills on a more advanced level in every chapter. There is an added focus on technology and writing for multiple media. Finally, we have included a fictional city directory that allows you to conveniently hone your investigative skills as you work through the exercises. It's up to you to determine when to use the directory in checking facts and investigating stories.

We have included many more exercises than one term can accommodate. Your instructor will choose assignments appropriate for your class; you may also want to seek extra practice. The resources for both are here. Your instructor may also alter or add to any of these exercises to fit local conditions or to include local examples.

These principles and exercises are well-tested. We use them in our own teaching. Hundreds of other instructors in courses throughout the United States (and beyond) have done the same. To all those colleagues who have offered suggestions and examples, we extend our thanks.

We appreciate the work done by the staff at Bedford/St. Martin's, especially developmental editor Linda Stern and editor Lai T. Moy. We extend special thanks to editorial assistant Ada Fung for all her hard work shepherding the manuscript through to production. Thanks also go to Emily Berleth, manager of Publishing Services.

Brian S. Brooks
George Kennedy
Daryl R. Moen
Don Ranly

Contents

Workbook for
News Reporting and Writing

1 The Nature of News

1. The criteria used by professional journalists to determine what's news can be summed up in three words: *relevance, usefulness, interest.* For your first assignment, put yourself in the role of media critic. Get the most recent editions of your campus newspaper and the city newspaper covering your area. Compare the news content.
   a. How many, if any, stories in the two publications cover the same event or issue?
   b. Now assess the relevance, usefulness and interest of each paper's content to you and your classmates.
   c. From reading the papers, and from what you have learned about how journalists try to reach their audiences, what can you tell about the different audiences of these newspapers?

2. Now broaden your survey. For the same day, compare the news content of a local news show on television to the content of the local newspaper.
   a. What similarities and differences in news judgment do you see?
   b. What can you tell about the relative importance the journalists in each news room place on *impact, conflict, novelty, prominence, proximity, timeliness*?

3. Turn from those traditional sources and force yourself to watch *The Daily Show* and *The Colbert Report.* What differences do you see between real news and the fake news on those shows? As serious journalists try to capture young readers and viewers, what lessons, if any, might they learn from Jon Stewart and Stephen Colbert?

4. Check out online news sites such as **CNN.com, MSNBC.com** and **nytimes.com**.
   a. Compare the content of newspapers and television news available in your community to what's available online. What do you find in one source that's unavailable in others?
   b. Which best satisfies your appetite for news?
   c. Which do you find most enjoyable to use?

5. Get copies of one day's newspapers from your town and at least one nearby town, plus a copy of *USA Today*, a national paper.
   a. Analyze the news decisions of the editors by applying the criteria discussed in Chapter 1.
   b. Of course, *USA Today* has no local audience. How does that fact affect its editors' news decisions? How do the editors attempt to meet "local" interests across the nation?

6. Journalists use the criteria of news value to help them come up with ideas for stories. As a reporter in your town, your assignment now is to generate five story ideas. Each story idea should be relevant, useful and interesting. For each idea, write a short memo to your editor explaining, in terms of the criteria, what makes it a good idea for your local paper.

7. **A.** What element or elements of each of the following events make it newsworthy?
   a. Police Chief Carlos Briceno is named Man of the Year by the local chamber of commerce.
   b. A store employee who reported a fire that did extensive damage to the store last night was taken into custody after police discovered that the store had been burglarized and found some of the merchandise in the employee's car.
   c. A national study found that the local cancer detection center has the highest rate of inaccurate diagnoses in the nation. The director of the center disputes the findings.
   B. Imagine that you are the news editor of your local newspaper. Rank the preceding events in order of their news value. Justify your decisions to the managing editor, your boss.

8. **a.** Imagine that your school has just announced that conservative spokesperson Patrick Buchanan and the national ACLU president will debate drug testing next week on campus. Your assignment as a reporter is to prepare a background story on the issue. Go to the library and find six sources of information. List them and note which, if either, side of the issue each source is likely to reflect.
   b. Now describe how you will find and evaluate local sources for the same story.

9. **a.** Your assignment as a reporter is a story on one of the following: religious conflict in the Middle East, capital punishment, the use of animals in laboratory experiments, air traffic safety. Use the library to find as many sources as you'll need for a story that will be fair and complete. Identify your sources and their likely viewpoints.
   b. How will you find local sources for that story? How might you evaluate the qualifications of such sources?

10. Put yourself in this situation:

    You are a reporter pursuing a story about the death of a child after an apparently simple operation at a local hospital. You establish that the incident happened, and you confirm enough details for a story. You are unable to learn the name of the surgeon who performed the operation, but you do learn the name of the nurse who was responsible for postsurgical care and who was on duty when the child died. You also learn that the nurse was transferred to another job immediately after the death. However, no one will say whether the transfer was related to the death.

    The question: Is it fair to publish the name of the nurse? Explain your response.

11. At the *Columbia Missourian*, an accuracy-checking policy requires that the facts in every story be double-checked with the sources who provided them before publication. Few newspapers follow such a policy. On many papers, editors do not allow sources to see or to be read stories before publication, for fear of improper influences on the way the stories are handled.

Discuss the advantages and possible disadvantages of accurately checking stories before publication by showing or reading them to the people who provided the information.

CHALLENGE EXERCISE

12. This chapter offers an explanation of the widespread perception of bias in the news. Put that explanation to the test. Study a day's worth of news on your favorite source. What, if any, biases do you detect? How well does the chapter's explanation fit your findings? If you don't like what the chapter suggests, propose your own explanation.

2 Redefining News: Citizen Journalism and Convergence

1. Each year more and more traditional media outlets are embracing citizen journalism. Write two pages comparing the coverage of a news event in a media outlet that has embraced citizen journalism to that of a medium that has not. Which do you prefer as a news source and why?

2. Find the online version of a college newspaper other than your own. Write two pages comparing the content of that newspaper with your own college or university newspaper. Does either contain content not found in the printed product? Does either use multimedia such as sound or video?

3. List two or three sources where you might find information on the number of newspapers owned by major newspaper companies in the United States. Using one of them, list the number of newspapers owned by the three largest companies. Also research the degree to which those companies have embraced online media.

4. Using online databases or the Internet as sources of information, list at least five media operations owned by Time Warner.

5. Write job descriptions for the following editors of your local newspaper or your college newspaper (if such positions exist):
   a. Editor

   b. Managing editor

   c. City editor

d. Sports editor

e. Lifestyle editor

f. News editor

g. State editor

h. Editorial page editor

i. Graphics editor

j. Copy desk chief

k. Online editor

6. Describe the functions of the following departments of your local newspaper or your college newspaper:

a. Advertising

b. Circulation

c. Business

d. Production

7. Write job descriptions for the following workers at a local television station or your local campus radio station:

a. News director

b. Newsanchor

c. News producer

d. Videographer

    e. Reporter

8. Examine the media operations in the large city nearest to your campus. Of the media companies located there, tell which one is doing the most with convergence and explain why you think so.

9. As citizens increasingly have opportunities to publish their views, the role of the editor as gatekeeper is diminishing. Explain the implications of this in your community. Is the trend positive or negative? Why?

CHALLENGE EXERCISES

10. Talk with a reporter from your local newspaper or broadcast station about the difficulty of adjusting to a reporting job that requires skills in online journalism and not just print, radio or television. What can you do to prepare for a cross-media career?

11. Evaluate the content of a participatory news site such as mymissourian.com or ohmynews.com. How does the content found there differ from that in your local newspaper? Are there gaps in coverage? Are there things there you would not find in your local newspaper?

3 Interviewing

1. Often the best interviews are determined by the amount of preparation the reporter does before the interview. One way is to prepare a memo for yourself. Write a memo of up to two pages to prepare for each of the following interviews. Don't restrict yourself to online sources.
   a. Your state's governor. Indicate the sources of your information. Concentrate on details that will allow you to focus on the topic of how the governor regards higher education.
   b. Your state's junior senator. Concentrate on details that will allow you to focus on his or her stand on gun control.
   c. Your congressional representative. Concentrate on details that will allow you to focus on his or her stand on abortion.
   d. The vice president. Concentrate on details that will allow you to focus on his or her stand on aid to higher education.
   e. The chief executive officer of your campus. Concentrate on details that will allow you to focus on his or her view of the role of fraternities and sororities on campus.
   f. The dean or chair of your journalism school or department. Concentrate on details that will allow you to focus on the role of professional experience in the training of an educator.
   g. The director of the local chamber of commerce. Concentrate on details that will allow you to focus on his or her views on promoting retail business.

2. If you don't phrase your questions properly, you may not be asking the questions you think you are.
   a. List five open-ended questions you can ask one person identified in exercise 1.

   b. List five closed-ended questions you can ask of the same person.

3. Assume that you will interview a public official who, your information indicates, may have embezzled $20,000. You don't yet have proof.
   a. List at least three open-ended questions in the order that you might ask them.

   b. List at least three closed-ended questions in the order that you might ask them.

   c. Evaluate the questions you listed above. Which ones are the most threatening? The most nonthreatening?

4. Assume that you have been assigned to do a story on a student who has been named a Rhodes Scholar on your campus. You haven't had time to find out much information about the student. List at least eight questions you would ask as you search for a focus. Identify whether they are closed- or open-ended questions.

5. List four ways to ask a candidate for student body president what his or her stand is on dedicating scholarship money to minorities. Arrange the questions from least threatening to most threatening.

6. Journalists must establish rapport quickly with sources.

    a. Watch one of the television news shows. Evaluate the rapport, or lack of it, between the interviewer and a source.

    b. How would you establish rapport with the source you reported on in the preceding question?

7. If you were assigned to do a feature story for the campus newspaper or radio station, on a campus instructor you haven't met, how would you establish rapport?

8. Describe how you established rapport with a source for a story you have done.

9. Interview another student in your class for a two-page feature story. After getting an overview of the person's life, you will need to hone in on some aspect of the person to create focus in your story. Before turning in the story, have the subject read the story and correct errors of fact and context. Check your notes again to try to determine how you made the errors. Ask the subject whether he or she agrees with your focus. Your subject should also write a couple of paragraphs about his or her reactions to how well you established rapport as well as the quality of your questions.

10. Select a story from your campus or local newspaper about a local source. (Do not choose a report of a meeting.) Mail or take it to the main source. Ask the source to identify errors of fact or context. Find out whether the interview was by phone or in person. If the interview was in person, find out where it occurred and how long it lasted. Critique the work of the reporter.

11. Interview a journalist from a local news organization. Ask the journalist to describe his or her most successful and least successful efforts at establishing rapport. Write a report.

12. Your instructor will read the class a prepared statement. Take notes. No questions will be permitted. Now reproduce the statement as best you can. Compare your version against the original. Is it accurate down to the articles?

13. Your instructor will invite someone to appear before the class to make a statement and to answer a few questions. The session will be recorded. Check your story against the recording for accuracy.

14. Using a database, find the original text of a presidential speech or a news conference. Then find two versions of the story published in newspapers. For instance, compare stories done by *The New York Times* and the Associated Press. Check the accuracy of the quotes in the stories against the transcript. Describe and evaluate any discrepancies.

15. Your editor calls you into the office to tell you that a source in your story claims he was misquoted. You show the editor the quote in your notebook. How does the editor know whether you or the source is right? How do you know?

16. To read about college costs at both two- and four-year colleges, both public and private, go to a report entitled "Trends in College Pricing 2006" at http://www .collegeboard.com/press/releases/150634.html. You have been assigned to do a story based on the national study but with a local focus.
    a. Whom would you interview at your local college?

    b. What further information would you want in hand before conducting any interviews?

    c. Prepare a list of questions for one of your key sources.

CHALLENGE EXERCISE

17. Last week, after an eight-year tenure, Barbara Behling resigned as chancellor of Springfield University. Behling took office at a time of waning state support. Her decisions on funding priorities and efforts to upgrade the physical appearance and integrity of the campus generated repeated controversies. Here is the interview you conducted with Behling:

Q: Think back. What was the university like when you came here? What were your primary challenges?

A: I wasn't really ready to leave Oklahoma, but a friend of mine had told me that this was a challenge that would interest me. What really intrigued me was the attitude of the search committee. It clearly portrayed an institution that was ready for some change.

The four earliest problem areas were the hospital, the physical plant, administrative structuring and minority recruitment.

The hospital was a big one. It was not in good financial shape. Bills were being delayed and not aggressively collected. The legislature was concerned about hospital financing. The place looked bad. There was no stopping and thinking about whether I had to do something; it had to be done.

Q: What did you do?

A: The first thing I did was hire a consultant to find out what was wrong with the operation. I learned a lot about hospital administration in a hurry. We made some personnel changes and recruited the current director, who came in with a lot of experience and put a plan together.

That first-year budget was about $50 million, with about a third of that coming from the state. Today, the budget is about $125 million, with only about 15 percent coming from the state. Remember, the hospital is there to serve the medical school. It's unique because it is a teaching hospital, but at the same time, it has to pay its bills. We constantly ask ourselves which is the tail and which is the dog.

Q: How about the physical renovation?

A: One of the first proposals made to me was for an addition to the law school building. I asked questions like "Do you need the space? Show me the documentation. Is other space on campus available? Is this the best solution?"

The point is, it made me realize how much work there was to do in the area of physical planning.

I divided the job into three parts. One was to hire a consultant to give me a list of highly visible projects that could be done at reasonable cost and would make a quick impression of progress to make the campus look better and make people feel better about it. Renovation of the south grounds of Jesse Hall and Jesse Auditorium were on that list.

The second part was to get good documentation on upkeep of the buildings, maintenance schedules and the like.

Third was to begin major planning for the campus. This plan is being used to guide about $145 million worth of construction that has been completed or is in process at a time when funds have been extremely scarce.

Q: Let's turn now to minority recruitment. Is part of the problem that there just aren't enough minority college students to go around?

A: Of the college-age minorities living in this state, we don't get our share applying to our school. This is a national problem. The population is becoming increasingly minority. It is the segment of the population that participates in higher education the least, and we will become increasingly dependent on them in the future to help run the society.

Q: Once all roadblocks are down and minorities are clearly encouraged to enroll, what else can you do?

A: Soon after I came here and had done a lot of inquiry into this, I used to say I did not know of anyone on campus who would willingly admit they were against minority participation, but they didn't make it a priority. We must continue to make it a priority.

Q: Is it a priority on this campus now?

A: It is in many areas—at least in some. Giving equal treatment is not enough. We need to do unusual things to recruit and keep minorities.

Q: Does this mean we need to practice affirmative action?

A: For years, minorities have had disadvantaged backgrounds. We have to give them extraordinary opportunities to succeed.

Q: Can you be more specific?

A: We are making a special effort to recruit minority faculty, to have minority speakers on campus, to recruit high school minority students, to give enough scholarship aid for minorities and to provide special academic support in the form of teaching study skills in math and writing.

Q: What was the problem you identified in the structure of the central administration?

A: I immediately found a problem with centralization in research administration. Too many approvals were required. There were too many stumbling blocks from the large structure at the central administration. I had a research position to be filled (graduate dean for research), so through that, I actually began to understand the university.

As is true on all campuses, as the student body had grown through the years, the administration had grown. It's very easy to put new people in without rethinking the total organization. As I recall, at the time I came, there were some 26 people reporting directly to the chancellor. There was considerable ambiguity about where decisions finally were made. I personally like to function with a smaller staff having broader responsibilities.

I had a lot to learn in a short time about the institution. I had to do a lot of listening. The basic thing I did was to think through what the campus is for. It's there to serve students academically, so I decided to reduce from three provosts to one provost for academics.

a. Write a 500-word story based on this interview.
b. List some of the follow-up questions you would like to have asked based on the answers Behling gave.

4 In Their Own Words

1. Rewrite the following passages as you think necessary. Pay special attention to the quotes.

   a. "We will be recording this spring," says John Dade, guitarist, singer and song-writer, who first began singing with Don Seiver about three years ago. "There will be a product on the streets—on the airwaves, we hope—by the end of the summer."

   b. "We did a show with Taylor Browne and John Barnes last summer in New York at a club called Trax," Dade says. "James has been a fan for a while and Jackson Browne turned into a real solid supporter."

   c. It took Seiver a long time to "shuck the robe of responsibility." "It took me a long time to shuck the robe of responsibility," recalls Seiver. "I fought it for three years saying, 'Well, I love to write songs, and I love to play guitar . . . but I don't think I can make a living doing it.' So I'm going to be an English teacher just in case.

   "I held on to this myth for a long time—that I could actually approach something involving my life with a just-in-case attitude—that I would settle for something less than maybe happy."

   d. Nobody settles "for anything less than the best," Dade says. The group squabbles "about the fine points," but the "creative tension" builds as the group molds a new song.

e. "They do nothing original," one critic said. "They steal all of their songs and the ones they do write are not worth hearing."

f. "It makes it more real," says Seiver. "It makes it feel like you're livin'. When I'm on the road, I'm always stayin' with friends. Travelin' can really git ya down."

g. "We love each other and we fight all the time," Dade says. "That's the way we work. It's all ultimately positive. Writing songs together ain't easy. We've written quite a few, but it's tough. But it's worth it."

h. "You don't have to live in Hollywood Hills. You don't have to drive a Mercedes-Benz. You don't have to hang out at the Rainbow Club," says Dade.

2. Write a news story from the following information. Be careful about the quotes you select.

A United Airlines jet with 61 persons aboard crashed while approaching Chicago's Midway Airport Friday afternoon. Most of the plane's passengers were killed when the airliner plowed through homes in a residential district south of the city.

One eyewitness said: "I saw the plane coming lower and lower. I couldn't believe it. I thought surely it would go back up into the air. But it kept coming down. I knew it would never make it to the airport. I was scared."

The National Transportation Safety Board in Washington immediately dispatched an investigative team to Chicago. Several board officials already were in Chicago conducting hearings into the Oct. 20 commuter train crash that claimed 45 lives. "We'll look into this thoroughly," an official was quoted as saying.

The plane's final destination was Omaha, Neb.

One of the survivors, Marvin Anderson, 43, of Omaha, said, "The last words the pilot said to us were, 'We are at 4,000 feet and everything is going well.' I knew something was wrong a few seconds later because he began to rev the engines."

Curtis Vokamer, deputy fire marshal, said his crew found most of the 55 passengers dead in the debris of the Boeing 737. "If hell has an address, this was the place," Vokamer said.

Holy Cross Hospital reported 16 persons, including the plane's three flight attendants, were admitted with injuries.

A United spokesman said, "The plane, Flight 553, was due at Midway at 2:31 p.m. CST. The plane was approaching the airport with a 500-foot ceiling and a one-mile visibility," he said.

"I hope this never happens to da great city of Chicago again," Alderman James Staley said. "And it ain't gonna happen. Not if I can help it."

The Cook County Coroner reported 42 bodies had been found. One of the victims identified was Rep. George W. Collins, D.-Ill., who was returning from Washington to "organize a children's Christmas party."

Another eyewitness said, "And to think, all this happened because the pilot probably had one too many cocktails during the flight."

John Eldon, of 234 Bixby Drive, said, "If dis is da way dis city is gonna run dere airports, we is movin'."

3. In the following exercises, delete or paraphrase (make more concise and clear) the direct quotations that are needless, wordy, unclear or in bad taste.

a.   "It's the American dream," Bill Buchanan says.

"There were some hard times I wouldn't want to repeat unless I was in need," says his wife JoAnne. "It was scary at first."

They are talking about owning their own business, a unique relationship that casts husband and wife in the roles of co-bosses.

The marriage survival rate and the small-business survival rate are bad. Trying to put the two together seems like asking for trouble.

"I feel like it's made it easier to work and be married. It brings us closer together," says John Pettey. Pettey and his wife own Pettey's Fashion Cleaners and Laundry, a business they have run together for eight years.

"It's great," Mr. Pettey says in a slow Southern drawl. "She does the books and I do all the work in the back. It's easy."

"It was unreal at the beginning," Mrs. Buchanan says in contrast. "The time we have to put in so we wouldn't have to hire someone else! We were open 9 to 9 and someone in the family had to be there all the time.

"It was really a strain on our family at the beginning. But the children were old enough to learn by it and it added to their education," she adds.

The Buchanans own Athlete's Feet, a store specializing in sports clothes. "They (athletic shoes) really took off as a fashion item. If they hadn't, we would have folded," Mr. Buchanan says.

Things are running smoothly, so to speak, in the athletic-shoe business now, and the Buchanans enjoy it. They started the business eight and a half years ago to have extra income to send their three children to college.

Mr. Buchanan likes sports and wanted to open a sporting-goods store. "I told him I didn't think I could handle guns and all that," Mrs. Buchanan says. Mr. Buchanan works at Monsanto, working at the store in the afternoons and on Saturdays. He does inventory chores at home in the evenings.

Mrs. Buchanan works from 10 a.m. to 2 p.m. in the store, then does out-of-store errands.

"She manages the store and takes care of writing checks, making orders, keeping books. I decide what to order, what styles of shoes and how many. JoAnne, of course, advises me, particularly in tennis clothes, socks, warm-up suits," Mr. Buchanan says.

"It's helpful to separate duties," Mrs. Buchanan says. "You can devote time to special duties and not have to worry about the whole thing."

Doug and Patti Lambert own Patti's, a gift shop that began as a plant shop and gradually expanded. They say a division of labor such as the Buchanans have is essential to making a husband-wife business work.

"We have to separate duties because we take everything so seriously," Mr. Lambert says. "We fight about where to display something, even if it's only six feet apart."

"Violently," Mrs. Lambert adds, smiling. "He and I fought like cats and dogs over Doug's Christmas tree. So he decorated it his way. (A light green tree with only light green decorations.) Everybody that comes in says 'Oh! I love that!' And he makes sure they say it again so I can hear it.

"There's a lot of stress we wouldn't have if it was just boss to employee. I'd just say, 'Put this here.' As co-bosses, we argue frequently.

"The biggest drawback is taking it home," Mrs. Lambert says. "It's our breakfast and dinner conversation."

Still, having different opinions can help the business in the long run, according to Mrs. Lambert.

"We have different tastes. We like different colors, textures. Doug's very formal, I'm very casual. It gives us more mass appeal."

"And makes it impossible to get along," Mr. Lambert adds. "It takes an extremely strong marriage to survive it, unless one is subservient, one is boss, the other is servant.

"But we're doing fine."

b. SPRINGFIELD—The death of his close friend, Jack Springer, more than two years ago may have led Donald Oaks to take his own life, say close friends and family. But nobody knows for sure.

The 17-year-old Springfield youth died at 6 a.m. May 21, about 15 hours after he had graduated from Springfield Central High School. He celebrated the event at a party with friends and later that evening was on his way to Jack Springer's grave.

"Donny said before the night was over he wanted to go see Jack," said Tanya Oaks, Donny's sister.

But on his way to the grave Oaks lost control of his car and went into a ditch, according to his friend Greg Manning, a passenger in the car. Manning said Oaks then pulled out his knife and was going to slit his wrists. Manning calmed him down and Oaks put the knife away.

"Man, he was acting strange," Manning said. "Crazy as a loon."

Oaks was driven home by the police. He walked straight into his room, loaded his .410 shotgun and shot himself in the head with it. Sheriff Sue Fuller arrived and declared it suicide. "God, it was awful," Fuller said. "There were blood and brains splattered all over the room."

Those who knew Oaks say the suicide might have been linked to remorse over the death of Springer, who was killed in a truck accident. Oaks was with him at the time.

He never came to grips with his friend's death, both Miss Oaks and her mother said.

"He never came to grips with his friend's death," his sister said. "That's why he probably done it."

"I guess he just couldn't take it no more," his mother said.

According to Miss Oaks, Oaks and Springer were inseparable. They fished, hunted, rode bikes and did everything together. And when Springer died, Oaks "really never understood why. Why Jack?"

"Donny would let it build up in him," his sister said, "and then he would take it out on things by hitting them. At parties, he'd get upset with it and start hitting things . . . walls, posts, people, whatever."

Oaks' girlfriend, Linda Turner, said that he had been upset the whole week before he died. Oaks told her that he was going to kill himself that Saturday. "I'm going to get the job done, one way or another, and nobody's going to stop me," he told his sister.

She didn't take him seriously. "I didn't take him seriously," she said. "I just didn't give it much thought."

Other friends of his saw no signs. "If he was having depressed feelings," Darin Schmid said, "he sure weren't showing them. Donny was usually cheerful. He most of the time had a screwy smile on his face—like he was a bit queer or retarded. He seemed to be in a good mood on graduation night."

Another friend, Brad Baumer, said Oaks talked about Jack Springer a lot. "He talked about Jack a whole lot," Baumer said. "He was always having these memories."

But for Oaks the memories weren't enough, so he decided to join his friend since his friend couldn't join him, his family sadly concluded.

"After the accident, he just didn't care," his sister said. "He wanted Jack there no matter what."

Oaks was buried May 23 in the Walnut Ridge Cemetery, across town from where Jack Springer is buried, but Miss Oaks and her mother believe the two are together again at last.

"If it's got to be this way, I hope they are together again at last," his mother said with a teary-eyed smile.

"They're probably a helluva lot better off up there than we are down here," his sister said.

c.   Brennan Scanlon hit four 3-pointers in the third quarter, as Springfield's boys' basketball team overcame a 32-25 halftime deficit en route to a 54-43 victory Saturday night in the MFA Oil/Break Time Shootout.

Scanlon, a sophomore guard, finished with a game-high 23 points—14 in the second half. Bruins senior forward Travis Rudloff scored 12 points and had eight rebounds.

"We did a nice job of taking away what they did the first half," said Jim Scanlon, Springfield coach and Brennan's father. "There weren't any secrets. We went with a quicker team and increased our pressure a little bit, and it paid off for us."

Hickman (9-9) hit 5-of-17 shots (29.4 percent) for the final half.

"Our seniors—Skyler (Graves), Travis (Rudloff) and Demetrius (Thompson)—really stepped up and played big for us," Coach Scanlon said. "I'm happy for all the kids."

Senior center Jason Meyer and junior guard Shaun Coleman led Hickman with seven points each.

"Our guys didn't suck it up," Hickman coach David Johnson said. "We forgot to guard Brennan Scanlon and he just lit it up on us. We just totally broke down in every phase of the game in the second half. We didn't execute in our half-court offense and didn't play any defense. Those are the things that win ball games."

With 4:15 left and Springfield leading 45-39, Meyer drove the baseline from the left for a layup. But he was called for charging and the basket did not count. Johnson said that missed opportunity snapped the Kewpies' momentum.

"It stopped our momentum because I felt we were getting right back in it," he said. "As a coach, I thought he had a good shot. I thought he was in good position. He had the right to the hole. But the referee saw it differently."

The lead never was larger than six in the first quarter, and both teams led.

The second quarter was a quarter of runs. Hickman had an 8-0 run to lead 23-19. Then Springfield regained the lead 25-23 with a 6-0 run. But the Bruins (9-5) didn't score again in the half.

"It was very obvious they hurt us on the offensive boards the first half," Coach Scanlon said. "That was probably the difference in the first half."

d. SPRINGFIELD — The purple color of Flat Branch Creek near Fourth and Locust streets probably will pose no environmental hazard.

Firefighters were alerted to the water's color by an unidentified neighbor about 9:30 a.m. Wednesday. Fire Chief Bernard Perry of the Springfield Fire Department said the stream was contaminated by neutralized muriatic acid, which is a dilution of hydrochloric acid.

Perry said the contamination had been emitted from MSA Inc. at 201 S. Seventh St. The corporation used the chemicals to clean its air-conditioning unit, and the residue flowed into the creek by way of a storm drain.

"Muriatic acid it was," Perry said, "and MSA is to blame."

Bob Channey, a university professor of chemical engineering, said muriatic acid is extremely dangerous. "Muriatic acid is very hazardous," Channey said. "It can burn your skin off. Those fools over at MSA are always pulling stuff like that. This time I hope they get them."

Even the fumes are dangerous. "I hope some of the fumes drift over to MSA and wipe out a few of those clowns."

However, Perry said neutralized muriatic acid probably poses no danger to human health. The purple color, the battalion chief said, was the result of a warning chemical that was mixed with the acid; once the dye is in the purple stage, the hazardous qualities of the acid normally are no longer present.

"The liquid changes into purple when it does everything it can do," Perry said. "Actually, the purple is kinda pretty. I don't know why everyone is getting so worked up about it."

Another professor of engineering, John Connors, agreed with Perry. "It's still an acid, but once it's in a stream, the water neutralizes it. Any beginning chemistry student knows that. Our students conduct lots of experiments like that. Actually, they get that information in about their third semester of chemistry. Or it might be their second. No one has died from the experiments yet."

"From what I understand, it's not caustic," said Mike Bangle, MSA's communications coordinator. "If anyone's at fault, it's the Ed More Co., the company that cleaned the air conditioner."

"It ain't certain whether anybody broke the law here," Art Growner of the state Department of Natural Resources said. "If anyone did, you can be sure that we will make the proper arrests. After all, that's our job. First, of course, we are going to make an investigation and really look into the matter. That might take a few days at least — maybe a week or more."

Perry said the city's drinking water is not in danger. "Understand, we get our water from wells, not from Flat Branch Creek. Thank God for that!"

4. In the following exercises, change the wording and the placement of the attributions wherever you think necessary. You may also wish to delete or paraphrase some of the direct quotes.

a.   All they are saying is give peace a chance.

Committed to the teachings of Jesus Christ, Pax Christi is a group of people who aim to contribute to world peace through prayer, reflection on Scripture and service. The Catholic organization was founded at the end of World War II by a French bishop named Theas.

The local chapter of Pax Christi began over two years ago.

Members are involved in various service ministries, such as St. Francis House, a hospitality center, and Loaves and Fishes, a soup kitchen.

"There's a real neat network of people in Springfield that help people through the different organizations in the community," claims Amy Schmidt, local Pax Christi contact.

"It's the type of group that can attend to the needs of local people."

The group's members also address broader issues.

"We balance what we do in peace work with work in social justice," maintains five-year member Lana Jacobs, who also volunteers at Loaves and Fishes.

Pam McClure, who has been involved with the group for a year and a half, agrees:

"The whole thing is an idea of service, self-knowledge . . . putting meaning where it is needed.

"I think it is meaningful to take prayer to missile silos, and take prayer and work to St. Francis and the soup kitchen."

Although Pax Christi works for social justice, the group does not directly engage in politics.

"Many groups are politically affiliated, but that's not where I come from at peace," Schmidt contends.

"We don't look at what is politically effective, but what's felt in the heart as prayerful," Jacobs explains.

"We do what we feel called to do by our spirituality."

Jacobs, who has been involved in the peace movement for 20 years, says politically oriented groups burn out quicker than those based on religious tradition.

"People get their strength from their spirituality, be it Buddhist, Christian or whatever," she confides.

Although Pax Christi is a Catholic organization, Schmidt says its catholicity is essentially in terms of "universal."

It is a broad coalition of persons concerned with justice who support non-violence as an alternative to war and violent resistance.

McClure, an Episcopalian, says there are no real differences in perspective because she is not Catholic.

"We're very committed to being rooted in Christ.

"The call of the Gospel is to preach love, justice and freedom — to help bring the Kingdom of God."

Schmidt says this call has ramifications for the community, the state, the country and the world.

The Bible indicates that all things will be in harmony and all relationships will be in order when the kingdom arrives, Schmidt says.

"When we become equals, when we're treated equally no matter who we are, that's when the kingdom will be here.

"We're so far from that view . . . that we're one people."

Along with a just world order, Pax Christi's priorities are disarmament, primacy of conscience, education for peace and alternatives to violence.

Disarmament and primacy of conscience, which is mainly concerned with conscientious objection, are the two primary concerns of the local chapter of Pax Christi.

"If you don't address those, you won't have a world left to address them in," claims Jacobs.

Although members wish to avert nuclear war, they are concerned mainly with the poor being currently hurt by the arms race.

"Our focus on disarmament is not because of fear of nuclear war, but on the harm it's doing to people now.

"When you see people suffering and you realize nuclear arms are expendable, you know things need to change," Schmidt states.

According to Pax Christi literature, 50 million malnourished children in developing countries could be adequately fed for the estimated cost of the MX missile. In addition, 65,000 health-care centers and 340,000 primary schools could be built.

Although many of the organization's concerns have political dimensions, Pax Christi members concentrate on witnessing and prayer, rather than appealing directly to government officials.

The group's members realize that much work remains to be done regarding their objectives.

"There's still injustice in correctional institutions, the arms race is still going on, there's still capital punishment and the draft," Schmidt says.

"But I know people have been touched and changed," she says.

"The group's members have major faith in prayer, and they consider it the key to facilitating social and spiritual change."

b.   The early morning sunlight casts his shadow on the ground, as OATS driver Carl Hockman conscientiously checks under the hood of bus 175 and inspects its engine.

Glancing at his watch to ensure punctuality, Hockman boards the bus. After adjusting mirrors and latching his seat belt, he turns the ignition key and begins his route through central Logan County.

With a secure grip on the steering wheel, Hockman adeptly avoids potholes as the bus rolls over the gravel of the winding country roads.

This particular yellow bus, labeled OATS in blue, is only one of the 160 vans that provide rural transportation service to 88 counties.

OATS, formally called Older Adult's Transportation Service, is primarily a rural system designed to meet the needs of low-income, elderly or handicapped riders. The service is open to the general public as well.

Entering the driveway of his first passenger of the day, Hockman honks his horn and brings the vehicle to a halt. At each stop, he gets out of the van, preparing to aid his rider in any way he can.

With a pleasant "good morning to ya" and a wide smile, Hockman escorts Mabel Caldwell to the bus door.

"Now Carl, you know that you don't need to get out and help me," she scolds appreciatively.

Refusing to deny his rider the usual courtesies, Hockman opens the door and helps her board the bus. The door of the bus is shut, but only after it is apparent that her seat belt is secure and that she is seated comfortably.

"I look after these women like an old hen with her little chickens," Hockman states proudly.

Guaranteeing personalized service to all their riders, OATS drivers assist passengers in boarding and disembarking.

Drivers are given initial orientation on the needs of the elderly and the handicapped.

In addition to being trained to handle wheelchairs, they learn defensive driving, first aid and cardiopulmonary resuscitation.

"Oh, Carl, Bonnie's not going today," Caldwell contends. "She says she's got the sniffles," she adds.

Hockman patiently revises his route and then maneuvers the bus throughout central Logan County to pick up other passengers—Ruth Jones, Maxine Bombauer, Enid Stephenson, Vera Craig and Nancy Exposito.

Jones, who is waiting patiently inside, hears the horn blow and hurries out to the bus. As she climbs aboard, her dog yelps loudly, objecting to its master's departure.

"That's OK," maintains Hockman, assuring the barking dog. "We'll be sure and bring her back safe and sound."

The riders are gradually picked up and greetings are exchanged between friends, as the bus is transformed into a moving social center with women discussing events of the past week.

News about a friend in the hospital generates immediate concern among the riders, and plans are made to buy her a card. The group waves as it passes by the house of a woman who was unable to join them that day.

The brightness of the sun that is peeking out from behind the over-shadowing clouds complements the good cheer of the talkative women. Birds chirp loudly and green buds indicate spring's arrival.

"Praise the Lord for this beautiful day," Hockman shouts as he inhales the fresh country air.

"Isn't it wonderful to hear them old frogs a-croakin' again?" Maxine smiles.

Heads nod in agreement; it's good to be "out and about" on such a nice day.

"The OATS buses mean so much to so many people," Hockman shouts over the rumbling of voices in the background. "It's the only form of transportation that some of these people have," he says.

OATS helps the elderly or handicapped individual meet his or her transportation needs independently, without having to burden friends, relatives or neighbors. For some elderly, this door-to-door bus service serves as an alternative to a nursing home.

Offering the chance to meet new people, OATS also helps to alleviate the loneliness that often results from living in isolated, rural areas.

"Some passengers own a car but like to ride along just to see their friends," Hockman says. "It's a form of therapy and breaks the monotony of looking at bare walls," Hockman says.

As the bus enters the city limits, the women skim through newspaper ads in order to determine where the best bargains can be found. Hockman attempts to make sense out of the confusion as six women blurt out the various errands to be done.

"Now, do we have any doctors' appointments today?" Hockman says with clipboard in hand.

Much to everyone's relief, none have been scheduled for that day. The trip becomes lengthy when several passengers have appointments to meet.

"Oh, Carl, I need to stop at the pharmacist's to get some prescriptions refilled," Stephenson confides.

Regular service includes trips for shopping, medical or essential business purposes, and to visit senior centers and nutrition sites. Today, stops are made at two banks and grocery stores, and the Biscayne Mall.

"You can go this trip a dozen times, and none would be the same," Hockman asserts, as he drops Exposito off at Nowell's. The others discuss plans for lunch.

"I'll pick you up at 1 p.m.," Hockman assures Exposito.

"Now is that going to give you enough time to do all of your shopping?" Hockman says.

Hockman helps Exposito off the bus and into the store. Meanwhile, the decision about lunch is proving difficult; six different people opt for their favorite restaurants.

The deliberations continue as each rider presents her preference. The compromise is made. The group will eat cafeteria-style in order to satisfy everyone's palate.

"There's times when you just have to bear with the crowd," Hockman laughs, attempting to comfort those who didn't get their choice.

After lunch, the riders stop at Biscayne Mall and are given a designated time to meet. All go their separate ways, weaving in and out of the shops, purchasing what they need.

At 3 p.m., Hockman's bus waits at the front of the mall. Five weary shoppers, laden with packages, come filing out and approach the bus.

"What did you get today, Enid?" Jones asks, as the two women discuss the sales they came across.

In order to account for all of his passengers, Hockman begins to count heads. "One . . . two . . . three . . . four . . . five . . . ?"

It soon becomes apparent that No. 6 is missing, so Hockman heads out to round up the last member of his crew.

"Carl is so patient with us," Stephenson maintains.

The women agree and then try to determine the whereabouts of their missing friend. After 10 minutes of searching, Hockman returns with the late rider.

"It's a good thing we found her," Hockman teases.

"I was about to drive home without her," Hockman states.

On the way home, the bus is crowded with groceries and other cumbersome packages. The once-bright sunlight has dimmed and reflects the flagging energy of the women.

Gradually, the bus empties and the cheerful voices of the passengers are replaced by the sound of gravel spitting out from under the tires.

c.   When it comes to a person's family tree, many of us are content with a sapling.

But there are some who want to know their roots.

Virginia Nichols of U.S. Lake St., a descendant of Cedric, King of West Saxony, A.D. 519 to 534, is one of those people.

She became interested in her genealogy in 1990 following the death of her father. While checking his safe-deposit box, she came across an application for the Daughters of the War of 1812 that her maternal grandmother had partly filled out.

Nichols is currently a member of about 20 genealogical organizations. They include Daughters of the American Revolution, National Society of Americans of Royal Descent, Dames of the Court of Honor, Magna Carta Dames, Descendants of Emperor Charlemagne, Order of the First Three Crusades and Daughters of the War of 1812.

A friend who had done some research on Nichols's ancestors helped her get started on what now is an impressive collection of names and dates.

"He supplied me with some information but no proof, so I had to start backtracking in order to get proof.

"One thing led to another and I began to work on my husband's (Lawson) lines at the same time. My ancestors came to the Ashland area in 1818 and his in 1823. We have not one mutual ancestor as far as I've been able to trace," Nichols believes.

Nichols explains that in order to get into each genealogical society, one must have proof of an ancestor from the particular time periods. Often one ancestor will get an individual into more than one organization.

Organizations generally require a copy of an individual's birth certificate and marriage license as well as his or her parents' marriage license, in addition to a copy, if possible, of a legal document proving the ancestor's existence. Nichols says most organizations will accept a published listing that includes the ancestors as proof.

"The ultimate organization to be able to join was the Order of the First Three Crusades," she says. "I have five ancestors who were members of the first crusade. You could only file on one, so I filed on Hugh Magnum, who was a duke of Normandy and the son of King Henry II of France," Nichols says.

Nichols has also proved to be a descendant of 14 of the barons who signed the Magna Carta in 1215. She explained that 17 of those who signed have descendants and added, "I'm still working on the other three."

"King John Lackland of England was forced by the barons to sign the document and I have proved I'm a descendant of his, even if he was a scoundrel," Nichols laughs.

Opening one of her many historical books, she flips to a page listing the council of 1619. Beside the name Edward Gourgany she has written the word "mine."

"I'm basically just trying to find as many names as possible," she claims, "husbands and wives, where they were born, where and when they died. In other words, to establish the surname line.

"The way things are going now, many places are destroying records. If you don't get this down somewhere, it's going to be lost to future generations."

Having experienced the process of tracing her family tree, Nichols offers some advice for the beginner.

"Begin with yourself and work backward. You don't want to start with an important person and work down. So many people want to belong to someone famous like George Washington, and of course he didn't have any children so you'll be stymied right there.

"You must prove each step. You'll have blank spots, but you don't guess. If you do, put it in pencil, which says, 'this is an idea, but it may not be right.'"

Nichols says that locally she had found the State Historical Society to be helpful in her endeavors.

James Goodrich, associate director of the library, says the library is a key depository for individuals who want to begin researching their family tree.

"We have over 400,000 volumes of history," he explains. "This includes many books on the history of different countries and cities as well as family histories."

The library also has the largest state newspaper collection in the nation. Its collection of state census records from 47 states can obviously be of great use to those who want to learn of their past.

Nichols says in addition to reference materials, she gets much of her information from published inquiries she submits to different publications.

"I also write letters to people all over the United States," she says. "I even correspond with people in Alaska and Hawaii. I help them and they help me.

"Through these years I have had a lot of hits and misses and so have done some unnecessary work and still do," Nichols says. "The nice part is I feel like I've made so many friends by correspondence."

5. You are writing a story about the following speech by William B. Walstad, professor of economics and director of the National Center for Research in Economic Education, University of Nebraska. It was delivered to the American Economic Association. Write out the words from the speech that you will quote directly in your story. Then explain in two or three sentences why you chose to use each of those direct quotations.

There is one major finding that I wish to present in my remarks today: *our schools are producing a nation of economic illiterates!* Now if you don't believe me, then just go out and ask high school students some questions on basic economics and see how they respond. That's the type of study that I conducted with Dr. John Soper of John Carroll University. My conclusion is based on that research and related work.

The Test of Economic Literacy

Here's how it was done. First, the *Test of Economic Literacy*, a standardized multiple-choice test for eleventh and twelfth graders, was revised by a working committee of high school teachers and university professors. Then, each question was reviewed by a "blue-ribbon" national advisory committee that included Nobel laureate James Tobin, former AEA president William Baumol, bank president Karen Horn, and other top economists. Finally, the *Test of Economic Literacy* was administered by the National Center for Research in Economic Education at the University of Nebraska-Lincoln to a representative, national sample of 8,205 senior high school students.

The items in the test focus only on basic economic concepts as described in the *Framework for Teaching Economics*. This Joint Council publication was written by a distinguished group of economists and educators, and it outlines those essential ideas that should be included in the economics curriculum for our nation's schools. Using the *Framework* as the guide meant that the test measures knowledge of economic concepts and related issues that are discussed daily in the national media: tariffs and trade; economic growth and investment; inflation and unemployment; supply and demand; the

federal budget deficit; and the like. It is these economic topics that people are likely to read about or hear about in the news. I firmly believe that our high school students need to understand these ideas if they are to be able to function with any degree of economic literacy in roles as citizens, consumers, workers, or producers.

The Findings

What do the results show? Overall, typical high school students could correctly answer only 40 percent of the items. To put this in perspective, on a four-option multiple-choice test we would expect a 25 percent correct score just by guessing. So typical high school students score only about 15 percentage points above a chance score on this test. Clearly, 40 percent correct represents a failing grade under even the most liberal grading standards. *This level of economic knowledge among most high school students is shocking!*

Students showed especially poor understanding of questions related to the national and the international economy—subjects often discussed in the news and in Congress. Senior high schoolers were correct only 34 percent of the time on the national economy questions and only 36 percent of the time on international economic questions. To illustrate, consider the following:

1. Only 25 percent could correctly answer questions on inflation;

2. Just 27 percent realized that an increase in U.S. tariffs would have an adverse effect on our international trade;

3. Only 30 percent recognized that increasing investment could stimulate economic growth;

4. Just 39 percent knew what the Gross National Product measures; and

5. Just 45 percent recognized that a government budget deficit is produced when government spending exceeds tax revenues.

Student knowledge of the other areas—fundamental and microeconomic concepts—was only slightly better. On fundamental economic items students got 44 percent correct. On microeconomic items students scored 43 percent correct. The following performance on selected items indicates the extent of the economic illiteracy problem:

1. Only 27 percent could figure out the economic cost in a simple question about going to college;

2. Less than 30 percent recognized that a major cause of low incomes in the United States was lack of labor market skills;

3. Just 34 percent knew the definition of profits;

4. Just 47 percent knew the reason for a progressive income tax; and,

5. Just half understood that high wages usually depend on worker productivity.

Solutions

Well, we know what the problem is, but can anything be done to improve the level of economic understanding? The extensive body of research that has accumulated over the years indicates that three actions need to be taken to reduce the level of economic illiteracy in our schools.

First, school districts need to make a commitment to economic education from the elementary grades through high school. Instruction in reading, math, and science starts at an early age, and so should the vital subject of economics. Many research studies show that students do better in school districts where there is an established economics curriculum for all students across all grade levels. Currently, 28 states have made this commitment and require that economics be included in some form in the school curriculum.

Second, students should take a course in economics before they graduate from high school. Numerous research studies show that if students take a separate economics course in senior high school, this course is one sure way to improve economic understanding. All too often economics is simply left out of the list of required subjects in recent calls for educational reform. Our schools provide separate courses to make certain that kids learn math and science. The same will be necessary for economics. To date only 15 states in the U.S. have a mandate for students to take a course in economics before high school graduation.

Third, and the most critical, is to have teachers who are well-prepared to teach economics, whether they teach it as a separate course or include it in other subjects. Economics is a challenging subject and it must be taught well for students to improve their understanding. Teachers must know more economics than the students. In fact, teachers might be more willing to teach about the national and international economy if they had more knowledge of these areas. National research studies show that there is a direct link between the number of courses in economics a teacher has taken (or teacher knowledge of the subject) and the amount of economics that students learn. This means that if teachers understand the subject, then they are more likely to do a better job of teaching it.

Implications

Our nation cannot afford to have high school students who lack the basic skills to understand vital economic issues. Most high school graduates never go to college and even those who attend college may never take a course in economics. Without a solid education in economics at the pre-college level, many adults will never have the slightest chance of learning how the economy functions and their roles in the wealth-creating process. No wonder a national survey by the Hearst corporation concluded that "a large segment of the American public is sadly deficient in its knowledge of basic business and economic facts of life." The short- and long-term costs from economic illiteracy and poor economic decision-making are too great to be ignored by this nation.

Economic knowledge is also critical for maintaining a competitive position in a world economy. Japan clearly recognizes this relationship. All high school students in Japan are required to take economics. The course work is more intensive than in the U.S. and focuses more on national and international economics—the very areas where U.S. students do the worst and which are not stressed in our school curriculum. Our next generation of voters, consumers, producers, and investors will need a better economic education than past generations if they are to be prepared for the challenges of competition in a world economy. To do so, we must take the actions that are needed to correct this failing grade in economics.

6. Find three stories by three different authors or wire services covering a speech or a news conference by the president of the United States. Compare and analyze the use of direct and indirect quotations. Write 200 words about your findings.

CHALLENGE EXERCISE

7. **a.** Attend a meeting that you know your local paper will cover. Take down the direct quotations that you would use in a story. Then compare your quotes to those used in the report of your local paper. Write 200 words on the subject.

b. Do the same for a news conference.

c. Do the same for a speech.

5 Gathering and Verifying Information

1. You are writing a story about U.S. immigration policies and their impact on the work force. Find the mailing address, e-mail address and phone number of the closest field office of the U.S. Citizenship and Immigration Service, which would be a primary source of information for such a story. List at least five other possible sources.

2. You are writing a story about flood control along the major river in your area. What would be the primary source of information for such a story? List at least five other possible sources.

3. Your instructor will give you the names of 10 local people. Using reference materials available in your college, public library, or newspaper, determine the occupation of each.

4. Using online reference materials, write a half-page biographical sketch of each of the following people as if you were preparing a story for an impending visit of that person to your campus.
   a. Henry Aaron
   b. Ruth Bader Ginsburg
   c. Tom Harkin
   d. Katie Couric

    e. Kasey Kahne
    f. Venus Williams
    g. Barbara Boxer
    h. Al Sharpton
    i. Maya Angelou
    j. Jay Leno
    k. Sheryl Crow
    l. Helen Thomas
    m. Selena Quintanilla-Pérez
    n. Tiger Woods
    o. Andrea Mitchell

5. Using reference materials available online or located in your college or local library, answer the following questions:
    a. What was the final popular vote in the 2004 presidential election?

    b. What was the electoral vote in the same election?

6. Who are the U.S. senators from the following states?
    a. Florida
    b. Kansas
    c. Tennessee
    d. New Mexico
    e. Washington
    f. California
    g. Illinois
    h. New York
    i. Maine
    j. North Carolina

7. List the largest city in each of the following states:
    a. New Hampshire
    b. Connecticut
    c. Mississippi
    d. Utah
    e. Colorado
    f. Alabama
    g. Iowa
    h. Ohio
    i. Kentucky
    j. North Dakota

8. List the five most recent prime ministers of Canada:
    a.
    b.
    c.
    d.
    e.

9. What are the primary cash crops of the following countries?
    a. India
    b. Germany

    c. Kenya
    d. Romania
    e. Canada
    f. Colombia
    g. Argentina
    h. Egypt
    i. Mongolia
    j. New Zealand

10. Determine when your city was incorporated and what its population was in 1960, 1970, 1980, 1990 and 2000.

11. Without talking with your mayor or town supervisor, where would you find the following information about him or her?
    a. His or her address and telephone number.
    b. The amount he or she paid for his or her house.
    c. The number of cars he or she owns.
    d. The names and ages of his or her children, if any.
    e. What other property, if any, he or she owns.

12. Using the U.S. Securities and Exchange Commission Web site (www.sec.gov) or a similar financial database, determine the names of the principal officers of the IBM Corp. and their salaries. List at least the five top officers.

13. Using Morningstar (www.morningstar.com) or another online database, determine the closing price of a share of stock in the following companies for each trading day during the past week:
    a. Tyco International
    b. Texas Instruments
    c. R.J. Reynolds
    d. Apple Inc.
    e. IBM Corp.

14. Using any online service, call up the major news story of the day from the Associated Press and any other wire service (such as Reuters) and compare the two. Tell which is the better story and why.

15. Which database would be most useful in helping you locate magazine articles on the rising cost of newsprint? Why?

16. A local supermarket has just gone out of business. After interviewing the local managers of that store and the remaining stores, you decide that your story needs background information about trends in supermarket marketing. Determine what traditional sources of information you would use for background data or insight. Then outline a search strategy you might use to conduct a database search of material related to the topic.

17. You receive a press release stating that a local McDonald's hamburger outlet is the second most profitable in a six-state region. Determine what traditional sources of information you would use for background data or insight. Then outline a search strategy you might use to conduct a database search of material related to the topic.

18. Read the following stories, and then make a list of the obvious sources the reporters used to develop each story. List at least three other sources that could have been used to improve each story.

A. Farming is at the top of the state's killer occupation list. And if anyone is going to knock it from the top, it will probably be a mom.

Bad prices and competition from an increasing number of larger producers have put the squeeze on farmers, who are forced to maximize their land, capital, labor and time. The pressure, in turn, eliminates timeconsuming safety practices.

The Springfield University Extension Service has developed a three-year safety program that targets women, who are the best at starting safety practices on the farm and in the home, said David Baker, University Extension safety specialist.

Among dangerous occupations, farming ranks high, due to long hours, neglected machinery, farm animals and a wide range of ages among farmers, Baker said.

The job of safety guard is usually included in women's daily farm and housework challenges. Women teach values and attitudes to the next generation. They think more about safety and health because they deal with it every day, Baker said.

Women throughout the state, like Jan Hedeman, are doing farm work they may not have been trained to do. They have become truck drivers, grain haulers, tractor drivers and machinery operators.

They are also learning more efficient ways to protect their families from possible tragedies using these machines.

Hedeman is the president of the Dade County Extension Council. She and her husband, Terry, sponsored a Farm Women's Safety Seminar in February.

The seminar was the third in a series of one-day workshops scattered throughout the state in 11 counties from February to April. The seminars give the state's women hands-on experience with machinery and teach them how to prevent accidents. They also discuss various health issues.

Of 38 farm deaths in the state in 1999, 35 involved machinery, said Rusty Lee, an extension associate. Twenty-eight farmers were killed on tractors, five on mowers, two on other machinery, two by electrocution and one while tree cutting.

At the workshop on the Hedemans' farm, two emergency medical technicians showed the women how to perform first aid and contact emergency vehicles.

"You always know safety is important, but it's hard to

remember and practice all the time," Hedeman said. "These seminars are a good reminder.

"We own a mixture of tractors and other equipment, so the women were exposed to different brands and types of machinery. We learned bush hogs can be the most dangerous machines on the farm. We also went over tractor controls and PTO shafts."

Bush hogs are farming implements that hook onto the back of a tractor and are used to mow grasses. The tractor driver must be extremely careful. The spinning blade can spit out rocks like bullets and take out small trees easily.

The PTO, or power take-off, is a shaft that rotates at about 540 revolutions per minute. When not properly guarded, a person's clothes may become entangled in the shaft in a fraction of a second.

"It's obvious women are concerned about farm safety," Lee said. "We have been welcomed with open arms in every county."

Support for the program is coming from women's groups, including the Farm Bureau, the Agricultural Machinery Dealers Association, county fire and rescue personnel, community nurses and the University Extension staff, Baker said.

The National Institute for Occupational Safety and Health will fund the three-year project at a cost of $350,000. The workshops are only one part of the program.

The next women's safety seminar is March 5 in Lawrence County. To learn more, contact David Baker or Rusty Lee of University Extension at 555-2731.

B.   Red Cross officials are helping a Springfield family whose home was destroyed by fire Saturday, but they say they can't do it alone.

Springfield's Red Cross organization is asking for food, new or used clothing and household items to help the Heaster family of 1804 Grindley Ave.

The family's mobile home was destroyed by fire late Saturday afternoon. Although the blaze was under control within 10 minutes, structural damage was estimated at $8,000 and damage to the contents at $15,000. The fire started in the bathroom and was caused by faulty electrical wiring, Fire Marshal George Glenn said.

Shirley Heaster, her boyfriend, her brother and her four children, ranging in age from nine months to 10 years, were not in the home at the time of the fire. The family's cat and dog were killed in the fire.

Heaster and her family are staying with friends and family.

Red Cross officials visited the Heasters on Sunday and learned that the family needs more help, said Gena Pliske of the Red Cross.

Donations will be accepted at the Red Cross at 1805 W. Wartley St. from 9 a.m. to 4:30 p.m.

C.   The closing of Eighth Street between Walnut and Ash streets is one step closer to reality, as are plans for a town square and county administration building.

Some Springfield City Council members wanted to wait for a traffic study before making a decision on the county's request to close the block, but the study would have delayed plans for up to four months.

Now City Manager Diane Lusbey wants to bypass the study, which was the only thing delaying a decision on the street.

In a recommendation to the council tonight, Lusbey will tell members that once a decision is made, the city staff will work around any problems that may develop.

Lack of information about the impact on downtown traffic patterns and the future location of a new downtown fire station were some of the concerns council members voiced last Monday at a joint meeting between city and county officials.

Lincoln County Commissioner Nicole Ziden said closing Eighth Street is essential to the design of the new administration building.

"What we do with Eighth Street will determine what type of building and its placement," she said. "It's a fundamental question to this project."

Also affected by the decision are plans for a town square, which Commissioner Andrew Kramer said Springfield does not have.

With the courthouse addition nearly complete, now is the opportune time to address landscaping needs, he said.

"We may never have an opportunity like this again, or at least not for a long, long time," Kramer said.

Besides providing a public gathering place and a much-needed green space downtown, closing the block will provide a safer way for county employees to move between the courthouse and their new building.

Area business people also support closing the block, thereby removing the hazardous intersection at Eighth and Walnut streets.

"I'm in that intersection daily, and I am amazed that people don't get killed every day," said Jeanne Matten, who has an office in the Guitar Building.

The New York architectural firm of Les Dally, which was selected to design the administrative building, may be assisting local architects with designing the plaza, Ziden said.

Dally has experience with adding new government buildings to existing structures and planning green space areas. Dally was responsible for the veterans' memorial and state information center in the state capital.

Kramer said closing the block would not create much of a problem if the city considered changing some one-way streets to two-way streets again.

"It's one of the deals where you have to decide what you really want in the downtown area and then do it and make traffic work around it," he said.

Jose Rodriguez, assistant city manager, said the city is still reviewing sites for the new downtown fire station. He said the station will probably be located north of Broadway between Sixth Street and College Avenue.

19. Prepare a complete dossier on the life of movie director and producer Steven Spielberg as if you were about to interview him for a major story.

CHALLENGE EXERCISE
20. You have been assigned to write a business article on the endorsement income of basketball star Shaquille O'Neal. Find all the information you can on his various endorsement deals.

6 Reporting with Numbers

1. A local college releases figures showing that its total budget is $120 million. Of that total, $80 million comes from the state budget, $6 million from student tuition and the remaining $34 million from fees, grants and gifts.
   a. Figure the percentage of the college's budget that comes from each source.
   b. Identify the significance of each funding source.
   c. Using plain words instead of numbers, explain the proportion of funding that comes from different sources.

2. Springfield Mayor Juanita Williams speaks at a campaign rally for a Democratic candidate for Congress and criticizes the incumbent member of Congress, a Republican, for missing 53 roll-call votes last year.
   a. What facts about Williams and the Republican and Democratic candidates would you need to know to write a balanced story about roll-call votes? What sources would you need to contact?
   b. Using the Internet, find out how many roll-call votes were held in the U.S. House of Representatives during the last congressional session. Figure the percentage of votes the member of Congress from your district missed and attended. How does that attendance record compare with that of other members of the congressional delegation from your state?

3. Area school committees are releasing their annual budget figures after the beginning of the school year, and you are the education reporter. Here are some base figures:

	Students		Budget	
	2006	2007	2006	2007
Springfield	4,650	4,724	$23,250,000	$23,620,000
Newburg	2,325	2,362	$12,787,500	$12,991,000
Hampton	1,211	1,101	$4,450,425	$3,496,000
Middletown	1,004	1,213	$ 7,530,000	$7,530,000

   a. Figure the per capita spending in each school district in both budget years.
   b. Figure the percentage change in per capita spending in each school district.

4. Using the data from exercise 3, identify the following trends in the four school districts:
   a. Figure the percentage change in the number of students from year to year.
   b. Figure the percentage change in budgets from year to year.

5. Again using data from exercise 3, identify some of the basic financial issues facing the different school districts. Outline additional information that would be needed to write a balanced story about school funding. Suggest probable sources.

6. A group of resident advisers in the dormitories at Springfield University asks to meet with the editorial board of the campus paper about conditions on the job. They complain that many RAs have seen their adviser-to-resident ratio increase 200 percent since last year, although their pay rate has remained the same. In preparation for the meeting, you phone the university's Campus Living Office. The director tells you that some resident advisers have seen their workload increase because several wings of single rooms have been converted to double rooms to allow for lower prices for students living on campus. She also says that resident advisers in some dormitories have even higher workloads. The director has scheduled a meeting with the advisers for next week. The number of resident advisers affected is seven out of a total of 42. The seven resident advisers now serve 36 residents each, instead of 18 each. The total number of students living on campus is 1,357.

   a. To prepare for the editorial board meeting with the resident advisers, prepare the numerical figures necessary to ask appropriate questions. Outline additional financial information that would help you determine if the university and the resident advisers are being reasonable.

   b. Craft a tentative lead for the next day's paper using words, not percentage figures.

7. Your editor assigns you a story about prison sentences handed down in cases of aggravated assault. He gives you the following figures from an anticrime group that is lobbying for tougher sentencing guidelines. The cases represent the people convicted for aggravated assault in Springfield during one month in 2007.

Name	Sentence
Donald Kimball	1 year prison, 2 years probation
Christian Pelletier	1 year prison, 1 year probation
Robert Mitchell	14 months prison, 1 year probation
Nancy Newberry	1 year prison, 1 year probation
Mitchell Smith	1 year prison, 2 years probation
Lyle Rothstein	8 months prison, 1 year probation
Michael Hamlet	7 years prison, 5 years probation

   a. Calculate the average prison term for people convicted of aggravated assault, taking care to convert some of the terms to figures that will compare properly (months versus years).

   b. Calculate the median prison term for people convicted of aggravated assault.

   c. Explain why the average or median figure is the most accurate description of prison terms.

8. Local millionaire David Dankowski announces that he will provide low-interest loans of $1,000 for local low-income teenagers who go to college. He will charge a simple interest rate of 3 percent per year, the amount of interest he paid his uncle when he borrowed $100 to start his toy business in 1957.

   a. If a student accepts a $1,000 loan from Dankowski for just one year, how much will the student owe Dankowski after one year? After graduating in five years?

   b. If the student accepts a $1,000 loan for each of her five years in college, how much will she owe after graduation?

9. Joe's Cafe, a local coffee shop, raises its price on a cup of coffee from $1.00 to $1.25. The café had charged $1.00 since 1990.

    a. Calculate the percentage increase in the price of a cup of coffee.

    b. Adjust the $1.00 price for inflation in 2007. Is Joe's Cafe charging more in real dollars for a cup of coffee now than it was in 1990?

10. Mayor Juanita Williams says in a campaign speech that she is proud that starting teachers' salaries in Springfield have increased from an average of $20,000 per year in 1988 to $30,000 in 2007. Across town, Republican Jesse Abraham accuses Williams of coddling Springfield teachers with a 50 percent pay increase during her 19 years on the City Council in order to win votes.

    a. Using an inflation calculator (see site listed in your textbook), calculate how much the 1988 starting salary would be worth in 2007 dollars.

    b. Explain whether Williams' statement about starting salaries is accurate and fair.

    c. Explain whether the numbers behind Abraham's statement about Williams are accurate and fair.

11. Some officials are proposing a county sales tax of 1 percent on top of the state's 6 percent sales tax. Salespeople in businesses from boutiques to auto dealerships claim that shoppers will avoid their stores and shop in another county if the tax is imposed. You want to test those claims by examining the difference in costs caused by the higher taxes.

    a. Calculate the dollar increase in a consumer's cost in the county for a $25 shirt.

    b. Calculate the dollar increase in a consumer's cost for a $1,540 computer.

    c. Calculate the dollar increase in a consumer's cost for a $15,000 car.

    d. Explain the credibility of the claims about the sales tax and suggest possible sources to interview about the issue.

12. The state legislature is considering exempting restaurant food sales from the sales tax in the same way grocery sales are exempt.

    a. Explain how much fast-food patrons who pay $5 per meal would save in a year if they go out once a week for a year.

    b. Explain how much money people would save if they spend $20 per meal once a week for a year.

13. The local paper mill files forms with the city declaring that the mill is overvalued and should be assessed at a value of $80 million instead of the $136 million appraisal determined by the city.

    The millage rate is 23.80.

    How much tax revenue will the city lose if the paper mill wins the decision?

14. Refer in *News Reporting and Writing*, Ninth Edition to text pages 125–26 for Table 6.1 "General Fund — Summary" to answer the following questions, which require the kind of simple arithmetic that any reporter should be able to perform even without a calculator.

    a. Which category of appropriations shows the greatest percentage increase between the revised 2006 fiscal year expenditures and the 2007 budget? What is the percentage?

    b. In percentage terms, did the Police Department or the Fire Department receive the bigger increase between actual 2006 and adopted 2007?

c. Under Appropriation, note that personnel services appropriations have increased from $9.5 million in actual fiscal year 2006 to $12.2 million in adopted year 2007. Is personnel services' share of the total operating budget going up or down? Explain.

CHALLENGE EXERCISE

15. As Springfield becomes a more attractive place to live and as business grows, people have watched their property values increase. The millage rate is 18.75 and has remained the same since 1990.

    a. Calculate how much property taxes would go up for Springfield's median home, which the property appraiser valued at $65,000 in 1990 and at $100,000 in 2007.

    b. Adjust the tax and property value figures for inflation and calculate how much property values and property taxes have increased after accounting for inflation.

7 The Inverted Pyramid

The six questions that journalists traditionally ask themselves when categorizing information for leads are *who? what? when? where? why?* and *how?* For each of the following leads, identify the answers to the questions. Then indicate which two questions the writer believes to be the most important.

1. NEW YORK—A scientist dismissed from an Environmental Protection Agency panel on secondhand cigarette smoke after vigorous lobbying by the tobacco industry says he will fight to be reinstated.
   a. Who?

   b. What?

   c. When?

   d. Where?

   e. Why?

   f. How?

   g. Which does the writer believe are the two most important questions in this lead?
      1.

      2.

2. Springfield police arrested a local woman Thursday for allegedly filing a false police report of a rape last month.
   a. Who?

   b. What?

   c. When?

   d. Where?

   e. Why?

f. How?

g. Which does the writer believe are the two most important questions in this lead?
 1.

 2.

3. Rewrite the lead in exercise 2 to emphasize why.

4. The United Way Board of Directors will announce how it plans to allocate $425,000 when it meets at 2 p.m. tomorrow at the board's offices.
 a. Who?

 b. What?

 c. When?

 d. Where?

 e. Why?

 f. How?

 g. Which does the writer believe are the two most important questions in this lead?
 1.

 2.

5. After 400 students protested a proposed tuition increase at Springfield University on Friday, University President Michael Quinn agreed to reconsider his recommendation.
 a. Who?

 b. What?

 c. When?

 d. Where?

 e. Why?

 f. How?

 g. So what?

6. Here are the leads for the same story as they appeared in four newspapers:

      A. ST. LOUIS—The USA's top earthquake scientists are hooting at a prediction that a major earthquake will strike the Midwest in early December.

      B. ST. LOUIS—A national panel of earthquake experts ripped on Thursday the track record of Ibex Browning, the New Mexico climatologist who predicted a greatly increased chance of a quake around Dec. 3 along the New Madrid fault.

      C. ST. LOUIS—The nation's experts say that you, too, can predict the date of the next big earthquake in the Midwest with all the accuracy of the famed Ibex Browning. Just start throwing darts at a calendar.

      D. ST. LOUIS—Predictions of a major earthquake in the Midwest in early December are without scientific basis and could even be dangerous, experts said Thursday.

    a. Which of the four leads answers more of the six questions basic to all stories? Which questions does it answer?

    b. What is the first question answered in each of the four leads?
      A.
      B.
      C.
      D.

    c. Which is the best lead and why?

7. Search the Internet and find three stories on the same subject distributed on the same day. Identify the answers to the seven basic questions. How many paragraphs do you have to read to find the answers? If the "so what?" is missing, can you figure out what it should be?

8. Here are leads for the same story as they appeared in three newspapers:

      A. WASHINGTON—The USA's 40 million Social Security recipients will get an unexpected benefit from the inflation: fatter checks.

      B. WASHINGTON—The nation's 40 million Social Security beneficiaries will receive a 5.4 percent cost-of-living increase in January, the biggest boost in eight years, the government announced Thursday.

      C. WASHINGTON—The nation's 40 million Social Security recipients will receive their biggest increase in 81½ years in January, a 5.4 percent increase that will average an extra $31 a month.

a. Which of the three leads answers more of the six questions basic to all stories? Which questions does it answer?

b. What is the first question answered in each of the three leads?
   A.
   B.
   C.

c. Which is the best lead and why?

d. Write a "you" lead based on the information in the three leads.

9. Here are the facts: The Springfield University Faculty Council Monday approved a plan to convert to plus/minus grading from the standard A/B/C/D/F plan in existence. At other universities that have adopted the system, students' grade point averages declined. The proposal will go to the university provost for final action.

   Write a lead for your campus newspaper to emphasize this story's relevance to your readers.

10. Here are the facts: The university provost has announced that beginning next semester, students will be able to register for classes on the Internet. Unless they are on probation, students will no longer have to obtain advisers' signatures.

   Write a lead for your campus newspaper to emphasize the story's usefulness and relevance to your readers.

11. WHO: Duane La Chance, 55, Springfield, a pipe fitter employed by Gross Engineers, a company based in Springfield.
   WHAT: Suffered third-degree burns and was listed in serious condition Tuesday night in the intensive care unit at Springfield Hospital.
   WHEN: 3 p.m. Tuesday.
   WHERE: Springfield Municipal Power Plant, 222 Power Drive.
   HOW: La Chance was installing new pipes on the roof of the power plant when he accidentally touched with a piece of angle iron a power line carrying 15,000 volts.
   SOURCE: Henry Rosen, project manager for Gross Engineers.

a. In 35 words or fewer, write an immediate-identification lead using the preceding information.

b. Using the same information, write a delayed-identification lead.

12. WHO: James W. Cunning, 20, 505 W. Stewart Road, and Wayne Clay, 19, Route 1, Springfield.

WHEN: 11:45 p.m. Saturday.

WHERE: On U.S. 63, one-tenth of a mile north of Blue Ridge Road.

WHAT AND HOW: Cunning was driving south on U.S. 63 in a 1994 Chevrolet; Clay was driving north in a 1992 Ford. Clay apparently crossed the center line and struck the Cunning vehicle, according to an officer in the Lincoln County Sheriff's Department. Cunning is in satisfactory condition at Springfield Hospital.

a. Write an immediate-identification lead of fewer than 35 words.

b. Write a delayed-identification lead of fewer than 35 words.

13. WHO: Sheryl Crow, singer
WHAT: Appointed to Alumni Board
WHERE: University of Missouri
WHY: She is a famous alumnus.
WHEN: Yesterday.

Write an immediate-identification lead of fewer than 35 words.

14. WHO: Amtrak train called the Colonial.
WHAT: Collided with three Conrail locomotives on a switch that merges four tracks into two.
WHERE: Near Chase, Md.

WHEN: 1:30 p.m. yesterday.

WHY: Larry Case, Amtrak spokesman: The Conrail diesels, like the
         Amtrak, were northbound. The Conrail had apparently run a
         stop sign.

OTHER: At least 15 dead, 175 injured. Worst accident in Amtrak's
         history.

Assume that you are writing an article for your newspaper's Web site, which will publish it immediately.

15. An announcement came at the end of a news conference in Springfield City Hall yesterday. Mayor Juanita Williams was asked whether she had decided to be a candidate for re-election. Williams said that she would not. She said she would support First Ward Council Member Hong Xiang.
   a. Write a lead for your news organization's Web site.

   b. From your lead, identify:
   Who
   What
   Where
   When
   How

16. There are several topics on the agenda of the Springfield City Council tomorrow night. One is the proposed approval of an agreement negotiated with Local 45, which represents 90 percent of city workers. It provides for a 4 percent pay increase. Another is action on a proposed ordinance that would restrict commercial signs in the downtown district. Yet another is an ordinance regulating the amount of noise permitted. It was requested by residents who live near fraternity and sorority houses. As always, the council meets at 7 p.m. at City Hall.
   a. Write a lead for an advance for tomorrow morning's city paper.

b. Write a lead for tomorrow morning's campus paper.

17. The Springfield Board of Education met Monday night. Superintendent Max Schmidt reported that enrollment was 17 more than expected but that there were no other problems associated with last week's school opening. Schmidt said he would be negotiating with the Maintenance Workers Union next week. He said they have already agreed on binding arbitration if necessary. He then presented the board with a revision in the school manual. This is the first time the manual has been revised in 20 years, he said. "It's overdue. There have been several changes in the law and the mores that we must recognize." Board member Janet Biss said she opposed several of the changes. She particularly did not like giving students permission to wear their hair any length, to drive their cars to school and to carry cell phones. "These rules were good enough for my generation; they're good enough for the students now." Other changes were that teachers could not use physical punishment on students, teachers must report all violations of school policy to the building principal, students convicted of using any kind of drug will be suspended for no more than 20 days, and all students found with drugs in the school will be turned over to juvenile authorities. The board voted 5-2 to approve the new manual. Student Body President Ryan Rodriguez said he welcomed the school board to the 21st century. The board then accepted a low bid from Farmer's Dairy to provide milk at 3 cents a pint.

a. Write a summary lead for the high school newspaper using the preceding information.

b. Write a summary lead for the local daily newspaper's Web site using the preceding information.

c. Write a multiple-element lead for the school newspaper using the same information.

d. Write a multiple-element lead for the daily's Web site using the same information.

e. Write a "you" lead for the high school newspaper.

18. The two candidates for mayor debated last night at the high school. The debate was sponsored by the League of Women Voters. About 245 people attended. More than 300 were expected. Republican candidate Jesse Abraham said he would try to accomplish three things if elected: (1) He would widen and improve Main Street; (2) he would buy land to build a city park on the south side; and (3) he would streamline council meetings. Democratic candidate Juanita Williams, the incumbent, accused Abraham of logrolling. She said he was trying to give something to everyone. "The city tax base can't support the kinds of programs he is proposing," she said. She also revealed that she has learned that Abraham's largest contributors are merchants who own land along Main Street. "They're the only ones who would benefit from widening the street," she charged. Abraham said he had not received a single donation from the merchants. Questioned from the audience, he said he would not make public the names of donors in his campaign until after the election on Nov. 3. League President Sally Harm thanked the candidates for a good debate and said she thought the evening was a success.

a. Write a summary lead using the preceding information.

b. Write a multiple-element lead using the same information.

19. Gary Roets, 49, 6204 Ridge Road, and Duane Craig, 51, 6206 Ridge Road, collided when they backed out of their driveways Tuesday morning. Both were on their way to work. Damage to the Roets vehicle was estimated at $250; to the Craig vehicle, about $400. Information is from the Springfield police.

    Write a lead with a twist.

20. Identify the "so what?" information in the following excerpt. Is it sufficient? Explain.

    > Terry Woolworth lost her health and her car after a drunken driver smashed into her last December. Unable to work, she then lost her business and her house.
    >
    > Now she has lost confidence in the legal system.
    >
    > The 35-year-old Detroit woman learned recently that the drunken driver who hit her—and who now has at least five alcohol-related convictions—had his six-month jail sentence in her case overturned and never served a day behind bars.
    >
    > "This has destroyed my life, and the justice system has treated it like a joke," Woolworth said. "My God, look at his record, and he's still out on the streets."
    >
    > Woolworth is one of many who regularly lose in a drunken-driving numbers game that is stacked against public safety, some judges say.
    >
    > Woolworth's case lends weight to the debate about how Detroit's chronic drunken drivers should be handled when they enter the justice system.

21. Find three news stories on the same subject from different sources, such as a *Washington Post* version, an Associated Press version, and a *New York Times* version. Count the number of words in each of the first three paragraphs. Which version is easiest to understand? Which answers the seven questions? What are the differences in news judgment among them? If a news Web site such as CNN.com or MSNBC.com has its own version, include it in the news analysis. If the site is using an AP story, see if the site has edited it differently for a Web audience.

22. The paragraphs in the following stories have been arranged out of order. Renumber the paragraphs in the inverted pyramid format. The six key questions and the transition words in the story will provide the clues to help you put the paragraphs in correct order.

A. 1. Children also spend more time on homework because they learn how to study using the computer, he says.

2. NYU graduate students observed 40 families in New York, Connecticut and New Jersey who have home computers, and Professor Joe Giacquinta is analyzing their computer use.

3. "Families appreciate each other a bit more than when Dad was watching TV and the son was playing his guitar. They're spending more time together at home because they're having fun working on their computer," Giacquinta says. He plans a four-year study of 2,000 families.

4. Families with home computers spend more time together and watch less TV, and the children do more homework, say preliminary findings in a New York University study.

5. The Census Bureau says about 25 million families now have home computers.

6. As more and more homes get computers, the technological revolution "could alter the structure of the family," says Giacquinta.

The correct order:

B. 1. Some scientists are concerned that such gene manipulation experiments might create harmful organisms, which might then escape and infect the public.

2. "Scientifically, we're ready to go ahead," said Dr. Wallace Rowe of the National Institute of Allergy and Infectious Diseases. He said work could begin in January if not blocked by court action.

3. Ferdinand Mack, a lawyer who lives near the Frederick, Md., laboratory, is trying to block the experiment by lawsuit. But the government asked a federal court Wednesday to let the National Institutes of Health proceed.

4. The government hopes to conduct a unique animal experiment in a former Army germ warfare lab next month to assess the hypothetical hazards of gene transplant research.

5. The experiment will take genetic material called DNA from a mouse cancer virus and splice it to the hereditary matter of a common bacterium.

6. Scientists then will feed and inject the bacteria into germ-free mice and hamsters to see if they develop infections.

The correct order:

23. Using your *Associated Press Stylebook* or the abbreviated version of it found in Appendix 2 of *News Reporting and Writing*, Ninth Edition, correct the following for style errors. Also use the Springfield City Directory in the back of this workbook to check names and addresses.

Springfield University President Michael Quint said today that he will recommend to the Board of Curators that tuition be increased by 6% each of the next two years.

The Curators meet at 10 a.m. Friday morning in room 249, Student Union, 322 University Avenue.

Springfield Student Association President Milo Nishada said he would oppose the recommendation. "The University is trying to balance the budget on the backs of students, and it's not fair," he said.

24. From the following information, write a news story using the inverted pyramid style. Use the type of lead you think is appropriate. Again, use the Springfield City Directory to check names and addresses.

Springfield police were called to the corner of Ninth and Elm streets at 4:30 p.m. Monday to investigate a two-car accident. After arriving, they called for an ambulance because they had two people injured. Two people were believed dead. Witnesses told police that the car in which the injured persons were riding was heading south on Ninth Street and went through a red light. It hit the other car broadside. The other car rolled over three times and came to rest against a light pole. At the hospital, the victims were identified as James and Martha Westhaver. James was 55. His wife was 60. James Westhaver was president of the Merchants National Bank, the largest bank in Springfield. Injured were James West, 43, and Samuel Blackwater, 32, both city employees in the Parks and Recreation Department. West suffered a broken leg and possible concussion; Blackwater had two broken arms and a broken nose. Police ticketed West for careless and imprudent driving. But Prosecuting Attorney James Taylor said he would investigate before determining whether involuntary manslaughter charges should be lodged against West. A bank official said Westhaver had been employed there for 33 years. He was named president on Jan. 1, 1975. He was also chairman of the United Way this year and treasurer of the Chamber of Commerce. His wife hosted a talk show on KTGG, a local television station. Funeral arrangements are incomplete.

25. Monica Drummond, 26, of 4527 W. Fourth St., and Jim Poplar, 28, of 5642 N. 11th St., were arrested on burglary charges. Police said the two broke into 14 houses in three neighborhoods over a 23-day period and made off with 200 items valued at $43,000.
   a. Identify which numbers you would use later in the story and which you would eliminate completely.

   b. Write a lead focusing on the most important elements.

CHALLENGE EXERCISE

26. From the following sets of information, write two news stories, both using the inverted pyramid style.

    A.   Four o'clock this morning, one day before opening of racing season. Lincoln Downs Race Track, Springfield. A fire in a barn where 25 horses were stabled. Dead are 15 horses: 13 thoroughbred and two saddle horses. Ten escaped, including two who stampeded through the barnyard with their backs on fire. Arson is suspected as the cause. The barn had been a one-story wooden structure. Only several rows of charred wooden supports remain after the fire. An arson squad has been called to the scene. The fire smoldered until noon. A jockey, Albert Ramos, of Miami, Fla., watched workers as they cleaned up the area. "Those are my best friends," he said, pointing to the surviving horses. "I love horses more than I do people. I feel like I want to cry."

    Statements from officials: Dan Bucci, assistant general manager of the track: "It could have been of an incendiary nature because it started in the middle of the barn, not at the end. The only heaters and electrical outlets were in the tack rooms at the ends of the barn."

    Bernard Perry, fire chief: "The fire exploded near the center of the barn. Flames were shooting out of the building when we got here. The fire is definitely suspicious."

    B.   Randy Cohen, Christy Wapniarski, Daniel Perrin, Tammy Ennis—all students at Springfield University, at Daytona Beach, Fla.—went sailing yesterday in a 16-foot catamaran. About 5 p.m. the boat sprang a leak and capsized. The four hung on to one of the catamaran's pontoons through the night. They were wearing no life jackets, and the Atlantic Ocean's current was strong. At dawn they decided to swim to shore at Ormond Beach 4 miles away. Randy Cohen, 19, was about 20 feet in front of Christy Wapniarski, 19, when he heard her call for help. She said a shark had attacked her. Cohen called to Ennis, who was 10 feet ahead of him, to help, but she yelled, "Randy, don't go back there; you'll get eaten too." By the time Cohen had swum back to Wapniarski, she was unconscious and he could see no sign of a shark. He put his arms around her shoulders and began swimming for shore. Perrin, 20, had been swimming behind the other three. He swam to the aid of Cohen and Wapniarski and checked her pulse. He told Cohen that Wapniarski was dead, but Cohen refused to let go. He swam with her another 15 or 20 minutes until he was exhausted; then he let her go. It took the three students six more hours to reach shore. Cohen was bitten by dozens of Portuguese men-of-war. He is in Halifax Hospital, Daytona Beach. The others were examined at the hospital and released. You, as the reporter, talked to Cohen by phone in his hospital room.

8 Writing to Be Read

1. Choose precisely the right word in the following:
   a. What was the (affect, effect) of the victory?
   b. (Because, Since) he lied, he was expelled.
   c. A painful ordeal is (tortuous, torturous).
   d. Let's go four miles (further, farther) before we make camp.
   e. The parties signed a(n) (verbal, oral) agreement.
   f. The diver carried an (air, oxygen) tank to the water.
   g. The prisoners (alluded, eluded) the guards.
   h. Sentences with (less, fewer) words are easier to understand.
   i. The lawyer (convinced, persuaded) the jury that his client was innocent.
   j. They are putting up a (cement, concrete) building.
   k. Any spelling is (all right, alright).
   l. The speaker (eluded, alluded) to his opponent.
   m. The president expects to win the ERA voting (block, bloc).
   n. Seven (fliers, flyers) completed the mission.
   o. My desk is different (from, than) yours.
   p. The city plans to upgrade its (sewage, sewerage) system.
   q. (Because, While) that was not the case, John continued to believe it.
   r. The judge hopes the jury members are (disinterested, uninterested) in the case.
   s. The bomb squad was (sited, sighted) at the apartment complex.
   t. Union members said they would strike Saturday if their (demands, requests) hadn't been met.
   u. The whole is (composed, comprised) of its parts. The whole (composes, comprises) the parts.
   v. The weather changes (continually, continuously).
   w. The (council, counsel, consul) is the governing body of the city.
   x. The (council, counsel, consul) often works overseas for the government.
   y. I conducted an (exhausting, exhaustive) search for the information.
   z. I am (anxious, eager) to learn all I can.

2. Be clear. Rewrite the following:

   "It's the most comprehensive and complicated labor relations law in the country," John Brown, lawyer for the Brown and Jones law firm in Milwaukee, said about a recent amendment to Wisconsin Statute 111.70, the Municipal Employees Relations Act.

Brown was one of two speakers Tuesday at an arbitration workshop for school boards and district administrators sponsored by Cooperative Educational Services Agency District 12. The workshop was in Springfield.

3. Rewrite the following:

The party of the first part, hereinafter known as Jack, and the party of the second part, hereinafter known as Jill, ascended or caused to be ascended an elevation of undetermined height and degree of slope, herein after referred to as "hill."

Whose purpose it was to obtain, attain, procure, secure, or otherwise gain acquisition to, by any and-or all means available to them a receptacle or container, hereinafter known as "pail," suitable for the transport of a liquid whose chemical properties shall be limited to hydrogen and oxygen, the proportions of which shall not be less than or exceed two parts for the first mentioned element and one part for the latter. Such combination will hereinafter be called "water."

4. Rewrite the following sentences to make them clear.
  a. The car is in the garage which he smashed just a block from his home.

  b. There is a lecture tonight about juvenile delinquency in the student lounge.

  c. Everyone stared at the girl who was dancing with the dean in the lowcut gown.

  d. Having spilled paint all over the carpet, my wife was annoyed with me.

  e. He gave the sweater to a friend that he had won in track.

f. He was strangled to death in his bed.

g. Cooking in a fireplace is a good alternative energy source.

h. The Cardinals allowed James Carver to get loose on two punt returns of 35 and 16 yards to set up touchdown drives of 41 and 28 yards to turn a 14-3 halftime lead into a 24-point margin halfway through the third quarter.

i. He ripped his pants jumping over a fence.

j. The company said their earnings are down from last year.

k. The horse is an 8-year-old gelding trained by the owner who races with his wife.

l. Sheriff Burton Stephan entered a plea of guilty to charges of second-degree sexual abuse of a child under the age of 4 at his arraignment Friday.

m. The toddler sits in a high chair across the table, waiting patiently to begin drawing.

n. For the second time this week, Tampa police Friday shot and killed a man who they say pinned an officer between two cars.

5. The budget for Springfield University was $25 million in 2000 and $30 million in 2007. In-state tuition rose from $10,000 in 2000 to $15,000 in 2007. Enrollment remained virtually unchanged.

a. Figure the percentage of increase for the budget.
b. Figure the percentage of increase for tuition.
c. Identify the possible significance of those percentages.

6. Is the opening to this story exposition or narration? How do you know?

During his years as America's noisiest preacher, Billy James Hargis likened himself to the Old Testament prophet Ezekiel—a "watchman on the wall" ordered to "blow the trumpet" of warning against sin and evil.

And could he ever wail on that horn. In the fifties, the Tulsa evangelist launched a "Christian Crusade" against communism. His crusading culture warriors, including Youth Director David A. Noebel, climbed to the ramparts to sound one continuous air-raid siren against the barbarians at the gate.

In the process, Hargis, an imposing man with the physique of Oliver Hardy and the lung power of Ethel Merman, scared up enough money to travel the globe and amass fancy homes, summer retreats and expensive paintings.

No other preacher of his era possessed Hargis's combination of salesmanship, charm, fearmongering and oratory, which decades ago earned him the label "doomsday merchant on the far right" and today a reputation as one of the century's most effective orators.

And no other preacher self-destructed so spectacularly.

7. Is the opening to this story exposition or narration? How do you know?

Connie Pitts's voice quavers as she speaks into the emergency room radio. She has repeated the lines calmly many times before—but always to begin drills. "This is Deaconess Medical Center calling all Spokane area hospitals. This is your hospital control center. This is a disaster call."

Playing in Pitts's mind is the horrific warning just relayed to the hospital from a lieutenant at Fairchild Air Force Base: "We've got five . . . 12 . . . 17 wounded and two dead. They're all gunshot wounds."

Five nurses and Greg Jones, the only doctor in the emergency room, look at each other in disbelief.

8. This story contains dialogue:

The entry wound is deceiving, as if a pencil punctured the skin. The exit wound is jagged and deep. Bambino has seen nothing this gory—not even the patient with a hatchet buried in his back.

"I'll bet it was an AK-47," says Russell Oakley, an orthopedic surgeon. Sam's voice surprises the doctors: "I thought it was an M-16."

The boy is talking, but Bambino sees terror in his eyes. "I'm scared," he says. "Am I going to die?"

Bambino, thrilled that Sam can wiggle his toes, tells him he will live. "Just squeeze my hand when it hurts, and hold still."

a. What does the writer do to re-create dialogue? How does it change the scene for the reader?

b. Convert this example to traditional journalistic quotation. Which is better, dialogue or quotation, and why?

9. In the following excerpt, circle the concrete details the writer uses to recreate the scene she saw.

> Billy Ross Sims is handcuffed and sweating. Not an easy combination.
>
> As perspiration beads up on his forehead, then drips into his eyebrows, Sims—afraid of losing his train of thought, his rant—dips his head down to clear away the sweat by dragging his face across the lap of his white prison overalls.
>
> His head darts back up, and it's as though he never stopped talking. Talking and grimacing, talking and sweating—working himself up into an anguished frenzy, determined to recall and relay every detail of the interminably long story of his wrongful imprisonment.

Can you see Sims? Is it as if you are watching a video? Take out the concrete details. How much information is left?

10. Here are three ways to treat essentially the same information. Identify whether the sentence(s) is(are) simple, compound, complex or compound-complex and discuss how the sentence structure changes the relationship of the facts and ideas expressed in the clauses. Which of the three is the most explicit?

a. He tried to come back to work too soon, and a large blood clot killed him.

b. Because he tried to come back to work too soon, a large blood clot killed him.

c. He tried to come back to work too soon. A large blood clot killed him.

11. a. Rewrite the following into no fewer than four sentences. Each of the sentences should be between 10 and 15 words.

> Then, suddenly, the crowd perked up. Bush had emerged from the Senator Hotel and was coming up a sidewalk through the park of the capitol grounds. Secret Service agents accompanied him.
>
> He stopped to return greetings from the crowd.
>
> The spectators, restrained by a rope, pressed forward to say hello.

b. Is the rewrite as good as the original? Why or why not?

12. Change the length of the following sentences by breaking them up or combining them. Pay attention to the pacing and rhythm you are creating. You may add conjunctions.

> Once they found a dead man. The desert all around him was ripped up as if he'd gone berserk. They could see marks on the ground. He crawled on his belly, swimming across the sand. Sometimes they find people with their shoes and clothes piled neatly beside them where they decided to lie down and peacefully die. When the body temperature soars, the brain seems to cook; people pitch off their clothes. To escape the heat, they bury their heads in the sand in the hope of cooling their craniums, but still they keep coming, day after day. Night after night.

13. Count the words in each sentence in the following story. Rewrite the story to give it more sentence length variety. Now count the words in each sentence again. Which version is better? Why?

> Almost three times as many students as usual were absent from Shelton public schools Monday. It appears that a "flulike illness" may be at least partly to blame.
>
> Neither Sam Ford nor John Simmons is ready to declare a flu epidemic. Ford is city health director, and Simmons is assistant director of epidemiology for the state.
>
> Boone, Chippewa and Columbia counties have reported "very widespread cases of flulike illness," Simmons said. Tests that could identify the virus as an influenza strain will not be complete for several weeks.

The tests involve taking blood samples during and after a person's illness to isolate possible flu strains. But the patient must recover before a final determination can be made, Simmons said.

Positive identification of the flu virus has not been made yet, Ford said. "It is quite evident that incidents of flulike illness have increased recently. Some of it is probably real flu, but we have no proof of that yet."

Simmons said Monday that excessive absences had not been reported in any of the state's public schools.

But local public schools reported 1,869 students absent Monday, compared with an average of 450 to 600 children.

Some flu cases were reported earlier, but Simmons said the number of reported illnesses began increasing after the holidays. Holiday travel and increased contact with family and friends may be responsible for the number of illnesses, he said.

14. Underline the transitions in your rewritten response to the previous question.

15. a. Underline the transitions in the following excerpt. Then read it aloud without the transitions.

> Since 1949, the federal government has quietly spent hundreds of millions of taxpayers' dollars building—and then abandoning—nearly a dozen pilot plants and experimental facilities to produce synthetic fuels.
> Time and again, the plants showed that it was possible to turn coal into synthetic crude oil or natural gas.
> And time and again, the government and its contractors in private industry walked away from the plants, always stopping short of actual commercial production.
> Now, under the Energy Security Act that became law in June, the government intends to distribute not just hundreds of millions, but billions of tax dollars to oil companies to construct yet more pilot synthetic fuel plants and experimental facilities to conduct yet more tests.

   b. Add transitions to the following story to improve the flow and to make it easier to understand.

> The nation's largest teachers union issued a task force report today urging that public schools be "totally restructured" to meet the needs of tomorrow's students.
>
> The National Education Association's Blue Ribbon Task Force on Educational Excellence was established a year ago. Its 18-page report consisted mainly of a lengthy

list of suggested educational reforms, including better teaching conditions and sharply higher average salaries of $29,000 to attract better people into the profession.

"An Open Letter to America on Schools, Students, and Tomorrow" was being released at a news conference in Minneapolis two days before the 1.6 million-member teachers union begins a four-day annual meeting in that city.

"All the many national reports on education released so far have lacked one critically important element: the perspective of the men and women who teach and serve our nation's young people," NEA President Mary Hatwood Futrell said in the introduction to the report.

Education will start earlier, it said. New technology will enhance learning, but books, discussions, lab experiments, writing and lectures will still play major roles in learning. Adults will return to school and view learning as a lifelong activity.

  c. Underline the words and phrases used as transitions, both between paragraphs and within paragraphs.

Shaggy, suspendered and sporting a tatty aviator's cap with the earflaps lowered, George Ballis is a transplanted Minnesotan who moved to California's Central Valley in 1953.

Ballis has been asking barbed questions ever since. He lives in a rambling bungalow embraced by grapevines and orange trees, where he plots the latest assault on California's agribusiness establishment, or, as he prefers, "the biggies."

Depending on your point of view, Ballis is either a populist firebrand slugging it out for truth, justice and the American way, or he is simply a loud, misguided pain in the neck.

Either way, he is in the middle of the fierce and occasionally vicious skirmishing over government water subsidies 20 miles west of Fresno in the Rhode Island-size Westlands Water District. Last year, the district's cotton, tomatoes, barley, wheat, cantaloupes and other crops were cashed in for more than a half-billion dollars.

This cornucopia is made possible by the federally financed San Luis Unit, a reclamation project that began delivering rivers of water to Westlands in 1968. The project was designed to benefit small farmers—limiting water rights to 160 acres (320 acres for a married farming couple) with only a few exceptions.

However, according to government documents, roughly half of Westlands' half-million acres exceeds the acreage ceiling. The entire district is owned by about 250 landowners, including Southern Pacific Railroad, which holds 105,000 acres. Other large landowners include the Boston Ranch with 26,000 acres.

16. Identify the type of figure of speech in the following:
  a. Like the conductor of a 1,500-piece orchestra, Quinn believes his job as pastor is important, but he adds, "It's the people who live out the tunes."

b. The autumn trees are skeletons.

c. She doesn't realize that she's smacking her gum like a cow just introduced to a fresh field of grass.

d. The mother grinned like a 5-year-old at Christmas.

e. The black lampposts covered with snow are now Charlie Chaplin dolls.

17. Write a sentence or two describing each of the following. Appeal to one or more of the five senses. Use similes, metaphors and other figures of speech.
   a. Dynamite exploding inside a student's locker.

   b. Fingernails against a chalkboard.

   c. Children scrambling for candy thrown by Santa, who is riding in a sleigh in a Christmas parade.

   d. Thousands of dead fish washed up on shore.

   e. A rock hitting a plate-glass window.

   f. A cat howling.

   g. Garbage strewed about from a toppled can.

   h. A turtle's shell.

18. The university's budget is $228 million. It has 25,000 students. The national debt is $5 trillion. There are 283 million people in the United States.

    Explain the national debt using an analogy to these or other figures you might know.

19. The star of your college men's basketball team is 7 feet 3 inches tall. The average height for males is 5 feet 9 inches. The average height for a seventh-grade male is 5 feet 1 inch. The smallest man on the university wrestling team is 4 feet 11 inches.

    Explain the height of the wrestler by using an analogy to one or more of the facts given above.

20. Rewrite this lead to emphasize relevance and usefulness and clarity. You may use more than one paragraph if necessary. Assume you are writing for a newspaper in New Orleans.

    Hoping to prevent a recurrence of the wrongdoing uncovered during a recent nine-month undercover investigation at one of its main work sites, the New Orleans Sewerage & Water Board plans to hire a chief of security and devise a plan to prevent crimes by employees.

21. Rewrite the opening of this story, using more than one paragraph if necessary:

    A 10-year study of an increasingly popular surgical technique used to correct poor distance vision shows that the method is reasonably safe and effective but that it might lead to an accelerated decline in the ability to see things up close, researchers said Wednesday.

    The study, the longest and most detailed on the aftermath of the surgical procedure, radial keratotomy, concludes that it can have long-term benefits in correcting myopia, a common condition in which light from a distant object focuses in front of the retina to produce blurred images.

But a previously little-known effect of the surgery—gradual changes in the eye that result in progressively fuzzier close-up vision—should be a consideration in deciding whether to have the operation, the study concluded.

22. You read in Chapter 8 that the following excerpt was jammed full of detail. Now circle the concrete details in the story. Could you improve this passage?

Two people died Thursday when a backhoe fell off a truck's flatbed and sliced the top off an oncoming vehicle near Fairchild Air Force Base.

The top of the Suburban, from about hood height, was shorn off by the backhoe's bucket. The front seats were forced backward, and the dashboard, roof and steering wheel were torn off.

Parts of the car lay in a heap of crumpled metal and glass under the overpass. The silver Suburban was identifiable only by a 1983 owner's manual lying in the dirt nearby.

Both victims wore seat belts, but in this case, that was irrelevant, Sale said. Both suffered severe head injuries.

Sleeping bags, a Coleman cooler and fishing equipment scattered on the highway and in the back of the Suburban suggested a camping trip. Unopened cans of Pepsi were jammed behind the front seat of the car.

23. Good reporting makes good writing possible. From the following set of facts, write a news story.

WHO: Gary Evenson, 33, of Springfield, the driver.
WHAT: Ran into a road-construction barrier, went off the road, rolled
         over three times before the car caught on fire. Evenson rolled
         out of the car. Another motorist pulled him to safety. Evenson
         is hospitalized with a broken arm, a slight concussion and
         burns on 50 percent of his body. He is in satisfactory condition
         at Springfield Hospital.
WHERE: On Interstate 70, 20 miles west of Springfield.
WHEN: Monday at 3 p.m.
WHY: Evenson said he fell asleep.

24. Use the information from the preceding exercise and rewrite your story. Add the following information that a good reporter was able to obtain by asking more questions.

> Evenson was driving a new green-and-white Pontiac Bonneville and was on his way to Kansas City, where he was to be married next weekend. The wedding has been postponed. In order to get two weeks' vacation, he had worked 16-hour days for two weeks, and he was very tired. He had purchased the car just before he left St. Louis and was going to surprise his fiancée with it. He was so excited about showing it to her that he decided to leave right after work instead of sleeping first. "I didn't even have insurance on the car," Evenson said. "This is a terrible thing."
>
> His fiancée, Nancy Mohr, 33, of Lansing, Mich., said she didn't care about the car. "I'm just happy Gary is alive. We can always buy another car."
>
> Police said Evenson hit 24 barrels, which were on the road near the construction site. His car stopped 300 feet from where he hit the first barrel. He was ticketed for careless and imprudent driving.

25. From the following facts, write a news story.

WHO:	Marcelle Sosinski, 37, of 2990 W. Hanover St., DePere, Ill.
WHAT:	Has offered a $500 reward for the return of her dog.
WHERE:	The dog was lost or stolen in Springfield while the Sosinski family was attending the Lincoln County fair.
WHEN:	Saturday evening.
HOW:	The dog, a German shepherd, was sitting outside a restaurant while the Sosinskis were eating. When they came out, the dog was gone.

26. Use the information from the preceding exercise and rewrite your story. Add the following information that a reporter obtained by asking more questions.

> The dog was five years old. It was a guide dog for the Sosinskis' daughter, Mary, who is 12. It cost them $3,800 for the dog and its training. The money to buy the dog was raised by members of the Sosinskis' church, Sacred Heart Catholic Church. The church members also raised the reward money. Marcelle Sosinski thinks the dog was stolen. "Duke wouldn't leave. He was too well-trained. He loved Mary too much. He

had to be stolen. He had to be tricked," she said. The Sosinskis slept in their car that night and returned to the fairgrounds the next morning to resume their search. "We have to find that dog," Mrs. Sosinski said. "He's not just a guide dog; he's Mary's best friend."

27. What technique does the writer use to communicate action and tension?

> As the battered 16-year-old girl is moved onto the resuscitation bed in the emergency room at Poudre Valley Hospital, Dr. Lilly Conrad barks out orders.
> "Let's get her clothes cut off. Set up for a big central line. And a chest tube," she says, placing the stethoscope on the girl's ribs. "I don't hear any breath sounds on the right side. . . ."
> A neurosurgeon is called.
> Her right hip is injured. From the way her leg is shortened and inward, it's obvious that it has been dislocated.
> An orthopedic surgeon is called.
> She has received about half a quart of intravenous fluid in the ambulance, and still her blood pressure fluctuates. The grimace on her face when her stomach is poked means internal injuries are likely.

28. From the following facts, write a news story.

> Donna L. Neal, 18, of 34 Wayside Drive; Angela Kane, 18, of 263 Blue Ridge Road; Colleen M. Stark, 17, of 534 Grand Ave., all of Springfield. Neal, the driver, and Kane, a passenger, were killed at 1:30 a.m. Saturday. Their car went out of control on a curve near 8301 E. Stadium Drive on the north side of Truman Sports Complex in Springfield. The Neal car crossed into the westbound lane and hit the driver's side of a tractor-trailer. The truck driver was not hurt. Stark was seriously injured. All three were thrown from the car. All three were students at Springfield High School. They would have graduated in a few weeks. All planned to attend college.

CHALLENGE EXERCISE

29. Use the information from the preceding exercise and rewrite your story. Add the following information obtained by doing additional interviewing.

St. Regis Church is next to the school. Classmates reacted with great grief to the news that two of their classmates had been killed and one seriously injured. Many of them waited at the hospital where Colleen had surgery. She was still in critical condition.

Brother Mike Martin of St. Regis: "Donna Neal had to select her favorite hymns as part of a class assignment on funerals last fall. She selected 'Be Not Afraid,' 'One Body, One Bread' and 'On Eagle's Wings.' Those songs will be sung at a memorial to her and Kane Monday morning. She said, 'I want to be remembered as happy.' That helped us pick out the songs and the readings. The saddest part of her funeral is the gospel reading. It's about a widow asking Jesus to raise one of her children from the dead and bring it back to the family. Donna's mother is a widow and has 13 kids."

Brother Sidney Edmond: "I came in to grab a cereal bowl about 8 o'clock. One of the brothers said, 'I've got some bad news for you.' It was instant denial. I started saying, 'No, no.'"

Throughout the day, students came to visit with the brothers and to talk to them.

The class that Donna selected the hymns and gospel reading for was one on death and dying. Her teacher was Brother Martin.

9 Alternatives to the Inverted Pyramid

1. In each of the following examples, identify the type of alternate structure and, in the margin, mark the transition and the nut paragraph.

A. After 10 years at System Planning Corp. in Arlington, Sandra Wong had risen to the rank of administrative assistant, was earning a $40,000 salary and had just agreed to buy a townhouse. She was a seasoned professional.

So when her boss told her in August that she had been "surplused," she first thought she was being promoted.

Hardly. She was being laid off.

Unemployed, Wong could not go through with the townhouse purchase. Because she had already sold her condominium, she had to move into a rented apartment. Now, she must start job hunting.

Wong and thousands of professionals like her give a distinctive, white-collar shading to the ranks of Washington's unemployed.

As defense, real estate, retail and financial companies have laid off workers and otherwise shrunk their staffs, a growing class of unemployed managers, consultants, engineers, architects and real estate agents has emerged.

Type of alternate structure:

B. NEW YORK—Outlaw pocketed the roll of bills and walked back down Steeplechase Pier to the Coney Island boardwalk. He had just sold his .32-caliber nickel-plated automatic. Now he had $65 to buy clothes for his two-day-old son. At the end of the pier, a 15-year-old from New Jersey leaned over the railing and aimed his new gun at the water 20 feet below. The explosion scared two gulls off the side of the pier. The birds fluttered down to the hard sand, where shallow waves collapsed onto the beach.

Twenty-five years ago, Coney Island was a resort town. Each summer, millions fled the city's sweltering tenements for the three miles of beach, boardwalk and amusements. The summer bungalows that clustered around the three-story walk-ups north of Surf Avenue went for $500 a season.

Then the resort became a dumping ground. Winterized bungalows went to welfare families for $1,800 a year. The amusements area became a summer battleground for street gangs. The poor man's paradise had become the poor man's purgatory.

Type of alternate structure:

C. NEW YORK—By all accounts, it was the happiest day in the largely unhappy life of Joanne Bashold; not in all her 24 years had her family ever heard her so exuberant.

"I had a baby girl yesterday," Joanne announced on Sept. 2 from a pay telephone somewhere in New York's Bellevue Hospital. Her younger sister Barbara, receiving the call at the Bashold residence in Kirtland, Ohio, was astonished. The family hadn't known Joanne was pregnant and wasn't even sure where she was.

"How are you?" Barbara asked. But Joanne wanted only to talk about her baby girl, Cara. "She has tons of black hair. She's so little and so cute."

Four days after that conversation took place, the baby was dead. It was devoured and killed by a starving German shepherd, Joanne's own pet and sole companion in the East Harlem slum she called home.

As a result, Joanne was charged with criminally negligent homicide. But last Thursday, the charge was dropped at the request of the District Attorney's office. "We concluded there was no purpose to be served by prosecuting her," District Attorney Robert M. Morgenthau said.

Her story is the story of how a young woman—like so many thousands of other young women in this country—came to New York to find herself but was overwhelmed by a city where anonymity is worn like a badge.

It is a story of a woman from a small town with gentle, undulating hills where neighbors help each other—a woman who literally fell through the cracks of a complicated bureaucratic system that is supposed to aid people like her.

Type of alternate structure:

2 Let's look again at the opening of the series about Grandma Braun's kidnapping discussed in Chapter 9 of *News Reporting and Writing*. What does the author accomplish with this opening? Can you find specific foreshadowing?

By Helen O'Neill
The Associated Press

LITTLE PRAIRIE, Wis.—It was cold the night Grandma Braun was taken, that bitter dead-of-winter cold when the countryside is sheathed in ice and the stillness is broken only by great gusts of snow that swirl across the fields and back roads, erasing footprints and car tracks and all traces of life.

Eighty-eight-year-old Hedwig Braun was in bed reading when the lights went out but she didn't pay much heed. In her tiny farmhouse on Bluff Road, miles from the nearest town, power outages are not uncommon. Pulling on her dressing gown and slippers, she lit a candle and padded into the kitchen. She poured a glass of milk, settled at the table and continued her book about angels.

The clock was stopped at 12:50 a.m.

A sudden blast of wind. A shadowy figure in the doorway.

"Eddie!" she screamed as the intruder lurched toward her, throwing something over her head. "Eddie come quick."

But her 88-year-old husband, asleep in the other room, didn't stir.

At 5-foot-2, weighing 80 pounds, Braun is a slip of a woman whose toughness is all inside. She had no strength to fight off her abductor. She didn't even try. She just prayed as she was flung into the trunk of her 1992 white Cadillac, kept praying as they tore down the country road, screeching to a halt beside a ditch, prayed even harder as she was tossed into the trunk of another car and they sped away again.

In the darkness, wedged against the spare tire, she wondered, "Why me? I'm just a nobody. What does he want with me?"

3. A college student wrote this opening to a story about victims of a California earthquake. What does the foreshadowing promise? Are you interested in reading more because of it?

> The October afternoon was warm and muggy, and although no such thing exists, people called it perfect earthquake weather. Ruth Rabinowitz was anticipating a night out with her lover, Robin Ortiz, when they met at 4 p.m. at the Santa Cruz Coffee Roasting Company. "We had a date that night for dinner and a show," says Rabinowitz.
>
> Rabinowitz, a production manager at the company, had to work an extra hour that Tuesday evening preparing orders for the next day. Before leaving, she gave Ortiz a hug. It was the last time she would see her alive.

4. Find an example of foreshadowing in a newspaper or magazine and evaluate its effectiveness.

5. Circle the "so what?" in the following story opening:

> If you get sent to Student Judiciary for DUI, chances are your peers will suspend you while an administrator will allow you to stay in school.
>
> In fact, student justices are seven times more likely to suspend you than an administrator.
>
> An investigation of Student Judiciary DUI cases shows that Main Court student justices suspend student defendants 57 percent of the time, while administrators suspend only 8 percent of the time.
>
> The investigation was conducted by The Red and Black during winter and spring quarters, after the Georgia Supreme Court ruled in December 1993 that student disciplinary records were open to the public.
>
> The implications, according to experts, are obvious:
>
> Based on the percentages, two local attorneys and two of the three Judicial Programs administrators said if they were student defendants, they would pick an administrator to hear their case—not a panel of students.

In your opinion, is the "so what?" located correctly? If not, where would you put it?

6. From your campus or local newspapers or their Web sites, find and evaluate two examples of "so what?" paragraphs. Submit the tops of the stories with your evaluation.

7. Using the focus structure, write about three paragraphs on the following information:

> There are 20,000 injuries in high school football each year—12 percent of them permanently disabling the victims. Thirteen youths died last year. Thirty-five percent of the injuries are to the neck or head. Most critics blame the helmet. Pete Stenhoff, 16, a junior at Chula Vista High School in Redmond, Calif., was hurt in a game during his junior year. He rammed his head into the ball carrier's chest. Stenhoff cracked vertebrae in his spine and now is confined to a wheelchair for life. At the time of the accident he

weighed 210 pounds; now he weighs 172 pounds. He didn't graduate with his class and is trying to get his diploma by taking correspondence courses. He is not bitter. "I knew the risks involved when I decided to play football," he says, and adds, "but I wish I would have known just how bad it could be."

8. Using the focus structure, write about three paragraphs on the following information:

> About 44,000 workers who had been laid off from Chrysler put on a mock funeral on April 1 to draw attention to their plight. Next week they will receive their last supplemental unemployment checks, which give them 95 percent of their take-home pay. They have been out of work for five months. Fifty workers, their spouses and children attended the mock service. One beat a slow cadence on a muffled drum during the procession. They had a casket. After next week, the workers will have to live on state unemployment benefits. Some quotes: "They'll give us our jobs back after we've lost everything. They don't care." — Henry Westoff, 44, of Detroit. "My wife is handicapped and she's supposed to have an operation. Our medical coverage is running out. Tell me what I'm supposed to do." — Bill Klisch, 51, of Detroit.

9. Now using the same information from the preceding question, write the top of a news narrative story that would be published soon after the mock funeral.

10. Dexter Filkins of *The New York Times* won an award for deadline reporting from the American Society of Newspaper Editors for a series entitled "The Conflict in Iraq." In the first article, identify the type of opening and the nut paragraph. You can find the series at http://www.asne.org/index.cfm?ID=5600.

11. Write a soft opening of two or three paragraphs using the following information:

> There are 55 million women in the country who work. Lillian Garland worked at California Federal Savings & Loan. She was granted a pregnancy leave. When she wanted to return, she was not given her job back. She sued under a California law requiring employers to grant up to four months' unpaid disability leave to pregnant workers and to guarantee a job for them when they return. The U.S. Supreme Court voted 6-2 Tuesday to uphold the state law. The ruling came five years after Garland had her baby.

12. Write about a memorable moment in your life as an anecdotal introduction to a story about how you came to be the person you are today. Continue through the transitional paragraph.

13. Find and evaluate two anecdotes in a newspaper or magazine.

14. What are the service journalism aspects of a story about an upcoming city council meeting at which members will consider rates for garbage collection and sewer and water service? How do you make it useful? Usable?

15. Assume that you are devoting a couple of pages in your campus newspaper to information freshmen need to know when they arrive on your campus. Using a service journalism emphasis, create a story list and description. Then identify the parts of the information that would be presented in text, in lists and other formats. Identify those formats.

CHALLENGE EXERCISE

16. In the excerpt that follows, the writer, a college student, has re-created an event he attended. Analyze the writing techniques he used to take readers to the scene.

While roosters face off in the "pit," opponents and supporters of cockfighting throughout the state clash in their views about whether the legal sport is a rural tradition or simply a game of cruelty.

On a warm and sunny Saturday afternoon in April, the massive red barn outside Middletown begins to stir with activity. Pickup trucks turn slowly onto the gravel driveway. The entrance to the barn is prominently marked with two posts displaying statues of roosters. A sign on the barn reads "H & H Poultry."

It's been two weeks since the last cockfight. Twice a month, cockers and fans gather to witness this long-standing tradition. Supporters of cockfighting see this ritual as a cultural event involving fighting roosters, while opponents view it as a cruel massacre and blood sport between animals forced to fight to the death.

Inside the barn, the smell of country cooking permeates the air. A restaurant featuring homemade corn dogs and apple pies does a brisk business. Families sit at tables drinking soda and bantering about the latest controversy involving the president.

The barn is immaculate. At least 200 seats rise above the pit, the 20-square-foot area made of wood and surrounded on each side by wire. This is the ring in which the feathered combatants will face one another. The pit is covered in a mixture of dirt, peat moss and cottonseed hulls. It has been raked to perfection like the infield of a baseball diamond.

An announcer's box sits high above the pit on the far end of the arena. Each side of the barn displays large red letters stating "Absolutely No Gambling." Each row in the arena has several empty canisters for patrons to discard their cigarette ashes and chewing tobacco. Behind the stands, several rooms house the fighting cocks, which alert everyone to their presence by continually crowing.

It's 4 p.m., time for weigh-in.

The roosters, Red Hatch and Calcutta Gray Battle Cross breeds, are placed on the scales. Once the weights are ascertained, they are entered into a computer that matches opponents down to the ounce. This ensures that weight will not give any rooster an unfair advantage over an opponent.

Cockers—the men who own, raise and sometimes handle the birds during fights—have come from all over this Saturday night for the Missouri State Championship. The defending champion, Ron Griffin of Hannibal, has brought his prize roosters.

As 6 p.m. approaches, excitement mounts among the cockers and the crowd. The seats alongside the pit fill up rapidly. Across the pit, several high school students, sporting their letter jackets, occupy the front row, laughing and joking. Three young children chase each other up and down the aisles, firing spitballs through their soda straws.

A man at the north end of the arena writes down the names of the fighting cocks on a large board. Each cock will fight once.

The hour has arrived. Two handlers emerge from under a tunnel, each holding a bird. Immediately, the people in the crowd begin making wagers with one another. "Five dollars on the white shirt," yells one man, referring to the white shirt of one of the handlers. "Ten on the red hat," yells another spectator, deciding to back the other handler who dons a red ball cap.

As the handlers enter the pit, a referee draws chalk lines about eight feet apart in the middle of the ring. The handlers proceed toward the center. The majestic birds are Red Hatch Battle Crosses, possessing deep auburn plumage with streaks of blonde, hair-like hackle feathers surrounding their necks. The roosters' amber spurs have been cut to a stump and replaced with 2¼-inch, metal "gaffs," which are needle-like and curved at the ends.

Standing about two feet apart, the handlers hold the cocks within pecking distance of one another to stimulate their fighting instincts. Immediately, the birds begin pecking each other with voracious ire. The handlers separate, pulling one of the cock's beaks from the other's head. The birds are now ready for the main bout.

Each handler steps behind one of the chalk lines in the center of the pit while maintaining a hold on his bird. The crowd cheers as the feathered gladiators prepare to do battle. The referee yells, "Pit!"

With hackle feathers swollen like umbrellas around their necks, the roosters dash toward each other with the ferocity of football linebackers. The birds clash in midair, wings flapping furiously. Feathers scatter in every direction. The battle rages on, until both become hung on the metal gaffs, prompting the referee to yell, "Handle that bird!"

The handlers pick up their birds, gently massaging their legs and blowing on their heads. Round two is about to begin. Once again, the birds charge one another, producing clicking noises as the razor-sharp gaffs penetrate their feathered bodies. This continues for five more rounds. Finally, one of the roosters begins to stagger, a victim of the sustained gaff punctures he has received during the fight.

The referee signals for the cockers to handle their birds, and the handler of the badly wounded rooster tries to "warm" the bird's head and body by blowing gently (a process cockers say helps increase circulation). In the next round, the wounded rooster refuses to stand up, resting squarely on his belly, apparently conceding defeat. The cockers, however, are not ready to end this clash.

The winning rooster continues to attack his ailing opponent, who miraculously rebounds to try and defend himself. By this time, the injured bird has lost all offensive capacity and rests on his side as blood drips from his beak. The referee begins a 10-count. By the time the referee reaches 10, the fatally wounded rooster falls lifelessly onto his side.

After 12 minutes of courageous fighting, it is over.

The handlers pick up their roosters and shake hands. For the winning bird, it's back to the cages behind the stands, where the cockers will scrutinize its body for injuries. For the loser, it's off to the incinerator in the back of the arena. . . .

10 Obituaries and Life Stories

1. Which elements are missing from the following obituary information? List them in the space provided.

   a. John Jones died Saturday night at Springfield Hospital. Funeral services will be at 1:30 p.m. Tuesday. Friends may call at the Black Funeral Home, 2222 Broadway Ave., from 6 to 9 p.m. Monday. The Rev. Eugene McCubbin will officiate at services in the Faith Baptist Church. Burial will be at City Cemetery.

   b. Mattie Avery, longtime teacher, died at her daughter's home in Springfield. Services will be at 2 p.m. tomorrow at the Springfield Memorial Cemetery.

   c. Gary Roets of Springfield, died Jan. 30, 2007, at Springfield Hospital. He was 49. Funeral services will be at 2 p.m. Feb. 1. He is survived by his wife, Jan, and three children: Rebecca, 10; Nathan, 8; and Nicholas, 4. A graduate of the Marquette University School of Law, he practiced law in Springfield for 24 years.

2. Write a lead for an obituary for the *Springfield Daily News* from the following information. Assume the victim is local and will be buried in your city.

   a. Jenelle Crookstein, born Jan. 1, 1986, to Don and Jane Crookstein, in Omaha, Neb. The family moved to Springfield in 1989. Jenelle died in a freak skiing accident Sunday while at Vail, Colo. Funeral services will be Wednesday at First Methodist Church at 1 p.m. She was president of her high school student council and of the marching band at the University of Nebraska, where she was a sophomore. She is survived by her parents and a brother, Tom, 10.

b. Pearl Cornell, 73, Rt. 4, Springfield, died yesterday. Was director of Welcome Wagon from 1995 to 2007. Was a volunteer at the Springfield Hospital for 37 years. Was president of the volunteers for seven years. Will be buried today.

c. Jackson Adams died yesterday while watching a high school basketball game in which his son Edward was playing. Apparent heart attack. Jackson was 44. Has two younger sons, 5 and 2. Was a widower. Will be buried tomorrow.

3. Write an obituary from the following information. At the end, indicate what questions, if any, you would need answered.

    a. NAME OF FUNERAL HOME: PARKER FUNERAL SERVICE
        PHONE: 549-4153
        PERSON TO CONTACT: HAL RICE

        NAME OF DECEASED: Retired Lt. Col. Ronald H. Lache
        ADDRESS: Springfield
                104 Alhambra Dr.
        OCCUPATION: Retired from the United States Air Force
        AGE: Born November 3, 1950, at Philadelphia, Pennsylvania,
            to Harry and Thelma Curry Lache
        CAUSE OF DEATH:
        DATE AND PLACE OF DEATH: June 16, 2007, at his home in
                             Springfield
        TIME AND PLACE OF FUNERAL SERVICES: Jefferson Barracks
                                     National Cemetery—
                                     Graveside service at
                                     2 p.m.
        CONDUCTED BY: Rev. Michael Finney
        BURIAL: Jefferson Barracks, Springfield
        TIME AND PLACE FOR VISITATION: none

BIOGRAPHICAL INFORMATION: His wife, the former Delores Carney, died March 7 of this year. The family moved to Springfield 5 years ago from Dayton, Ohio. He was a member of the Newman Center and the Rock Bridge Lions Club.

SURVIVORS: Survived by his mother, Thelma Lache of Springfield
his son Ronald Lache of Springfield
three daughters—Barbara Ann Peck of Dayton, Ohio
Patrice Louis Wylie of Indianapolis, Ind.
Cynthia Lache of San Mateo, Calif.
one granddaughter, Jennifer C. Peck, Springfield

b. NAME OF FUNERAL HOME: RESTWELL FUNERAL SERVICE
PHONE: 588-4153
PERSON TO CONTACT: JOHN KRONK

NAME OF DECEASED: Raymond Lee Hope
ADDRESS: 1060 College Ave.
Springfield
OCCUPATION: Salesman for Springfield Auto Supply for one year—has been in the auto parts business since 1974
AGE: Born July 3,1932, in Chicago to Virgil W. and Flossie Dissart Hope
CAUSE OF DEATH:
DATE AND PLACE OF DEATH: June 17, 2007, at Springfield Hospital
TIME AND PLACE OF FUNERAL SERVICES: Tuesday, June 19, at Faith Baptist Church at 2:00 p.m.
CONDUCTED BY: The Reverend Eugene McCubbins
BURIAL: Memorial Park Cemetery
TIME AND PLACE FOR VISITATION: 7–9 p.m. Monday evening at Restwell Funeral Service, 10th and Walnut
BIOGRAPHICAL INFORMATION: He and Mary Alice Willett were married March 24, 1953, at Chicago, Ill. He lived in Springfield since.
SURVIVORS: Survived by his wife, Mary, of the home in Springfield
his daughter, Mrs. John (Raycene) Bach of Springfield
his brother, Earl Hope of Chicago
two granddaughters, Jacqueline and Jennifer Bach

c. Henry Higgins was the victim of a two-car crash Friday night at the corner of U.S. 63 and Route NN in rural Lincoln County. The driver of the other car, Thomas Henry, 32, is hospitalized with head and neck injuries in Springfield Hospital.

Although he was young, Higgins had accomplished much. He was president of his senior class at Springfield High School, he was a letterman for two years for the University of Illinois football team for whom he played tight end, and he recently earned his real estate license and was associated with the firm of West and Haver, Springfield.

He was a member of the Springfield Jaycees. Survivors include wife, Cloris, 209 Fourth St.; his parents, Ralph and Amy Higgins, of Columbia; a sister, Ruth, of Birmingham, Ala.; and a brother, Russell, of St. Louis.

Funeral services will be held Tuesday at the Newman Center with Father Ralph Green officiating. Burial will be in City Cemetery.

Higgins was born Sept. 24, 1979, in Springfield. He lived there all his life.

Friends may call at the Restwell Funeral Home, from 7 to 10 p.m. Monday.

4. The best-written obituaries often require additional reporting.
   a. The obituary notice from the funeral home contains all the basic information. However, under biographical information, it indicates only that the man worked at the local paper mill for 25 years. If you wanted to find out whether there was anything extraordinary about this man, whom would you call and why? Where might that call lead you?

   b. An obituary notice contains most of the basic information. The age of the deceased is 14. There is nothing under cause of death. Memorials are requested for the American Cancer Society. What angle does this information suggest may be possible? Whom would you call and why?

   c. The space under biographical information is empty. The deceased has no local survivors. Whom do you call, and what would you be looking for?

5. In Chapter 10 of *News Reporting and Writing*, students read about Amy Rabideau Silvers in the On the Job feature. She wrote the life story below. What distinguishes this life story from a normal obituary? She identifies two sources in the obituary. What are they?

   Arlowyn Keller didn't plan to drive a big rig, but she was proud to be a trucker once she got the hang of it.

   That was in 1949, when a female truck driver was news, complete with her height and weight and what she wore to work.

   "Ladylike, the 35-year-old Mrs. Keller was concerned that her asphalt smudged face might look grimy in a picture," declared a 1950s newspaper story. "But she looked nearly as fresh as some housewives whose biggest driving assignment is getting the station wagon out of the garage to go shopping."

   Her husband insisted that she help when a driver didn't show up.

   "My mother said she was shaking the first time she had to back up that truck and put up the box to let the asphalt out," said daughter Barbara Sutton. "Someone there said she did it better than any of the men."

   Keller suffered a severe stroke Wednesday and was pronounced dead the next day. She was 83. Keller lived on Milwaukee's south side.

   The former Arlowyn Ostrander—"Lou" if someone had trouble pronouncing her name—grew up in Seneca. She was a teenager, sitting on the porch with her girlfriend, when a young trucker would drive by and wave. One day, he stopped the truck and got out to talk. Soon, she was happy to hop in the truck for a ride. Not long after that, they began dating.

   "She didn't graduate from high school," her daughter said. "She got married in 1940, when she was 17."

"I wanted to get out of Seneca," she later told her family.

Her husband, Orlyn Keller, first worked for his father and then on his own, hauling gravel and working road projects in Southern states.

After she joined their little Keller Trucking company, they both drove rigs. They also hauled a small mobile home for their family, Sutton said.

"And that's where we lived," she said. "I used to tease my mom that they were like gypsies."

In 1951, they settled in Milwaukee. By then, Arlowyn Keller was used to handling a truck loaded with 10 tons of hot asphalt mix. Warm-weather months were spent working jobs in the Milwaukee area.

"She helped pave Wisconsin Avenue, Plankinton Avenue and lots of Milwaukee streets," said her son, Howard Keller.

When the weather turned cold, they drove oil tankers to Illinois and back every day.

Apart from the occasional wolf whistle or someone tut-tutting that she should be home, work proved fairly routine.

"The guys treated her with respect," Sutton said. "It was hot work, but she always wore black slacks and a sleeveless blouse—never shorts."

"I was a lady, and I had to act like one," Keller would say.

In 1958, the Kellers spent a hectic year trying to run a tavern above their south side home. They called it Orlyn & Arlowyn's Halfway Bar, closing it when two full-time jobs became too much.

In 1964, Keller decided that she'd had enough of trucking. She became a full-time homemaker until her husband's death in 1966, when she began working in customer service at the J.C. Penney warehouse.

"My mother was feisty," Sutton said. "She liked to laugh, and she was very opinionated. She loved the color red, and she loved Willie Nelson."

Sometimes, Keller would just head out to her car.

"Willie and I are going to take a little ride," Keller would say.

"Being behind the wheel, it never got out of her blood," Sutton said. "She was very proud of the fact she was a trucker."

In addition to her son and daughter, survivors include daughter Marilyn Rybacki and son Ronald Keller; brother Donald Ostrander; grandchildren, great-grandchildren and great-great grandchildren.

Visitation will be from 11 a.m. today until the service at 1:30 p.m. at the John J. Walloch Funeral Home, 4309 S. 20th St.

6. Important policy questions often arise when you are writing obituaries.
   a. If a private citizen committed suicide on the grounds of a local high school when no one was around one night, would you include the cause of death in the obituary? Why or why not?

   b. If the mayor died and you could quote other city officials as saying the mayor's drinking had interfered with his or her work in the last year, would you include that in the obituary? Why or why not?

   c. If a citizen who was an active member of several civic groups died and you had several paragraphs describing the work he or she did for the community, would you include the fact that he or she had died of AIDS? Why or why not?

CHALLENGE EXERCISE

7. Using information from a database search, write a two-page advance obituary for one of the following. At the end, list your sources.

   a. Daniel Inouye

   b. Germaine Greer

   c. Phil Collins

   d. Reggie Jackson

   e. Bill Cosby

   f. Henry Cisneros

   g. George H.W. Bush

   h. Your mayor

   i. Your college or university president

   j. Your governor

   k. Dale Earnhardt Jr.

11 Finding the News in News Releases

1. The text lists three categories of news releases:

— announcements of coming events or of personnel matters.
— information regarding a cause.
— information that is meant to build someone's or some organization's business.

First indicate the kind of news release each of the following is, and then list the questions you would ask before writing the story.

a.   NEWS RELEASE

The Board of Advisors for the Outstanding Young Men of America Awards Program announced today that the men named below have been selected for inclusion in the 2005 edition of "Outstanding Young Men of America."

These men were selected from nominations received from senators, members of Congress, governors, mayors, state legislators, university and college presidents and deans as well as various civic groups—including the United States Jaycees, which also endorses the Outstanding Young Men of America program.

In every community there are young men working diligently to make their cities, as well as their country, better places in which to live. These men, having distinguished themselves in one or more fields of endeavor, are outstanding and deserve to be recognized for their achievements. The criteria for selection include a man's voluntary service to community, professional leadership, academic achievement, business advancement, cultural accomplishment, and civic and political participation.

The men listed below, along with fellow Outstanding Young Men throughout North America, will be featured in this prestigious annual awards publication.

Our board of advisors and editors salute all chosen as Outstanding Young Men of America. We take great pride in bringing their accomplishments to the attention of the American public.

Clarence B. Wine	Bruce D. Ballard	James R. Oglesby
1909 Dartmouth	Route 2, Box 18227	1908 Iris Drive
Randall J. Scherr	Thomas C. Graham	Thomas M. Hinckly
301 Shepard Court	1204 Manor Drive	6 Edgewood St.
William H. Miller	Alan R. Everson	
1716 Bettina Drive	1704 Countryside Lane	

b. FOR IMMEDIATE RELEASE

McKinley, Soldan Seniors to Be Welcomed at Springfield University

Springfield—Eighty McKinley and 80 Soldan High School seniors will be welcomed to Springfield University Friday, Feb. 10, through the Student Affirmative Action Program.

"We think the program is an excellent opportunity for the seniors to learn first-hand what the campus is like and to meet university students, faculty and staff," said Jennifer Hill-Young of the Center for Student Life Office of Minority Student Affairs.

After a continental breakfast in Jesse Hall, students will meet with Dr. James Bates, vice chancellor for student affairs; University Students Association President Dave LaGesse; members of the Legion of Black Collegians; and Dr. Carolyn Washington, assistant professor of education and coordinator of the Black Studies program. Advisement in financial aid, admissions and housing will be completed in the morning session.

After lunch, the high school seniors will meet at the Campus Career Planning and Placement Center for a program on opportunities and center services. The afternoon concludes with students attending an orientation of their choice to one of the university's 15 academic divisions.

More than 1,500 minority high school students in the state will spend a day at the university through the Student Affirmative Action Program this year.

c. NEWS RELEASE

OPTIMIST BASKETBALL CONTEST TO BE HELD

The Downtown Optimist Club of Springfield will hold a Tri-Star Basketball skills contest at Springfield College on February 19, 2004, at 1 p.m. The contest is composed of three basic skill tests aimed at evaluating a contestant's skill in passing, shooting and dribbling.

Boys (and/or girls) will compete in six age groups, 8 through 13, against youth of their own age. All that is needed to compete is the desire and a pair of gym shoes, according to Jess Weaver, club president.

There will be plaques awarded to the winners in each age group. Every contestant will receive a memento scorecard. Entry blanks are available at MFA Employees Credit Union, 2909 Falling Leaf Lane, or at the contest site on the day of competition. They may also be obtained by calling John Sanders at 442-1458 (day), 449-6456 (evening).

2. Assume you are a reporter for the Springfield paper. Your instructor will answer any questions you have. Rewrite each of the following news releases as a story:

a.   ROBERT L. BARTLETT
APPOINTED CHAIRMAN
TO NATIONAL TOOL GROUP

McGraw-Edison
Portable Appliance and
Tool Group
McGraw-Edison Company
1808 N. Stadium Blvd.
(314) 445-8888
Contact Joan Jolly

FOR IMMEDIATE RELEASE

Springfield—(January 2007)—Robert L. Bartlett, director of tool engineering for McGraw-Edison's Portable Appliance and Tool Group headquartered in Springfield, has been appointed to a two-year term as chairman of the Joint Engineering Committee, Power Tool Institute, beginning this month.

The institute is a trade association representing 21 major corporations producing 95 percent of all power tools sold in the United States, according to Bartlett. The committee plays a major role in developing safety standards for power tools, in cooperation with the American National Standards Institute, Underwriters Laboratories and various government agencies.

McGraw-Edison's Portable Appliance and Tool Group, located at 1801 N. Stadium Blvd., manufactures and sells power tools, lawn and garden tools, portable electric housewares, fans, heaters, electric alarms, kitchen and decorator clocks, and automatic household timers under the brand names Toastmaster, Edison, Village Blacksmith, Shopmate, Manning-Bowman, Ingraham (Time) and McGraw-Edison, in addition to private labels.

b.   FOR RELEASE ON RECEIPT

JAMES TO VISIT SPRINGFIELD ON JANUARY 12, 2007

WASHINGTON, D.C.—Congressman Richard H. James has advised that he will be at the South County Bank in Springfield from 2 to 5 p.m. on Friday, Jan. 14, to visit with area residents and discuss any problems or pending legislation.

SCHEDULE FOR JANUARY IS AS FOLLOWS:

DATE	TIME	LOCATION
Friday, Jan. 12	9 a.m.-12 noon	Vienna Post Office
Friday, Jan. 12	2-5 p.m.	Community Room, South County Bank, Springfield

James has long stressed the importance of direct communication with his constituency and expressed the hope that many people would have time to stop by and visit.

On Saturday, Jan. 13, James will be visiting with constituents at the Alton Post Office from 9 to 12 and at the West Plains Courthouse from 2 to 5.

c. See page 87.

3. Read the following press releases carefully. For each press release write a paragraph describing a possible news story or local reaction story.

a.   FOR IMMEDIATE RELEASE

For further information, contact:

Daniel Hines
Edelman Public Relations
515 Olive Street
St. Louis, MO 63101
314/421-6460

RAIN? SUN? CROP PRICES?
FARMERS NOW ARE GETTING ANSWERS THROUGH
TELECOMMUNICATIONS

There's something new down on the farm.

A farmer sitting at his desk wants to know what beans for November delivery are selling for on the Chicago Board of Trade. He turns to a computer, punches in a request for information and immediately has not only the latest quote but can also call up charts indicating the price spread for beans (or any other commodity). Then, he can ask for a graph to indicate where, based on historical data, the prices might go and what would be the best time for him to sell his crop.

In a small town grain elevator, as many as seven aerials protrude from the roof, directing radio connections to several local farmers who use radios to get the latest cash prices being offered for crops.

And, even the oldest ally—and enemy—of the farmer is brought down to size somewhat as a farmer asks for the latest weather report not just for his locale, but the soybean-growing regions of Brazil.

Today, the traditional farm, a preserve of tractors, combines and farm implements, has a new tool. It is telecommunications.

Farmers are turning in increasing numbers to computers and other forms of telecommunications to help them with their critical business decisions.

One person who isn't surprised by this trend is Edwin Spievack, president of the North American Telecommunications Association (NATA), which will hold its annual exhibition and showcase at the Cervantes Convention Center in St. Louis, Nov. 4-7.

Spievack knows what he is talking about. He has been named one of the 25 most influential people in the telecommunications industry by a leading trade publication and is a leading industry spokesperson in his role as president of NATA.

"Agriculture . . . the farmer . . . is just another of a growing number of occupations which is finding out how telecommunications can help them do a better job," Spievack explains. "That is why we are so excited about our NATA convention in St. Louis. We believe that there is an increasing number of people interested in what telecommunications can do for them, and our more than 500 exhibits and seminars will offer them several new perspectives on the industry."

Spievack says that agriculture offers a prime example of the services telecommunications can provide.

"The American farmer today must compete on a worldwide basis," he notes. "More than ever, good information can help someone be a better farmer."

Spievack's contention is borne out by the fact that increased use of telecommunications has spurred competition among suppliers of equipment and services.

The result is that although computers and news service wires might seem exotic when contrasted with the traditional image of the farmer toiling in the field, new advanced telecommunications techniques are now becoming within the reach of more farmers.

For example, a computer network that offers access to the Chicago Board of Trade and offers other business analyses for the farmer once cost as much as $90 monthly. Now, some services are as little as $15 monthly. Also, the cost of sophisticated radio equipment has been cut in half.

The importance of this is that since planning has always been important to the successful farmer, increased and useful information will enable him to increase his returns. This is a highly important consideration in light of the many pressures facing American agriculture today, Spievack notes.

"It is this type of benefit to users that makes telecommunications valuable and will generate even greater use of it in the future," Spievack says.

"As that happens, the user—in this case, the farmer—will be faced with choices. It's true throughout our society, and that's why we've titled our St. Louis show 'Choices.'

"As the need for quick and reliable transmission of information increases, the telecommunications industry will be ready to fill the need."

Spievack admits there is one thing that telecommunications might not be able to do anything about for the farmer. That's the weather.

He recalls a discussion he had recently with a farmer who has a computer network with complete services—pricing, businesses' analyses, a worldwide newswire. But one thing hadn't changed.

"It was harvest time and the farmer was anxious to get into the fields to finish combining his beans, but an unwanted—and unneeded—rain that morning had prevented him from getting into the field. Some things will never change, I guess."

"Choices," the convention and exhibition showcase of the North American Telecommunications Association, will be held at the Cervantes Convention Center in St. Louis, Nov. 4-7. For additional information, call NATA at 800-LET-NATA or write to the North American Telecommunications Association, 2000 M Street, Suite 550, Washington, D.C. 20036.

b. See pages 88–89.
c. See pages 90–91.

4. You have been assigned to write a business brief based on the following news release from a manufacturing company in your town:

The Zerbe Co. had its most productive and safest year ever. Zerbe, the nation's leading producer of egg cartons, increased productivity by 23 percent while injuries dropped by 40 percent.

Zerbe cranked out 14,500,356 egg cartons in 2006, the most in company history and nearly 1 million more than the nation's second-leading carton producer. Meanwhile, injuries at the plant fell from 20 in 2005 to 12 in 2006. Company President Antonio Zerbe IV credits the efforts of all his employees for the successful year.

Zerbe, founded in 1905 by Antonio Zerbe Jr., is the largest employer in Lincoln County with 478 workers.

a. What figures should be checked with other sources, and how would you confirm them?
b. Assuming all figures check out, rewrite the news release in a two-paragraph story.

CHALLENGE EXERCISE

5. Make these press releases into news stories using local sources and resources.

a. FOR IMMEDIATE RELEASE

KANSAS CITY—What does "hardening the target" have to do with lessening the chances of a burglary at your home?

A lot, says the Insurance Information Institute. It involves making property harder to steal.

The Institute suggests these steps to make your home more secure:
- Install good-quality door and window locks.
- Install alarm systems.
- Provide outside illumination.
- Trim trees and shrubs.

What's the best strategy for your car? The Institute says many car thefts could be prevented if people would ALWAYS lock the doors and take the keys with them—even if for "just a minute."

By practicing "personal protection" avoidance techniques, you can reduce the three advantages held by a would-be attacker or robber—opportunity, surprise and fear, the Institute notes.

You can reduce a criminal's OPPORTUNITY to attack you by choosing travel routes carefully and by using well-lighted and well-traveled streets. Stick to routes you know and become acquainted with sources of help along those routes—buildings with doormen, police alarm boxes, telephone booths and businesses that are open late.

You can reduce or eliminate the criminal's element of SURPRISE. Carry yourself in a positive manner so that you don't look like a victim. Pay attention to your surroundings. Make yourself aware of people around you who might pose a threat.

A criminal's third advantage is your panic or FEAR. Remain calm. Assess the situation. Decide how you will act. Does the criminal want your valuables or is he after you? Is it a matter of losing replaceable property or are you in physical danger? Remember that no property is worth serious harm.

One way that citizens can help overworked police departments is through neighborhood watch programs in which people give the police information on suspicious activities in their own areas and promptly report any crimes they see to the police.

Some watch programs involve mobile patrols. Citizens in radio-equipped cars cruise the streets of their own area OBSERVING and REPORTING—the common thread of all neighborhood watches—and being seen by potential criminals.

Watches may cover a single apartment house, one or several blocks or an entire neighborhood.

Strangers loitering in the area and unfamiliar vehicles are noted or reported to the police. And volunteers keep tabs on the homes of neighbors who are away during the workday or who are on vacation.

But for any neighborhood watch to be effective, it requires organization, training, and coordination with the local police, the Institute notes.

If you're interested in forming or participating in an organized program to help make your community safer, the first step is to contact your local police. They can tell you if such a program is available or if one is already being planned and with whom you can work.

If you're breaking new ground in your town, let the police know of your interest and volunteer to work with them.

b. See pages 92–93.

c. See pages 94–95.

News release for Exercise 2.c. (page 83).

NEWS

FOR IMMEDIATE RELEASE   CONTACT: Jennifer Kelley

January 11, 2007

SPRINGFIELD UNIVERSITY FACULTY TEAM RECEIVES NATIONAL RECOGNITION

SPRINGFIELD—Two Springfield University faculty members recently received national recognition by their peers at the 51st Annual Meeting of the International Textile Apparel Association (ITAA) held at the Radisson Hotel Metrodome in Minneapolis, Minn. Fashion instructors Jennifer Tobias and Billie Kuntz received a $500 Special Recognition Award and a plaque from the American Textile Manufacturers Institute (ATMI) for their emphasis on internships, industry affiliation and international perspective in the Springfield University Fashion Merchandising Program curriculum.

ATMI, a national trade association for the domestic textile industry, has member companies operating in more than 30 states and accounts for approximately 80 percent of all textile fibers consumed by mills in the U.S.

Established in 1992 by ATMI, the Special Recognition Award recognizes clothing and textile educators for curricular developments, teaching methods and educational programs that promote an understanding of the U.S. textile, apparel and retail industries. ATMI developed the award program in cooperation with ITAA, which is comprised of textile, apparel and retail educators.

Award winners are judged on innovation in curriculum, a program's impact on students and the industry, and how well theory, research and industry initiatives were integrated into the curriculum.

-30-

News release for Exercise 3.b. (page 85).

Publisher of Consumer Reports

CONTACT: Rana Arons
              914-378-2434

CONSUMER REPORTS: TEENS HOOKED ON CIGARETTES

YONKERS, NY -- More than 3000 teen-agers a day become regular cigarette smokers. Kids who are legally too young to smoke -- it is against the law to sell tobacco anywhere in the United States to those younger than 18 -- light up an estimated 17 billion of the 500 billion cigarettes sold each year in this country. Following a comprehensive look at the nation's smoking patterns, published in the March issue, *Consumer Reports* magazine believes that halting the teen-age smoking epidemic must be a public-health priority.

To stop teenage smoking, *Consumer Reports* endorses three strategies recommended by a National Academy of Sciences panel: ban cigarette advertising and promotion, raise cigarette taxes to make smoking less affordable, and enforce the laws against selling to teens.

Adolescents start smoking for many intermingled reasons. Some factors seem to fortify children against tobacco experimentation -- for example, self-esteem, academic achievement, skills for dealing with peer influence, and a close parent-child relationship. These should be built up from toddlerhood on. They can't be provided overnight when a child reaches the high-risk age of 12 or 13. Still, if you're looking for ideas, *Consumer Reports* suggests several steps you can take to help your children shun cigarettes:

- **Talk.** Children whose parents don't talk to them regularly are at greater risk for experimenting with cigarettes. Make a point of discussing your children's lives and feelings. Make sure you know their friends (and the friends' parents). That will help you find out if a friend is smoking, so you can talk about it with your own child.

- **Make your feelings clear**. Children who understand the depth of their parents' opposition to it are less likely to smoke.

- **Help them decode ads**. Children first become susceptible to the images in cigarette ads in the fourth or fifth grade. Urge them to identify seductive images and ads targeted to different groups of people.

-- over

- **Give them a reality check.** Point out that, despite what the ads suggest, the vast majority of adults do not smoke and no longer even tolerate the practice in public.

- **Emphasize health.** Kids are notoriously unconcerned about getting sick. Tell them anyway that teenage smokers have weaker lungs, cough more, and suffer worse upper-respiratory infections. Young athletes don't perform as well if they smoke. And the more years a person smokes, the greater is the risk of lung cancer in middle age.

- **Emphasize addiction.** Nicotine is so addictive that some experts compare it to heroin. And, once hooked, kids find it just as hard to kick the habit as adults do. Trouble is, there's no way to predict which kids will become addicted. So it's best not to even experiment.

- **Help them say no.** This technique is used in many formal substance-abuse prevention courses in school but can easily be adapted at home. As best you can, play the part of an admired friend or acquaintance trying to get your teen-ager to try a cigarette. Help your child work out other ways to turn down the offer.

- **Don't smoke.** If you are a smoker and are unable or unwilling to quit, at least explain to your children that you are in the grip of a fearsome addiction -- and hide your cigarettes. Smoke less in front of your children and make their rooms smoke-free zones.

- **Impose consequences.** If, in spite of your efforts, you find your children experimenting with cigarettes, do not treat it as a minor "kids-will-be-kids" infraction. Treat it as what it is: an act that puts your child at very high risk of developing a life-threatening addiction. Impose whatever sanctions your family uses for a major misdeed -- and don't back down.

-- 30 --

Consumer Reports is published by Consumers Union, an independent, nonprofit testing and information gathering organization, serving only the consumer. We are a comprehensive source of unbiased advice about products and services, personal finance, health, nutrition, and other consumer concerns. Since 1936, our mission has been to test products, inform the public, and protect consumers.

News release for Exercise 3.c. (page 85).

AMERICAN BAR ASSOCIATION

National Conference of Lawyers
and Representatives of the Media
750 North Lake Shore Drive
Chicago, Illinois 60611-4497
(312) 988-6126
FAX: (312) 988-5865

Release: Immediate   Contact: Deborah Weixl
                            Phone: 312/988-6126

BUT, THE PUBLIC WANTS TO KNOW...

NEW BOOKLET FOCUSES ON FAIR TRIAL AND FREE PRESS ISSUES

Chicago, Jan. 6 -- When can court proceedings be closed
to the public? Can a reporter get in trouble if a story he
writes causes the court to change the location or delays a
trial? Is it permissible for media to use information provided
by a lawyer who has violated ethics rules?

Questions such as these, which illustrate the tension
between assuring a fair trial and a free press, have surfaced
during high profile cases such as the O.J. Simpson trial.

To clarify the rights and responsibilities of judges,
lawyers, reporters and court personnel in conducting criminal
proceedings, the National Conference of Lawyers and
Representatives of the Media has produced a new edition of "The
Reporter's Key."

The booklet, written in a question and answer format,
highlights ABA Criminal Justice Standards pertaining to issues
confronting reporters covering trials, especially high profile
cases.

REPORTERS KEY, Add One

The National Conference of Lawyers and Representatives of the Media is composed of representatives of the ABA, both lawyers and - judges and representatives of media organizations, including publishers, editors, reporters, broadcasters, news directors and cable operators. The book was produced to explain that the purpose of the ABA guidelines to those involved in the day-to-day administration of justice and those reporting on the justice system: to assist in public understanding of the criminal justice system.

To ensure accuracy, the booklet follows a proceeding from pretrial hearing through sentencing; through the "Key", a better understanding of the concerns for a fair trial and the role of judges, prosecutors and defense attorneys can be gleaned.

Credit for the booklet goes to Alice Neff Lucan, an attorney in private practice in Washington, D.C., who represents small media outlets. Co-editing the book and providing research assistance was Robert O'Neil, and his staff at the Thomas Jefferson Center for the Protection of Free Expression. Contributors included judges, lawyers and reporters who have participated in numerous proceedings relative to access in criminal cases.

Enclosed is a copy of the booklet for your reference. If you cannot use it, please pass it on to a colleague who can.

Single copies of the booklet are available through the American Bar Association Service Center at (312)988-5522. Additional copies are $10 each. For more information on using the booklet for seminars, programs and bench-bar-media conferences, contact Debbie Weixl at the ABA at (312)988-6126.

-30-

News release for Exercise 5.b. (page 86).

FACTS FOR CONSUMERS
FROM THE FEDERAL TRADE COMMISSION

FOR IMMEDIATE RELEASE

Holiday Shopping By Mail

Like many people, you may find advantages to ordering holiday gifts by mail. You can save time and energy and can give gifts that are not locally available. But if your order arrives late, damaged, or does not arrive at all, you need to know your rights.

During the post-holiday months of January and February, the Federal Trade Commission receives more letters about mail order problems than at any other time of year. Most consumers who complain are unaware of a rule that gives them certain protections when shopping by mail — the Mail Order Merchandise Rule. This Federal Trade Commission rule requires the seller to send your mail order goods within 30 days or when promised, or to give you the option of getting a prompt refund.

Here are some answers to questions you may have about shopping by mail:

WHAT CAN I DO IF MY ORDER IS NOT SENT WHEN PROMISED?

You can cancel your order for a complete refund. The rule requires that the seller mail you an "option notice" if the promised shipping date can't be met. This notice tells you the new shipping date and includes a postage free way for you to cancel your order for a complete refund or to agree to a new shipping date. If the company cannot meet the new shipping date, it must send you a second option notice. Your order will automatically be cancelled unless you sign the second notice and return it to the company.

IF I CANCEL MY ORDER AFTER RECEIVING AN OPTION NOTICE, WHEN SHOULD MY REFUND BE SENT?

If your order was paid by cash, check, or money order, the rule states that a refund must be mailed within seven business days. If the sale was by credit, the seller must mail the papers that adjust your account within one billing cycle.

WHAT IF NO SHIPPING OR DELIVERY DATE IS PROMISED?

Under the Mail Order Rule, if no delivery period is promised, the seller must ship the merchandise no later than 30 days after your complete order is received.

DOES THIS RULE APPLY TO EVERYTHING ORDERED BY MAIL?

No. The rule does not cover photo-finishing, magazine subscriptions (except for the first issue), COD orders, seeds and plants, or credit orders where your account is not charged before the goods are shipped.

WHAT SHOULD I DO IF MY ORDER ARRIVES DAMAGED OR DOES NOT FIT?

Instructions on how to handle such problems are often included with your order. If there are no instructions, write the company and explain the situation. In your letter, provide all the information that identifies your order, including your account and order number, and keep a copy of your letter. The company should let you know how to correct the problem. If your order has been damaged, you may want to notify the post office or the company that delivered the product.

WHAT PRECAUTIONS ARE ADVISABLE WHEN SHOPPING BY MAIL?

1. Note the delivery or shipping time stated in the ad. Order early to allow plenty of time for delivery before holidays.
2. Find out about the merchant's return policy. If it is not stated, ask before you order.
3. Note the merchant's name and address, and the date you sent your order.
4. Keep a copy of your order form, cancelled checks, and charge account records. These will be helpful if you have a problem later.
5. Check the reputation of the firm with your local Better Business Bureau or consumer protection agency.

WHO SHOULD I CONTACT FOR ASSISTANCE WITH A MAIL ORDER PROBLEM?

First, contact the seller and try to resolve the problem. If that does not work, the consumer protection office in your area or in the vicinity of the company may be helpful. Your local postal inspector may also be able to assist. The Direct Mail Marketing Association, an industry group, may help you resolve your dispute if you send them a letter explaining the problem and include copies of relevant documents. Their address is: 6 East 43rd Street, New York, N.Y., 10017.

The Federal Trade Commission enforces the Mail Order Rule. While the FTC cannot resolve your individual complaint, information about your experiences is important to the enforcement of the Act. Therefore, we appreciate receiving copies of your complaint correspondence. For more information, write for a free copy of "Make Knowledge Your Partner in Mail Order Shopping," FTC, Washington, D.C., 20580.

News release for Exercise 5.c. (page 86).

New For Consumers

Highlights of
New Federal
Publications

FOR IMMEDIATE RELEASE

WHAT'S IN YOUR
MEDICINE CHEST

Consumer
Information
Center

General Services
Administration

Washington, DC 20405
(202) 566-1794
GSA #1853
654K

On the surface of things, it might appear that the reason a medicine chest is thus called is that it's a good place to store medicines. Not so, according to the Food and Drug Administration. Potential danger lurks when there's medicine in the medicine chest. One reason is that bathroom medicine chests are usually right over the sink, and accessible enough to tempt the curiosity of children who live in or visit your house.

To help you know not only how to child-proof your medicine chest, but to keep it safe and up-to-date for adults too, the Food and Drug Administration has a free reprint from its magazine, the FDA Consumer. For your copy of What's in Your Medicine Chest, write to Consumer Information Center, Dept. 645K, Pueblo, Colorado 81009.

Even if there aren't any children in your household, the medicine chest is not a good place for drugs, since the warm moist atmosphere of the bathroom can cause some drugs to deteriorate. Ideally, both prescription and non-prescription drugs should be kept in a cool, dry place.

What else should be kept in that cool, dry place will depend on the makeup of the family. If there are young children in the family you're likely to need baby aspirin, anti-bacterial topical ointments, and medicine to treat the symptoms of diarrhea. Almost every family will want to keep aspirin or a non-aspirin pain reliever on hand.

No matter what the age of your family, avoid overstocking drugs. Some drug products lose potency on the shelf over time, especially after they are opened. Other drugs change in consistency. Ideally, supplies in the medicine chest should be bought to last over a period of no more than 6 to 12 months.

Be sure to review the contents of your medicine chest every 6 months and discard old supplies. Also be sure that any new prescriptions you get are clearly dated.

Tablets that have become crumbly, medicines that have changed color, odor, or consistency, or are outdated should be destroyed. Empty the bottle of medicine into the toilet, flush it down and rinse out the bottle. Don't put leftover drugs in the trash basket where they can be dug out by inquisitive youngsters. Newly purchased drugs that don't look right should be returned to the pharmacy. Drug products that have lost their labels also should be destroyed.

And, as a final safety precaution, always keep the telephone number of the local poison control center, doctor, hospital, rescue squad, fire and police departments near every phone in the house. And tape the emergency phone list wherever you keep medicines and emergency supplies, as well as inside the bathroom medicine chest door.

When you order What's in Your Medicine Chest (free) you'll also receive a free copy of the Consumer Information Catalog. Published quarterly by the Consumer Information Center of the General Services Administration, the free Catalog lists 200 selected free and moderately priced federal consumer booklets.

12 Speeches, News Conferences and Meetings

1. Toni Morrison is coming to town to discuss her literary work. Prepare to cover the speech. First list the sources you would consult to learn about Morrison. Then write down in note form what you have gathered from those sources that will be useful in covering the event and the content of the speech.

2. The secretary of the interior is holding a news conference before a meeting of local conservationists. The secretary is to discuss his views on offshore oil drilling and drilling in national parks. First, list the sources you would consult to prepare for this news conference. Then write down in note form what you have gathered from those sources that will be useful in covering the event and the content of the news conference.

3. Find out when your city council is holding its next meeting. Prepare to cover it. First, list the sources you would consult to prepare for this meeting. Then write down in note form what you have gathered from those sources that will be useful in covering the event and the content of the meeting.

4. **a.** Find a story about a speech in a newspaper. First look to see whether the reporter covered the *event* and the *content*. Then analyze and comment on the lead, the transitions, the use of quotations and the comprehensiveness of the coverage. Write 300 words.
   b. Do the same for a story about a news conference.
   c. Do the same for a story about a meeting.

5. Find three stories by three different authors on wire services covering a speech or a press conference by the U.S. president. Compare and analyze the stories. Write 200 words about your findings.

6. Write a story covering the *content* of the following speeches.

a.

Learn to Listen with Your Heart

Farewell to Graduates

By MARTHA SAUNDERS, *Dean, College of Arts and Sciences*
Delivered at the University of West Florida

In the Department of Communication Arts, we spend a great deal of time thinking and talking about words—the meaning of words, the persuasive value of words, the ethical implications of words and, generally, the impact of words as they are delivered in messages among people. Because of this, I was especially captured by a magazine article a few months ago that discussed how words influence people.

The article suggested that the most important messages that humans deliver to one another are usually expressed in very simple terms. I hope that doesn't shock you now that you've spent these past few years having your minds crammed with complicated thoughts. The article went on to suggest that the *most influential messages* in our language most often come in three-word phrases.

I had to agree that three-word phrases such as "I love you" or "There's no charge" or "And in conclusion" certainly were capable of prompting a strong reaction in me, and as I had hoped to impress you with profound thought today, I decided to share with you *three* three-word phrases that I have found useful as I have moved along in my life.

The first three-word phrase I've found useful in life is this: *I'll be there.* Have you ever thought about what a balm those three words can create?

I'll be there. If you've ever had to call for a plumber over a weekend, you know how really good these words can feel. Or if you've been stranded on the road with car trouble and used your last quarter to call a friend, you know how good those words can be. Think about them:

"Grandma, I'm graduating in August!" *I'll be there.*

"Roommate, I'm stuck at the office and can't get to the airport to meet my sister!" *I'll be there.*

"Mom, the baby cries all night and if I don't get some sleep I'll perish!" *I'll be there.*

Recently I was talking with a local business person who is occasionally in a position to hire UWF graduates, and she told me the single most impressive thing a job candidate can do is to demonstrate a real interest in the well-being of that business. Someone who will help further the objectives of that organization, whether or not he or she is "on the clock" is going to be a valuable person. In other words, *be somebody who will be there.*

One of my favorite stories about someone who knew how to "be there" is told of Elizabeth, the Queen Mother of England, who was asked whether the little princesses (Elizabeth and Margaret Rose) would leave England after the Blitz of 1940. The queen replied: "The children will not leave England unless I do. I shall not leave unless their father does, and the king will not leave the country in any circumstances whatever." *I'll be there.*

The second three-word phrase I want to present to you is perhaps the hardest to learn to say—I know it was for me and sometimes still is. It's *maybe you're right.* Think about it. If more people were to learn to say *maybe you're right*, the marriage counselors would be out of business and, with a little luck, the gun shops. I know from experience it can have a disarming effect on an opponent in an argument. In fact, one of my lawyer friends uses it often in his closing remarks—and he is a very successful lawyer. *Maybe you're right.*

It has been my experience that when we get so hung up on getting our own way that we will not concede on *any* point, we are doing ourselves a real disservice. Make life a little easier on yourself. Remember the old saying—"There are a hundred ways to skin a cat—and every single one of them is right." *Maybe you're right.*

The third phrase I want to introduce to you I must have heard a thousand times when I was a little girl. Whenever I faced a hard decision, I would turn to my caregiver and ask what I should do. Her response was always the same three-word phrase— *"Your heart knows"*—then she would go on about what she was doing.

"My heart knows?" I would think to myself. "What's that supposed to mean? I need advice here. I need for you to tell me what to do."

But as I was an imperious child, I would throw my hand on my hip and say, "Maybe so, but my heart isn't talking!"

To this she would respond— *"Learn to listen."*

This brings me to the point of my speech. You know, life doesn't come in the form of a degree plan. There's no Great Adviser out there who will give you a checklist and say, "Do these things and you'll earn your degree in 'life.'"

To some extent, the page is blank now. You may have a rough outline of where you're headed, but I can assure you, you won't get there without having to make some tough decisions—and decision making is never easy.

You may be able to find people to suggest what you should do, but for the most part, no one will be willing to accept the responsibility for your mistakes. You'll have to make your own choices.

My advice to you today is to *learn to listen to your heart.* The psychologists call this "turning in to our subconscious." Spiritual leaders call it "turning to a higher power." Whatever you call it, there is an ability in each of you to find the right answers for your life. It's there, and it's a powerful gift that all the education or degrees in the world can't acquire for you. You've had it all along—now, you're going to have to use it.

In *The Bending of the Bough*, George Moore wrote: "The difficulty in life is the choice." Choose well, graduates!

b.   The Ten Commandments of Corporate Communications

Better Management Understanding of the Communications Function

By FRASER P. SEITEL, *Senior Counselor, Burson-Marsteller*
Delivered at the Cincinnati Chapter of The Public Relations Society of America, Cincinnati, Ohio

Thank you. Good afternoon, ladies and gentlemen. It's a great pleasure to be with you today. I must say I was a bit taken aback when I arrived here late last night and turned on the radio and heard a report that "The U.S. planned to strengthen the blockade until the dictator agreed to leave." I said to myself, "My God, she's only been back several weeks, and already they're trying to get rid of Marge Schott!"

My job today, as described in the letter of invitation, is to discuss "the future of the practice of public relations and, in particular, how to build better management understanding of the communications function."

I might say that's a lot to ask for *free*!

But I'll do my best.

Let me begin by saying that the *potential* of the practice of public relations has never been brighter, because the *need* for positive communications among organizations and their publics in all sectors of society—government, business, nonprofit, the arts, sports, you name it—has never been more pronounced.

Consider the following:

In July, the chief executive officer of the United States of America—President Bubba—had no choice but to replace his *closest* and *most respected adviser*, George Stephanopoulous, as White House communications director. To make matters even more ignominious for young George, President Clinton named as his successor—horror of horrors!—a Reagan Republican!

Why did he resort to such cruelty?

The answer is simple. The job of public relations director for the president of the United States demands a *consummate communications professional*. George Stephanopoulous wasn't. David Gergen was. The president literally had no choice.

A few months later, when the chairman of the once-unparalleled IBM Corporation was forced to step aside, his successor, a man named Louis Gerstner, named, as his first official appointment, a new communications director.

The new chairman fired a woman who had been with IBM for two decades and replaced her with a public relations professional with whom he had worked before and in whom he placed his total trust. People at IBM are still shocked at the suddenness and severity of the beheading. But Lew Gerstner didn't have time to fool around. He needed a public relations pro.

Finally, in numerical terms—there are 200,000 people in this country who practice public relations, hundreds of colleges and universities that teach public relations, public relations agencies that bill their clients in the hundreds of millions

of dollars each year, and a growing number of practitioners in this field who earn six-figure incomes and at least one corporate communications director who earns seven figures.

So on the one hand, the practice of public relations has never been more *prominent*. But on the other hand, this field, like so many others, has been riddled by the wave of mergers and consolidations, downsizings and retrenchments that continue to rip through America and the world. The ranks of public relations professionals have been hit hard by the recession.

So *whether* the practice realizes its potential over the rest of this decade and into the next century is very much open to question. The *answer* will depend on how well each of us in this room and in this field impress upon the people for whom we work the *importance* and the *relevance* of practicing proper public relations.

We accomplish this, I believe, by embracing what I call "The Ten Commandments of Corporate Communications."

So if you will permit me to become a bit biblical, I will share these with you.

The First Commandment of Public Relations is to hold as our one and only God the spirit of Truthful Communications.

We must *want* to communicate, be pro-communications, be prone toward *disclosure* and not withholding. We must understand that *understanding* is the essence of what we do. And we must convince those for whom we work that if they are truly to be trusted by those with whom they deal, then they must *explain* to people not only *what* they're doing but, more important, *why*—that is, the *reasons* for their actions.

For example, Johnson & Johnson explained why it was removing Tylenol from the shelves. Pepsi-Cola explained why it wasn't removing Diet Pepsi. Both triumphed in the face of adversity. By contrast, NASA with the *Challenger* and Exxon with the *Valdez* said little and lost terribly.

The Second Commandment is to honor your Corporate Father and Mother.

This has two dimensions.

First, we in public relations must demonstrate an *understanding* of and *knowledge* about the business of our organization. Computers, insurance, banking, arts, education, whatever. Your employer or client won't and *shouldn't* accept—much less "respect"—your expertise as a communicator until you first demonstrate *your* understanding of the nature of his or her business.

Second, you must be an *advocate* for your organization. You must believe in the people who pay your salary. This is *critical* in public relations, because we are the "public face and conscience" of our organizations. So if we don't like what's going on, if we don't think the people we work for are *ethical* or *honest* or *reasonable*—then it's fair neither to them nor to ourselves to represent them in public.

Indeed, that's why Jerald Ter Horst resigned as spokesman for President Ford—because he couldn't support the decision to pardon Richard Nixon.

Extreme, perhaps. But in public relations, you must be an advocate for your employer or client.

The Third Commandment of public relations is to make no graven images, nor to bow down to false prophets—such as worshiping at the Altar of the Status Quo.

We must question the popular wisdom, not accept the notion that "We do things this way because we've always done them like this." (How many times have you heard that refrain in your organization?)

The one thing Bill Clinton has done *right* and for which he will receive high marks—no matter what happens to his plan—is his questioning of the status quo on health care.

So, too, must we in public relations hold as our mandate continually to *question*, to *challenge*, to *innovate*. This is particularly pertinent in a communications environment that will soon be dominated by *fiber-optic highways* and *digital infrastructures* and *global interactive media.*

Fourth is the Commandment of keeping holy the Sabbath notion of practicing with integrity, of upholding ethical values, of doing what is right.

Public relations must be the conscience of the organization. We must be the ones who ask management—before we ask anything else—the following question: "Is what we're doing here the *right* thing to do?" Few others will have the nerve to raise such an issue.

It's been my observation that with all the firings and dislocations and trepidation about *future* firings and future dislocations, the timidity factor in our organizations has increased. Most, in fact, seem to agree with the sentiment expressed once by the radical philosopher Saul Alinsky that "In America, people concerned about the morality of means and ends always end up on their *ends* without any *means*!"

We in public relations can't afford to think like that. As Dan Rather said once, "There's a big difference between doing well and doing right."

In public relations we must always do what's right.

The Fifth Commandment, in a related sense, says that we must never take the lord's name in vain.

Our "lord," as I indicated, is *truth*. And we must always tell it.

Should we always answer every question the media or the analysts or the legislators ask? No. There are some areas, because we are "advocates" for the organization, that we simply can't—and shouldn't—get into.

But we should never *lie* or *distort* or *confuse* or *obfuscate*. (That's the job of a lawyer! Only kidding!)

What this does mean is that in our jobs it is crucial that we always know where the truth lies. And that means that

management, if it wants us to represent the organization in the best possible manner, must confide in us.

The Sixth Commandment says thou shalt not kill—the competition.

Be competitive. But don't *demean* or *denigrate* or *bad-mouth* your competitors. Rumor-mongers, unfortunately, are rampant in a society where the line between legitimate journalism and self-serving entertainment has become a blur.

Some reporters today—not most, but some—feast on Geraldo-esque tidbits of gossip and intrigue and scandal.

But we in public relations should reject the temptation to win favor by fueling such stories. As NBC News learned, to its ultimate embarrassment, in its fabricated report on General Motors trucks—such *misleading* and *distorted sensationalism* can backfire catastrophically.

And we should have no part of it.

By extension, then, the Seventh Commandment says we should not bear false witness against our neighbors.

Indeed, we in public relations must respect the publics with which we deal. That means we must set *standards* and keep them high. We must take pride in the communications products for which we and our organizations are responsible.

This, too, is no easy task in a society where communications "standards" are defined by the likes of "A Current Affair" and "Hard Copy" and "Beavis and Butt-head" and this year's best-selling literary work, Howard Stern's *Private Parts* and next year's best-selling literary work, Robert Packwood's *Private Diary!*

Despite all this, we in public relations must adhere to a higher communications standard and resist succumbing to the pandemic popularity of *pandering* and *gossip* and *sleaze* that dominate the society.

Public relations Commandment Eight says thou shalt not steal. This is also known as the "Inaki Lopez Commandment"!

Commandment Nine says thou shalt not commit adultery. This, of course, is the Burt and Loni Commandment!

Both refer—if you'll permit me some poetic license here—to the kind of advice and counsel we must offer management. Such advice should not be stolen from others, nor should we cheat management by offering counsel that reflects solely what it wants to hear.

The advice we offer—and make no mistake, the *essence* of public relations practice is to counsel, *to give advice*—must be *our own*, based on our experience, our knowledge, our judgment.

It shouldn't be taken off some shelf. Your particular organization confronts problems and opportunities that are peculiar to it alone—its people, its culture, its special circumstances.

Original problems demand original *solutions.* And increasingly, today's CEOs will renounce the adviser who tells them only what he thinks they want to hear. Such a person, as Kennedy adviser Ted Sorensen has said, "is a bearer of consistently *good tidings* but frequently *bad advice*."

We, on the other hand, if we are to serve our managements well, must stand up for what we stand for.

Finally, the Tenth Commandment of public relations says thou shalt not covet.

This means you must be *true to yourself.* You must believe in yourself and in what you do for a living.

When I began in this field more than two decades ago, public relations was a much maligned and mysterious and misunderstood art form.

Today, professional public relations is not only an *accepted* profession but one *respected* by everyone from corporate CEOs to national legislators to university presidents to religious leaders, even to—albeit grudgingly—reporters and editors.

So I'm convinced that the halcyon days for this field lie just ahead.

And those who will lead our field into this golden age will be the ones who take seriously these Ten Commandments . . . and also who take to heart the words of the Rev. Dr. Billy Graham, who is fond of saying the following:

"Never give up. Never slow down. Never."

Thank you.

c. ## Journalistic Ethics, Machiavellian Style

By JOHN C. MERRILL, *Emeritus Professor of Journalism, University of Missouri*
Delivered at the National Conference on Ethics and the Professions, University of Florida

A very plausible theory of the American press is that it is Machiavellian. Throughout the years—even in the earliest days, when partisan politics dominated American journalism—there was a strong element of pragmatic or egocentric utilitist motivation in the press. Without using the name "Machiavellian," numerous critics and press observers have noted the strong hunger for power that has infected a succession of publishers and editors right up to the present moment. And along with this love of power, especially exemplified by such men as Horace Greeley and William Randolph Hearst, a certain foundational love for a good fight and fierce competition has characterized a very large segment of American journalism.

And since the fifties at least, with the advent of commercial television, personalities such as Edward R. Murrow, Walter Cronkite, Dan Rather, Ted Koppel, and Peter Jennings have put success and power alongside a competitive spirit in their desire to secure high ratings and a national following. Helping American journalists, or many of them, in their often irresponsible (or at least dubious) techniques has been the tradition of freedom assured by the First Amendment. Often news directors and editors have justified their actions by appealing to constitutional guarantees of freedom. In the minds of many, "freedom" seems to have become synonymous with "proper action."

It is not [my] purpose to document various types of Machiavellian practices in the American press. This has been done many times and reverberations of such practices are found all around us. What I intend to do is to provide a glimpse of what "Machiavellian journalism" is about, provide a statement by a well-known American journalist that is obviously Machiavellian, give some instances of reactions to this statement by modern journalism students, and come to a few conclusions.

Even if you reject the thesis that American journalism is Machiavellian—or even largely so—you cannot ignore the strong element of student sympathy that I found in samples of opinion from a number of journalism classes at Louisiana State University in the spring semester of 1991.

Let me hasten here to quote from an article by Robert Sherrill, an American journalist writing in the 1980s, who sets forth what I believe to be a significant—and even growing—philosophical perspective in American journalism. I quote from his "News Ethics: Press and Jerks," in *Grand Street* 5, No. 2 (Winter 1986), p. 117:

> Do journalists sometimes write fiction and pass it off as fact? Do they use stolen material? Tape phone conversations without telling the person on the other end to beware? Misrepresent themselves in order to pry information from reluctant sources . . . ? Does this mean that journalists are unethical? As one who has done all of the above at one time or another, seldom with a feeling of shame and sometimes with a feeling of satisfaction for the results, I am inclined to pass over the ethical question entirely. If it works, I am generally for it. . . .

> So long as reporters, vastly outnumbered and outgunned, are expected to penetrate these hostile areas [government and corporations] to obtain useful information, they can, I think, be forgiven for using almost any device or tactic so long as it enables them to bring back the bacon.

Now, so far as I am concerned, that is a statement of pure Machiavellian essence. I have heard journalists through the years say much the same thing, but with not quite the bluntness and honesty of Sherrill's words. For a long time I have been a student of Machiavelli, have devoured his works—especially his *Discourses* and *The Prince*—and believe that Sherrill has neatly wrapped up his "achieve your ends by any means" or "nothing succeeds like success" philosophy in blunt Machiavellian language. He even brings in the pragmatic ("if it works, it's OK") element of Machiavellianism.

Perhaps you are saying that Sherrill does not represent American journalism. Of course he doesn't. No one journalist does. Without a doubt there are principled, formalistic and altruistic Kantians out there among American journalists. All I am saying here is that Mr. Sherrill has nicely encapsulated Machiavellian journalism for us. And the new breed of "investigative reporters" and success-intoxicated journalists out to win prizes, get promotions and public attention seem hellbent to join Old Nick in his pragmatic grab for success and power.

At any rate, I decided to see what our modern journalism students thought of Sherrill's position, hoping that they would repudiate it. Was I surprised!

I supplied the above quotation from Robert Sherrill to three different classes of journalism students. All the students were juniors and seniors. I asked the students to take the discussion forms and write their reactions and their agreement or disagreement with Sherrill's position, and bring them to the next class. Of the 74 forms returned to me by the students here are the numerical results as to agreement-disagreement with the Sherrill position:

Agreement: 66.
Disagreement: 6.
Ambiguous: 2.

Those results were not very reassuring to me. Those among you who are scientifically inclined, let me assure you that I had a couple of fellow faculty members read the student responses, and they agreed with me on the direction of student opinion. And as you will shortly see from the samples to be provided, the student opinion was rather clear-cut.

Let me now provide some of the student reactions:

"As Sherrill states, sometimes unethical practices are necessary to get to the truth, which in turn brings high rewards to the 'go-getter' journalist. All journalists want to succeed, to go upscale in their careers, and they would be smart to get the right, accurate news, but they should be sure they aren't caught doing it unethically." — Y.S.

"I agree with Robert Sherrill when he says that journalists will get a story by any means. I think the question of whether or not it is ethical can only be expressed by each individual. I believe in situational ethics. What is appropriate for one story may not be appropriate for another. There are liars in every profession; the only reason journalists seem to take more heat is that their information is in the public's hands." — P.S.

"I believe pragmatism is crucial and necessary in all facets of life. For every problem you encounter, it is your option to do it the right way or the wrong way. If you solve your problem with a method that works, you will gain very much. To me, if it works, keep it; if it does not, throw it overboard." — P.G.A.

"I believe most journalists do what it takes to get their story. I don't believe that this is being unethical—

this is their job. There are certain reasonable boundaries, of course, but it takes crossing these boundaries every once in a while and it is a *must* to get their story completed." — G.G.

"I agree with Sherrill's position. It is the journalist's job to get the story, no matter how they do it. I think that media ethics and personal ethics should be kept at a distance from one another. For example, I think it would be all right to take a document that could prove to be important to the story, but I don't think it would be all right to steal something from someone for your personal satisfaction." — S.C.

"I think Mr. Sherrill's position is valid and can be justified, but not for the reasons he presents. I believe that sometimes a journalist has to go to extremes in order to get a story or even a tip to a future story. I believe that in order to serve the public interest some unusual methods are necessary." — D.M.

"I agree with Sherrill's position because I think most journalists are in the business for the money. I think journalists are willing to break the rules of ethics to get a story because if they get a story no one else can get, they will be recognized and praised for it. It is also true that journalists are unethical and get away with it because their bosses are the same. That's probably how they got to the top. Some probably won't ever admit it, and others will probably admit it with pride. Sometimes it seems like the only way to get ahead in a business that is so competitive." — J.C.

"It is the job of a good journalist to find out and report the truth. Oftentimes there are serious barriers standing in his way. Journalists should use whatever means necessary to find out the facts of a story. They shouldn't operate every day with blatant disregard for the privacy and trust of public officials and citizens, but if the situation requires it, the journalist should not hesitate to use all of the means at his disposal to find out and report the truth. The public's right to know supersedes most arguments for "ethical" newsgathering. The journalist should not purposely abuse people's privacy, but he should not be afraid to use all of his talents and methods to do his work." — K.W.

Now that we have had a look at a sampling of student comments about the Sherrill quote, let me conclude with a few remarks. We can see in the comments a rather wide range of ethical sophistication. Some of the comments contain nuggets of philosophical insights, from whatever source they may have been obtained. Others are simply surface opinion devoid of much thoughtful consideration. This is perhaps to be expected. But it must be pointed out that these students had not had a course in journalism ethics [none is offered in the School of Journalism] and had perhaps had fleeting references to ethics in various of their courses. This would account for some of the students who were able to use such terms as "teleological ethics" and "situation ethics."

Some of the students were familiar, probably without realizing it, with the concept of principled or Kantian ethics with its "a priori" guiding maxims and also with its opposite ethical theory based on consequentialism.

But one thing is certain. Somewhere—from some journalism course or from some journalist—most of the students had received the idea that the journalist's duty or responsibility is to get the story out to the public. And it seems to follow for most of these students that such a duty dictates a policy of success or of getting the story "by any means."

Such comments, as we have seen from the students, certainly offer reverberations of Machiavellianism. One has a duty to succeed, to use the tactics necessary to achieve desired ends. Hide your deceit if at all possible. Get that story. Or as Sherrill wrote: Bring home the bacon.

As I have just finished my fortieth year in journalism and journalism teaching, during which time I have tried to instill large doses of principle-based ethics into my students, I must confess that it was painful to find students writing such comments as we have seen above. And I'm afraid it doesn't bode well for American journalism of the future—at least from an ethical perspective. It may well be that in journalism as well as in politics, Machiavellianism has found a new birth of energy and will dominate journalistic activities into the new century.

The new crop of journalists, if they resemble the sample of journalism students included [here], will be driven by pragmatics rather than ethics and will put success in getting a story above moral considerations. Of course, they will say in defense of their actions that what they are doing is, indeed, ethical in the "big sense"—in the sense of letting the light shine in, in granting the people's right to know, in simply doing their job as reporters. And, they will undoubtedly say, doing their job as reporters, being good reporters—that is, getting the facts out, period—is journalistically or professionally what is called for.

A rather dismal journalistic image seems to be coming over the horizon: the journalist inspired by Machiavelli rather than Kant. An enterprising journalist, no doubt, but a sly and even ruthless one, out to succeed at any price. This is not a pleasant picture for the person concerned with ethics; it is a downgrading of the humanities at the expense of the practical and hardnosed utilitarian world.

It may well be an indication that professionalism in education for journalism is getting out of hand and that journalism needs to retreat from this growing concern with success-oriented professionalism and step into a kinder, gentler world of humanistic and liberal education.

7. The dean or director of your school or department of journalism has resigned her position. She has charged that the college or university has provided insufficient funding for the school or department to function properly. Her name is Jessica Jergens, and she had been head of journalism for five years. She holds a news conference. Write a story for your local newspaper covering the content of the news conference. Do not exceed 1,000 words.

Opening Statement

Ladies and gentlemen, I have called this news conference to announce that at the end of this school term, I shall be resigning my position as head of journalism. It has been no secret that I have had some serious differences with the administration of this university over how the journalism program continues to be funded. The faculty in journalism are too few and too poorly paid. The facilities are pathetic by anyone's standards. This university does students no favor by sending them out into the world of journalism improperly prepared. I can no longer in good conscience head a program that has so little support.

When I came on board five years ago, I thought we had an understanding that I could bring on one new person each year for at least five years. In those five years, our faculty has increased by only one. Although we acquired some new equipment, our newswriting lab still has manual typewriters.

Although the administration can cite lack of funding generally, it cannot explain how one can run a program successfully without proper support.

Questions and Answers

Q. Dr. Jergens, are you recommending that the journalism program in this university be dropped altogether?

A. I am not saying that. Perhaps my departure will help the administration see the seriousness of the situation and do something to remedy it. I personally think it would be a tremendous loss to the university not to have a journalism program.

Q. Are you merely resigning your position as head of journalism, or are you also leaving the university?

A. I am leaving the university.

Q. Do you have any future plans?

A. Well, I am going to take it easy for at least a year. I have some writing to do and a lot of reading to catch up on.

Q. What is your primary complaint? What didn't you get that made you resign?

A. I thought I made myself clear on that.

Q. But what was the final straw? What made you quit now?

A. Well, I had set certain goals for myself. When I came, I realized the journalism program needed strengthening in many areas. If we were going to be a well-rounded program, we needed courses added. You need qualified faculty to teach courses. It all starts with qualified faculty. I guess I had something of a five-year plan. If I didn't get to a certain point in five years, I thought it would be a pretty good indication that this university was not serious in its commitment to a quality journalism program.

Q. If the situation is so bad, how do you expect the university to recruit a new head? Who would take this job?

A. Hope springs eternal. There's always someone out there who would like to have a shot at this.

Q. Is there someone on the faculty now whom you would recommend?

A. I am not sure I would wish this job on anyone who knows the situation here well. But if you are asking whether anyone on this faculty is capable and qualified to handle this position, of course there are several. Any of several could succeed—if the administration comes through with more support.

Q. What is your proudest achievement as head of journalism?

A. The curriculum is stronger now than it was five years ago. The faculty is stronger as well. I also believe we have attracted a better brand of student.

Q. Is there any truth to the rumor that lack of cooperation among your faculty is the real reason you are stepping down?

A. That would be news to me. I have had my differences with one or two members of this faculty, but I cannot complain about a lack of faculty support.

Q. What about the rumor that the administration has asked you to step down but gave you a chance to resign?

A. That is altogether incorrect. Perhaps my resignation will cause some joy in the halls of the administration, but no one has asked me or even suggested that I resign.

Q. Dr. Jergens, you are not denying that you have at times engaged in open warfare with the president of this university, are you?

A. I have not been asked that question. All I am saying is that no one has asked me to resign. And that includes the president of this university.

Q. Do you think you have enjoyed wide support among this student body? Hasn't there been a great deal of student dissatisfaction?

A. I will leave that to others to answer. However, you may consult a student survey conducted less than a year ago that indicated that students gave me an above-average rating. You may compare my rating to the heads of other areas that have taken such a survey.

Q. What is your single biggest regret?

A. Well, it has to be that times and people are such that proper funding is simply not forthcoming. Perhaps I and others have failed to impress this university and people in general of the importance of journalism in a free society and how badly we need to train people well.

Q. What one thing would you most wish for the journalism program?

A. Better writing classes. The biggest complaint in any area of professional journalism is that we are not turning out good writers. Writing classes must be taught by qualified faculty, and those classes have to be small enough for the professor to be able to give the kind of attention students need. Everything begins and ends with writing.

Q. Will you return to teaching, or will you seek work in the real world of journalism?

A. I don't think I have ever left the real world of journalism. But yes, I can't imagine that I will leave teaching.

Q. What about another administrative post?

A. For the time being, no, thank you.

8. Your mayor, James Alton, holds a news conference twice a month. Here's a transcript of one of them. Write a story for your local newspaper on this conference. Do not exceed 1,000 words.

Opening Statement

Ladies and gentlemen, I have no startling announcement today or any shocking news. I am pleased to tell you that local crime is down 9 percent from last year at this time. I believe our efforts to strengthen the police force and to make neighborhoods aware of their responsibilities to combat crime are paying off.

We must all continue working to make the streets of our city safe. That includes safe from traffic accidents. Unfortunately, five more people have been killed in traffic accidents in our city than were killed a year ago.

Not surprisingly, alcohol was involved in four of those fatalities. We will crack down even harder on drunken driving and will continue to push for a tougher ordinance on first- and second-time offenders.

What's on your minds today?

Questions and Answers

Q. Mr. Mayor, what kind of ordinance would you like to see enforced regarding drunk driving?

A. Well, I have been thinking about this for some time now, and it seems to me that first offenders should spend a night in jail and have their licenses revoked for 90 days. Second offenders should spend 30 days in jail and have their licenses revoked for one year. Three or more offenses should carry a mandatory sentence of six months in jail and license revoked for five years.

Q. Don't you think you are being a bit severe, especially with first offenders?

A. No, I don't. Drunk driving kills. If someone drives while intoxicated, that person is a potential killer, a threat to every citizen. That person is similar to someone going around with a loaded, cocked gun. But even the person with the gun might have some control. The drunk driver is out of control.

Q. You speak of sending a lot more people to jail. Where do you propose to put them? Our jail is already too crowded.

A. You're right. We have a serious problem there. The voters of this community have turned down the means to enlarge our jail three years in a row now. Somehow, we have not found the way to get citizens to see how desperate the situation is. The crowded jail is a disgrace to this community. Even more disgraceful is that we have released prisoners only because of lack of space.

Q. Isn't it true also that some have clearly received lighter sentences because of a lack of jail space?

A. I don't want to comment on that. I would have to know of specific examples. Right now I don't have one.

Q. Here's one. The police chief's son was just sentenced to serve six months in jail on three charges of driving with a revoked license and one charge of driving with a suspended license. Don't you think that is a light sentence, and do you think the jail situation has something to do with it?

A. Let me answer the second question first. No, I think the jail situation had nothing to do with the sentencing of that young man. . . .

Q. What was it then, the fact that he is the son of the police chief?

A. Answering your second question is a bit more difficult. Was it a light sentence? If I remember the facts correctly, he was sentenced to serve one year for driving with a revoked license, but that sentence was suspended. Instead he was placed on two years' probation and ordered to perform 40 hours of community service and to pay court costs. He was then given three concurrent six-month terms in jail on three other charges: two counts of driving with a revoked license and one of driving with a suspended license. So he has six months in jail, plus community service.

Q. But surely this sentence does not speak well for improving the safety of drivers and pedestrians in our community. Why haven't you been vocal in urging stronger sentences in cases like these?

A. I don't know that it is my place to second-guess a judge.

Q. Mr. Mayor, do you or do you not think the police chief's son got off too easy?

A. Yes, I do.

Q. Well, which is it?

A. I think the sentence was light.

Q. There has been a blight of school bus accidents around the country. Some have pointed to the young, inexperienced drivers of these school buses. This community has 12 drivers below the age of 20. Three of them are 18. Do you think we should be entrusting the lives of our children to 18-year-old drivers?

A. I am not sure that age has much to do with driving skills. You could argue, I suppose, that experience helps. After all, the jet fighter pilots of our Air Force are often under 20, I'm told. Young people have quicker reflexes, and they can be excellent drivers.

Q. But what excuse can there be to let inexperienced drivers drive our school buses?

A. Money.

Q. You mean we can't pay mature, experienced drivers enough, so we have to hire kids?

A. Of course.

Q. But that's outrageous.

A. Tell the taxpayers that. You have to understand that a bus driver's hours often make it impossible for that person to hold down another job. People with solid, well-paying jobs are not likely to become school bus drivers.

Q. The vice chairman of the Springfield Tomorrow Committee resigned this past week because he was unable "to stand the pettiness of the press." What is your reaction to that?

A. Well, I guess I have known you folks to be petty from time to time. I'm sorry Gerald Nicklaus felt that way. Any public position demands that we put up with you people.

Q. Is that your understanding of the press, that you have to "put up" with us?

A. Of course not. You know that I know that we can't exist without you people.

Q. Let's return to Mr. Nicklaus. You must have known that he ordered a committee selection meeting to be held Tuesday without public or media present. Did you approve of this order? Or did you ask for his resignation?

A. I neither approved of the action nor asked for his resignation.

Q. Why didn't you ask for his resignation?

A. Well, I would have at least given him a chance to change his mind on the subject. Had he persisted on closed meetings, I don't suppose there was any choice but to ask him to step down.

Q. His letter of resignation also cited poor health. Do you believe that was the reason?

A. I only know what he said, and I have no reason to disbelieve him.

Q. When will you name his replacement?

A. I hope by the end of the week.

Q. Mr. Mayor, what about the rumors that you and Mrs. Alton are living in separate residences?

A. Thank you, ladies and gentlemen.

CHALLENGE EXERCISE

9. Using computer databases to search for information, prepare for, cover and write:
   a. A speech story.
   b. A news conference story.
   c. A meeting story.

   Then compare your stories to those appearing in the local paper.

13 Other Types of Basic Stories

Crime Stories Reporting

1. Write a story based on the following information obtained from police and other sources:
   a. The Black Derby Liquor Store, 2311 Ripley Way, was robbed at gunpoint.
   b. The clerk was Seve Bellinos of 4673 Bellinghausen Court. His age is 28.
   c. A man with a pillowcase over his head entered the store at 7:12 p.m. He pulled out a pistol and demanded that Bellinos empty the contents of the cash register into another pillowcase.
   d. Police officers Anne Fulgham and Jose Lopez answered a silent alarm triggered by Bellinos at 7:16 p.m. They arrived at the store at 7:19 p.m. as the gunman was leaving the store.
   e. The man fled as he saw the police car. Officer Fulgham shouted a warning and fired a shot at the man, but she missed. The man ran into an alley, and the two officers followed. He finally escaped.
   f. A witness, John Paul Reinicke, 35, of 109 Ninth St., Apt. 3C, was walking down Ripley Way when the incident occurred. "The officers did a great job," he said. "The guy ran so fast he looked like a track star."
   g. The owner of the liquor store, Ralph Martinson, 53, of 109 Lincoln Terrace, said about $2,845 was taken.
   h. Police Chief Antonio Grasso said a routine investigation of the incident would be made by the Police Internal Security Squad. Such investigations are conducted each time an officer fires a service revolver.
   i. The clerk said the robber was about 6 feet tall and weighed 155 pounds. He was wearing blue jeans and a dirty white T-shirt with a torn right sleeve.

2. Write a story based on the following information obtained from police and other sources:
   a. Danielle D. Drummond, 19, of 209 Rodgers Hall on the local campus, was raped.
   b. Location was by the Chemistry Building as Drummond was walking back to her dorm after going to a movie downtown. She was alone.
   c. A man with a stocking mask displayed a knife and forced her into an alley beside the Chemistry Building. He threatened to kill her if she screamed.
   d. She described the man as 6 feet 4 inches tall, 210 pounds, athletic appearance, blond hair, blue eyes, scar on the left side of his neck.
   e. Police said the description was similar to that given by two other victims of rapes in the campus area in the past six months. In all, there have been four rapes in the area during that period.

f. One of the other victims also said the man wore a stocking mask. In the two other assaults, no mask was used. All involved the use of a knife.

g. The reported rape is the 16th in the city this year, compared with two during the same period last year.

h. Police Chief Grasso said he is forming a rape task force composed of police, rape crisis center officials and others to determine what can be done about the series of rapes.

i. College officials say they will install emergency telephone lines in outdoor areas around the campus and review street lighting in the area.

3. In almost any crime story, there are three major sources of information. List those sources and briefly describe what kind of information you would expect to obtain from each.

4. You are sent to the scene of a bank robbery, where you find that the police and FBI are still investigating. Describe what steps you would take to get as much information as possible for an early edition of your newspaper.

5. Obtain from your local police department crime statistics for the previous year as reported to the federal government. Using *Crime in the United States*, published annually by the Federal Bureau of Investigation, write a story comparing crime in your city with overall U.S. figures.

6. Murders in Holyfield, Kan., rose from one in 2005 to seven in 2006, but rapes fell from 35 to 27, robberies from 97 to 86 and assaults from 302 to 280. Meanwhile, burglaries rose from 576 to 603 and larcenies from 3,404 to 3,420. Auto theft remained the same at 172.

a. Write a news story based on these crime statistics.

b. Create a simple chart to accompany your story.

Accidents and Fire Stories Reporting

7. You have been sent to the local river where a young girl is believed to have drowned. From whom would you try to obtain information, and what would you expect to get from each of them?

8. You have covered a tornado and would like to include damage estimates in your story. From whom would you obtain those estimates?

9. You have covered a house fire that resulted in the loss of housing for a family of four. You would like to find out what relief help will be forthcoming. From whom would you obtain that information?

10. Write an accident story from the following information extracted from a police accident report:

   Vehicle No. 1: Car driven by Kelvin L. Bowen, 16, 513 Maple Lane. Son of Mr. and Mrs. Lawrence K. Bowen. Passenger: Brad Levitt, 16, 208 Maple Lane.
   Vehicle No. 2: A school bus driven by Lindell B. Johnson, 24, 3033 Jellison St. No passengers.
   Vehicle No. 3: Car driven by Ruth L. Anderson, 42, 88 Jefferson Drive. No passengers.
   Time: 9 a.m. today.
   Location: Thompson Lane and Lindbergh Avenue.
   Police reconstruction of event: Bowen was driving west on Thompson Lane. He passed another westbound car that was stopped for a stop sign. Bowen then made a left turn into Lindbergh Avenue into the path of the school bus. The bus was headed north on Lindbergh. The left side of Bowen's car was struck by the front of the school bus. After the collision, the bus and Bowen's car crossed into the southbound lane and traveled 54 feet north of the intersection, where Bowen's car hit the front end of Anderson's car, which was moving southbound on Lindbergh. That car was forced off the road and into a ditch.
   Damage estimate: Vehicle No. 1 destroyed. Vehicle No. 2 damage estimated at $1,000. Vehicle No. 3 damage estimated at $250. All estimates by police.
   Dead: Kelvin L. Bowen. Died at Springfield Hospital at 7 p.m.
   Injured: Brad Levitt and Ruth L. Anderson, both in satisfactory condition at same hospital.

11. Your instructor will provide you with an accident report or will instruct you to visit your local police department to get one. Write a story from the report. Then prepare a narrative explaining what you would do to prepare a better story if it were to appear in print. Be sure to include information about whom you would contact for more detail and what questions you would ask.

12. Write a fire story from the following information obtained from a fire report:

> Building burned: T&L Electronics Co., 4404 U.S. Highway 90.
>
> Pertinent times: Fire reported at 9:23 p.m. Wednesday. First units arrived at 9:27 p.m. Second alarm issued at 9:42 p.m. Fire under control at 10:56 p.m.
>
> Person reporting fire: Fernando Lopez, 27, of 209 E. Watson Place, night watchman for the company.
>
> Injuries: None.
>
> Estimated damage: $1.2 million to building and contents.
>
> Probable cause of fire: Electrical short in main building power supply, according to Capt. Anne Gonzalez, fire marshal.
>
> Additional details: Fire Lt. Stephen Gorman, public information officer, reports that the owner of the business, George Popandreau, is on vacation in Florida. Reached by police by phone, he said the building and contents are fully insured. He will return to town tomorrow to begin making arrangements for moving the business to another location and restocking the lost inventory. The Fire Department used eight vehicles and 45 men in battling the fire. Low water pressure in the area hampered firefighters. New water mains are to be installed in this older area of the city next year.
>
> Quotes from Lopez: "I was making my routine rounds when I noticed that it was unusually hot in the rear of the building. Then I turned the corner and saw flames leaping out from a room that contains the electrical circuit breakers, the water heaters and that type of stuff. By the time I got to the phone, the whole back part of the building was on fire. I didn't know a fire could spread that fast."

13. Write a fire story from the following information obtained from a fire report:

> Building burned: Residence of Albert Stone, 2935 Parkway Drive.
>
> Pertinent times: Fire reported at 3:11 a.m. Wednesday. First units arrived at 3:18 a.m. Fire under control at 4:23 a.m.
>
> Person reporting fire: Rowena Stone, daughter of home owner.
>
> Injuries: Albert Stone treated for smoke inhalation at Baptist Hospital and admitted for observation. Condition: stable.
>
> Estimated damage: $25,000 to building and $20,000 to contents.
>
> Probable cause of fire: Careless smoking (Source: Capt. Anne Gonzalez, fire marshal).
>
> Additional details: Rowena Stone, daughter of the injured, was returning home from a date with her boyfriend and noticed smoke coming from the house. She entered immediately and found the house full of smoke and fire in the living room area. She and her boyfriend, Tim Stookey, 21, 309 Lake Lane, were able to get to the bedroom and carry out Albert Stone, who had passed out from consuming too much alcohol, the fire marshal believes. They were able to get Stone out of the house and call the Fire Department and an ambulance at the home of the next-door neighbor, John Perkins, 2933 Parkway Drive. The fire marshal said there were signs that a cigarette had been left burning in the living room. "The cigarette could have fallen from an ashtray and ignited the nearby curtains," he said. Mrs. Stone is estranged and believed to be living in California. Her first name is Dorothy. The fire marshal said a full investigation is being conducted.
>
> Insurance details: House insured by Dominic Prado, agent for Property and Casualty Co., Inc., 303 First Ave. Building insured for $79,000 and contents for $30,000. House valued at $75,000.

14. List all the sources the reporter used to prepare the following stories. List other sources that you might have used had you been covering each story. Finally, critique both stories, paying particular attention to clarity, conciseness and writing style.

A. Horses pull buggies down roads unmarked by tire tracks. Men till fields with horse-drawn plows while the women and children work in the garden. The Amish community near Springfield is a quiet and peaceful island in a hectic and sometimes violent world.

The peace was shattered in May when the Amish community received news of a tragic accident in Fredericksburg, Ohio, that claimed the lives of five Amish children aged 2 to 14 and injured five others. The 10 children were walking home from a birthday party when an 18-year-old driver going 65 mph attempted to pass a truck and barreled into the huddled children.

The Ohio tragedy was a shocking reminder to the Amish here that the refusal to conform to the 21st century can be more than just inconvenient or uncomfortable. On a highway, it can be life-threatening.

Ten members of the Amish in Audrain County, about 20 miles north of Springfield, made the 700-mile trip by van to Ohio.

Valentine Schettler had lived in the Ohio community for 47 years before moving here. He and his son-in-law, Jon Miller, were related to 10-year-old Ruby Troyer, who died in the accident.

About 2,500 Amish from across the nation came to mourn—but not to condemn.

"As Christians, we feel that if we can't forgive, then the Lord can't forgive us," Schettler said. Having to forgive is nothing new for the Amish. Schettler's son lost his wife and daughter in a similar accident in Wisconsin. The families of the children in Ohio have already forgiven the driver, who is charged with five counts of aggravated vehicular homicide. The Amish do not believe in prosecution through the legal system.

"It would not be a very good token of forgiveness," Miller said. Mary Gingerich, who has lived in the local Amish community for 27 years, said the Amish are rarely harassed by local residents. Once, however, she was riding in a buggy when someone in a passing car hurled a soda bottle and hit her in the head. She was holding her year-old baby at the time.

"When things like that happened, we didn't get angry," Gingerich said. "We were just scared."

What really sets the Amish apart is not the refusal to conform to 21st-century technology. It is their ability to forgive those who do them harm, to turn their anger into Christian forbearance.

"I am not angry," Schettler said. "Most of us think it happened for some reason."

B. Lynn Woolkamp knows better than most parents how cars and teenagers can be a tragic combination.

With more than 15 years of experience with the Springfield Police Department and the Lincoln County Sheriff's Department, Woolkamp has seen his share of cracked-up cars and injured teenagers.

The youngest drivers are the ones most often involved in accidents, Woolkamp said. Last year more than 1,100 Lincoln County drivers under 21 were in wrecks, according to the Highway Patrol.

"With the younger drivers, a lot of it is just inexperience," Woolkamp said. "It's kind of a power feeling—you get your license and you've got a little more freedom."

But Woolkamp is doing his best to make sure his own teenage daughter, Kelley, doesn't become part of the statistics.

Since the Rock Haven High School student got her learner's permit in June, her father has given her several hours of behind-the-wheel driving instruction each month. Last week, she turned 16 and picked up her license.

There's some good news and bad news for young drivers like Kelley and her parents.

More young people are in car wrecks, but fewer are dying in the accidents.

Since the state's seat belt law took effect in 1987, traffic deaths of Lincoln County teenagers have decreased by more than half.

From 1988 to 2000, 12 Lincoln County residents aged 15 to 19 died in traffic accidents, according to the state Division of Health Resources.

"We have noticed more use of seat belts by our children, and we believe that is why they are walking away," said Don Needham, director of the state's Division of Highway Safety.

Even those who still don't wear seat belts seem to know their own mistake, he explained.

"You'll go to an accident and people will admit to a traffic violation, but not to not having their seat belts on," Needham said. "There'll be a goose egg on their head and a crack in the windshield, and you know they weren't wearing one."

But seat belts don't prevent accidents.

This year, Lincoln County recorded the ninth-highest accident rate for young drivers out of the state's 96 counties, according to the Highway Patrol.

The trend is statewide: In 2000, the number of fatal accidents involving young drivers fell by more than 20 percent, despite a 3 percent increase in total auto accidents.

"I think they're starting to depend on the safety devices," Woolkamp said. "Now it's like they think, 'I've got an air bag, so it'll protect me.' With males, there's also a macho thing."

Males account for more than 70 percent of all traffic deaths in the state involving young drivers.

The gender gap is even wider for alcohol-related traffic fatalities.

More than 80 percent of 31 young drivers killed in alcohol-related traffic accidents this past year were male.

"That's staggering considering there are laws that they shouldn't even be purchasing it (alcohol)," Needham said.

Young drivers are involved in alcohol-related deaths at a higher rate than others, according to the National Highway Traffic Safety Administration.

Recently, the state scored a D-plus on a Mothers Against Drunk Driving survey of state efforts to prevent alcohol-related accidents.

But the state Division of Highway Safety disputes the grade. Officials claim the group received inaccurate accident and fatality rates for the state.

But the state doesn't dispute one of MADD's claims: Un-like a growing number of states, this one doesn't have a zero tolerance law.

In states with such laws, underage drivers with alcohol on their breath can be charged with driving while intoxicated.

"We are hoping to have something introduced in the up-and-coming legislature," Needham said. The proposed measure would classify youths with blood alcohol concentration of .002 or more as driving while intoxicated.

Woolkamp said it's hard to get young drivers to take safety seriously.

Once he pulled over a young woman for expired plates and wrote her a citation for not wearing a seat belt.

Her father—who had been following behind—pushed back the girl's hair to show scars on her forehead from when she hit the windshield in a previous accident, Woolkamp said.

"He said, 'You'd think she would've learned.'"

Court Stories Reporting

15. Analyze the following court stories and write critiques of them. Pay particular attention to the flow of the story and the attention to detail. Also, describe how the stories might have been improved.

A.   Friends of a murdered man gathered Monday in the Lincoln County Courthouse to hear a life sentence pronounced for Lilah Butler, convicted in February of conspiring to kill her husband.

Judge Linda Garrett denied her motion for a new trial and ordered her to spend her first night behind bars Monday.

Lilah Butler has been free on a $500,000 bond since a jury convicted her of first-degree murder and recommended a life sentence without possibility of parole.

Danny Johnson admitted killing Alfredo Butler but said he did it at Lilah Butler's urging, convinced by her promises of a life together and $200,000 in life insurance money.

The crowd of Alfredo Butler's friends and co-workers stirred and murmured as defense attorney Joel Eisenstein asked Garrett to allow his client to remain free on bond. Even before the murder, they said, Lilah Butler had ruined her husband's life.

"He changed from one day to the other" after his marriage, Heinz Albertson said. Albertson moved from Switzerland in 1981 with Alfredo Butler, but Butler stopped seeing his friends after the marriage, and "his smile disappeared."

Another Swiss friend, Rudi Bieri, described Lilah Butler as a "spoiled brat." He said Alfredo Butler told him that his wife had threatened his life more than once.

"He knew it was coming," said Jane Welliver, a co-worker of the victim. Two weeks before the murder, she said,

Alfredo Butler told her that his wife was going to kill him, that she had held him at gunpoint several times, once waking him with a gun at his head. Coworker Marcus Polzner said he felt relieved at the sentence. "It's long overdue."

The case has also been a tragedy for the family of Lilah Butler, many of whom attended Monday. Her mother broke down as the defendant was turned over to uniformed court officers. Her father is the presiding circuit judge of Dent County, and her uncle is a judge there.

Two brothers, both attorneys, watched as Eisenstein argued two hours in his attempt to convince the court that Lilah Butler deserved a new trial. He requested a postponement of the sentence so he could gather more evidence that one of the state's most damaging witnesses had perjured himself during the trial.

Eisenstein maintained that the prosecution had a secret deal with Billy Goodwin, who testified that Lilah Butler told him she wanted to get rid of her husband and she knew how to get away with it because she was trained as a police officer. Lilah Butler had been an officer on the St. Francois police force.

The investigator for the prosecution flatly denied any such deal Monday. The only evidence Eisenstein offered was that an outstanding warrant against Goodwin had been dropped. His motion was denied.

B.   No lights, no cameras, no action.

Two months after the state Supreme Court's decision to experiment with cameras in some circuit courtrooms, the idea seems to be stalled in the talking stages.

Although the two-year experiment is still in its early stages, only one media request for coverage of a trial has been filed in the 13th Judicial Circuit, which includes Lincoln and Callaway counties, said media coordinator Carlos Fernandez.

The state Supreme Court appointed Fernandez to handle all media requests for judicial proceedings in the circuit.

With 46 states already allowing still cameras, audio equipment and video cameras in their courtrooms, this state lags far behind. The conservative makeup of the state Supreme Court might be partly responsible, some observers say. The change of judges within the past few years, however, gave the idea new life, said Roger Cruise, executive director of the state Press Association.

"Cameras in the courtroom have been talked about here for years and years," Cruise said. "But it took a change in the Supreme Court."

Lincoln County Presiding Circuit Judge Robert Wagner agreed: "I think it is just a change in philosophy among the people on the bench," he said. "We have a different court in the state capital."

Courtrooms have been off-limits to electronic media coverage, but the state Supreme Court in October approved the experiment for the high court and the appeals courts. On Jan. 13, the high court announced that some trial courts—including the 13th Judicial Circuit and 10 other circuits—would be part of the experiment. Wagner co-chaired a 17-member statewide task force to investigate and oversee the experiment.

"Assuming that the coverage is done correctly," Wagner said, cameras will allow the public "to better understand what goes on in the courtroom."

Even advocates of the change harbor reservations. "My primary concern is to see to it that the defendant gets a fair trial," Wagner said. "This is not a First Amendment right; it is a Fifth Amendment concern."

Wagner listed potential drawbacks to cameras in the courtroom, especially in areas involving victims of sexual assault. Lincoln County Prosecutor James Taylor agreed that witness testimony is a primary concern.

"I wouldn't want to have a situation where a victim of a crime, who did not want to be publicly identified, was subjected to that," Taylor said.

Part of the experiment, titled Administrative Rule 16, provides for crime victims, police informants, undercover agents, juveniles and relocated witnesses to object to being filmed. The trial judge makes the final decision.

Dzuigas Kramer, a KBCD-TV editor and media coordinator for the 8th Circuit in Boonville, said he previously worked in Florida and California, where cameras in the courtrooms "were just a matter of fact." The procedure in those states is to contact the judge and fill out a request, both of which can be done the day of the judicial proceeding, Kramer said.

The experiment, in most cases, requires a request 14 days in advance to the media coordinator, who must file with attorneys and the judge at least 10 days before proceedings.

Judges can alter the rules. Television coverage of a Boonville murder trial in February—which would have been the first TV trial in the state—was stymied by restrictions outlined by the judge, Robert Dowler.

After several television stations requested permission to cover the Eaton Fleming case, Dowler ruled that the coverage would be severely limited and that he would preview the videotapes, Kramer said. "Television stations declined under the conditions that the judge stipulated. We felt we could not abide by them," he added.

The defense attorneys and the prosecutors in the Fleming case were also opposed to camera coverage, Kramer said.

Cruise said he believes an agreement can be reached between the judges' concerns for a fair trial and journalists' desire to cover it. "The judge has to have some control. On the other hand, if media follow the guidelines set down, they should be able to use the material without review."

The Supreme Court's Task Force on Cameras in the Courtroom is monitoring both the appeals courts' and the trial courts' experiments and will report its findings to the high court at the end of the year. Then the Supreme Court will apply the rule to all state courts permanently, continue the experiment or reinstate the statewide ban on electronic coverage.

16. John R. Wallinger, 29, of 202 Park Place, has been arrested in connection with the robbery in exercise 1. He is taken to Magistrate Court and enters a plea of not guilty. He claims to be indigent, and the judge, Darla Mickelson, appoints Linda Treator as his court-appointed attorney. Write a story about the court appearance.

17. Write a story based on the following information obtained from police and other sources:
   a. John A. Intaglio, 22, of 2909 Richardson St., has been arrested in connection with seven burglaries of homes and businesses during the past year.
   b. The burglaries took place on the following dates at the indicated locations:
      1. Roger's Liquors, 202 Delmore St., $250 in cash, Sept. 8.
      2. Bill Rhone Texaco, 1212 Fifth St., $23 in cash and calculator, Sept. 17.
      3. Linda Poole residence, 2000 Dickerson Ave., $200 in cash and $300 in jewelry, Sept. 20.
      4. Ron Doyle residence, 2180 Dickerson Ave., $2,000 fur coat, Sept. 26.
      5. Denny Doyle residence, 209 Drolling Place, $10 in cash, Nov. 12.

6. Miller Bros. department store, 209 Main St., $2,800 in merchandise, Feb. 18.
7. Don and Linda Hopson residence, 333 E. Briarwood St., $20 in cash and coins valued at $2,900, July 19.

c. Police Chief Antonio Grasso said, "We think this guy could be involved in as many as 40 other burglaries during the past year."

d. Grasso said investigators started checking on the suspect after he sold some of the stolen items to a well-known fence. The fence has fled town, and a warrant for his arrest has been issued. The warrant is sealed.

e. Other items were found in the suspect's home to link him to some of the burglaries with which he is charged.

f. Prosecutor Ralph Gingrich said the suspect will be charged with seven counts of burglary, seven counts of stealing and four counts of selling stolen merchandise. Other charges will be filed as burglary cases involving the suspect are cleared.

g. Chief Grasso would not comment on whether this suspect may have been involved in an attempted burglary last month in which a 34-year-old woman was shot to death by a burglar.

h. That incident occurred when Barbara Dueringer was awakened in her room at 3335 Grossman Lane. She screamed, the man fled and shot her roommate to death on the way out of the house. The roommate was Mary Dillinger.

i. Recovered items will be returned to the owners after the trial.

18. John A. Intaglio is being tried in Circuit Court on seven counts of burglary as described in exercise 19. Using the supplemental information obtained in the courtroom appearance, write a court story:

a. Intaglio's lawyer is Richard Delano, 2020 First St., a well-known criminal lawyer. He handled the infamous murder case of John D'Aquisto, who was found innocent of murdering First Ward City Councilman Roger Baker last year.

b. Delano called for a mistrial on grounds that the judge, Thompson Dickerson III, is prejudiced against Italians. Intaglio is Italian. The judge, Delano claims, has tried 14 cases involving Italian defendants in the six years he has been on the bench, and all 14 were convicted. The judge dismisses the motion and says, "You would be wise, Mr. Delano, to concentrate on defending your client. Leave the rest to me. I can assure you that I like Italians, and I like pizza, too."

c. Police Detective William O'Shaunessy testifies that the merchandise found in Intaglio's home was positively identified by the owners. He says that Intaglio admitted to stealing the items. Delano objects to the testimony about the confession and requests a mistrial. The motion is denied, but the judge orders the statement stricken from the record and tells the jury to ignore it.

d. The judge adjourns the trial for the day. The jury is dismissed.

19. John A. Intaglio is acquitted. Write a story using the data in exercises 19 and 20 and the following information:

a. Delano, the defense attorney, says, "Justice has been served. My client has been persecuted by the police, the prosecutor and the judge. A wise jury saw through all that."

b. Prosecutor Gingrich says, "I'm appalled. It all goes to show that sometimes the system doesn't work. I thought our case was airtight. We'll have another chance, though. We plan to try him in connection with some other burglaries. This man (Intaglio) should be off the streets."

c. The jury deliberated only 20 minutes before returning its verdict. None of the jurors would comment.

20. Define the following terms:
    a. misdemeanor

    b. felony

    c. preliminary hearing

    d. arraignment

    e. probable cause

    f. grand jury

    g. true bill

    h. not true bill

    i. indictment

    j. information

    k. plea bargaining

    l. change of venue

21. You are assigned to cover a preliminary hearing in a murder case. What information would you expect to obtain at such a hearing?

22. The trial in a major kidnapping case begins tomorrow, and you have been assigned to write a pretrial story. With whom would you talk and why?

23. Attend a session of traffic court in your city and write a story based on one of the cases heard. If none is particularly interesting, write a story that describes how the traffic court operates.

24. Attend a trial at your local courthouse and write a news story based on the testimony there. Check newspaper clippings that reported on the incident at the time to help you develop proper background.

25. List all of the sources the reporter used to write the following story. Also list additional sources that might have improved the story.

The trial date for Angelica Jackson, the Mississippi woman charged in the stabbing death of her boyfriend, has been reset for May 25. Judge Todd B. Schwartz granted the extension to allow the defense more time to conduct investigations.

Jackson, 20, had testified that she stabbed her boyfriend, Mark Thomasson, also from Mississippi, on Dec. 13 while the couple was visiting relatives in Springfield. Jackson said Thomasson accused her of having an incestuous affair with her father. She is charged with second-degree murder, which carries a sentence of 10 years to life.

Associate Public Defender Rahsetnu Miller said Jackson is a victim of battered woman syndrome. Miller has been investigating information on Thomasson's possible criminal record. He hopes to interview about 10 witnesses. "It's my understanding that he (Thomasson) has had some scrapes with the criminal justice system down there," Miller said.

Thomasson was awaiting trial on a drug case before his stabbing death, he said. Miller hopes to find additional evidence that Jackson was abused by an "intoxicated man with a past violent record."

26. Using online database services, make a list of the key figures for both the prosecution and the defense in the trial of O.J. Simpson, the former football star acquitted of murdering his ex-wife and her male friend.

CHALLENGE EXERCISE
27. Search your library for information on the 1954 murder trial of Dr. Sam Sheppard in Cleveland, Ohio. Compare the free-press, free-trial issues raised in that case to those raised in the case of O.J. Simpson. Describe both the similarities and differences.

14 Covering a Beat

1. In this era of convergence, beat reporters are expected to use all the tools available both to report and to tell stories. Log on to the Web sites of two local news organizations—one that is primarily print and the other primarily broadcast. Analyze what tools their reporters have used to gather and report the news. Standard interviewing? Video? Sound? Use of electronic records? Others?

2. Read the last several issues of your campus newspaper. Now answer these questions:

   — Does the paper have reporters assigned to beats? If so, what are the beats?
   — Who are the most-quoted sources? Why?
   — Do the reporters rely on campus officials for their stories, or do you see nonofficial sources?
   — For whom do the stories seem to be written—the sources or the students?
   — What's your assessment of the overall quality of the paper?

3. Now what about the newspaper's Web site? How complete is it? How interesting? How current?

4. You've just joined the staff of your campus media. Your first reporting assignment: Cover the central administration. The assigning editor asks how you'll carry out this important responsibility. Reply in a memo.

   — What sources will be most important?
   — How will you go about earning the confidence of these sources?
   — What will be the topic of your first story? Why?

5. You have been assigned to cover your county government. Do some background research online and in your local newspaper. Then write a memo describing what you expect the most important issues to be on your new beat and whom you expect to be your most important human sources.

6. Do the same for the local public school system. In both cases, make note of the opportunities, if any, for using your sound and video recorders. What about live webcasts of meetings?

7. Acknowledging your success in covering local government and schools, your editor asks you to take on the environment beat. Unlike the others, this assignment doesn't offer regular meetings or officials' offices to cover.

— How will you prepare for this beat?
— Who will be the most likely sources in your town?
— Which Web sites and online databases might be useful to you?
— Which three publications will you find most helpful? Answer in a memo to your boss.

8. On your daily rounds at city hall, you are handed this press release:

> Mayor Juanita Williams announced today that the city and the Downtown Merchants' Association have hired a consulting firm from Washington, D.C., to devise a master plan for redevelopment of the city's central business district.
> The cost of the plan, estimated at $200,000, will be borne by the city.
> Mayor Williams said the firm, DHR Inc., was chosen over five other applicants, despite its slightly higher bid, because "the chemistry seems right to us." Mayor Williams said that, as a realtor and downtown businesswoman herself, she knows that the return to the city from increased property taxes and revitalized business will return the consultants' fee "10,000 times over."
> Williams also announced that she would meet with opponents who claim mistakenly that the taxpayers are subsidizing downtown merchants by the city's picking up the whole cost of the study.

   a. Describe the reporting you will need to do in order to write a complete story on the subject of the press release.

   b. How will you keep your readers abreast of the project's developments after that original story?

9. Describe five stories about religion that could be done in your area of the country. What sources would you use for each?

10. Do the same for possible stories about science, medicine or the environment. Include documentary as well as human sources.

11. Your instructor will assign one of the stories you described in exercise 7 or 8 and give you a deadline. Report and write the story.

CHALLENGE EXERCISE
12. Often, the most useful stories a beat reporter writes are done in advance of meetings at which important issues will be decided. Such advance stories permit readers to take part in the decision-making process, if they so desire. Then, of course, you'll describe the outcome in a story after the meeting. Here's an example of an advance and the account of the meeting that was previewed. Using these as a model, prepare for and cover an issue before your school board, zoning commission or city council.

(advance)

By MARY LANDERS
staff writer

Residents of Tanglewood and Deerfield subdivisions treasure the wooded stretch of Bear Creek behind their homes. But while they love nature on their property, they don't want the government or strangers there.

They fear the city's proposed greenbelt will bring both.

Tonight, the city council votes on a greenbelt plan that aims to preserve green space along portions of Hinkson and Bear creeks.

Thirty-three of these northeastern Springfield neighbors gathered recently to tell Juan Guttierez, Second Ward councilman, that they oppose the plan. Tanglewood and Deerfield residents note that floodplain requirements already prohibit certain types of construction in these stream corridors.

And the homeowners have also worked to protect the area. One day last year, Tanglewood residents planted 1,800 pine tree seedlings in the woods. They want to know why the council needs to legislate what they're already doing.

"We're keeping a greenbelt for free for the city," Doris Sears said.

She and her Tanglewood neighbors boast of the deer, raccoons and even coyotes in the woods.

"Everybody in our neighborhood is interested in preserving it as it is," said Kim Cottey, a Deerfield resident.

The Mid-states Greenbelt Coalition has encouraged the council to create a greenbelt. The group's priorities are providing flood control and preserving green space and natural wildlife corridors along streams.

Coalition President Chris Davis calls for pro-active measures in protecting streams. He said that although current residents might be voluntarily protecting the areas, future residents might not.

"Good intentions may be there, but if hard times fall on somebody, you'd be amazed at what they'd do," Davis said.

(meeting story)

By JESSICA WAGNER
staff writer

Preserving land along Hinkson and Bear creeks was the intention of the Springfield City Council last night when it passed the greenbelt policy resolution by a 6-0 vote.

However, greenbelt residents were more concerned about the possibility of a trail in their backyards.

Currently, the resolution does not include a public trail, but a trail could be added later, following a public hearing. According to the resolution, a pathway is only a secondary goal.

Bill Johnson, 2120 Smiley Lane, had previously submitted a 28-signature petition on behalf of the Deerfield subdivision residents against the idea of a trail in their eight-acre area. They also were concerned about private land being made public.

"We enjoy the green space every day," Johnson said. "We feel like we live in the country. We don't want to see our backyards turned into public trails."

Doris Sears, 1805 Lovejoy Lane, said the greenbelt could be preserved by private land ownership.

"I don't know where this idea came from that we can't take care of our own land," she said. "We are for preservation, but not for the trail along private land."

Fifth Ward Councilman Jun Ping Yang said the resolution would restrict the property rights of the residents. However, Juan Guttierez, Second Ward member, said that it doesn't give the city any more rights.

The greenbelt plan is meant to protect large areas of green space in the urban area from construction and other development.

15 Business and Consumer News

1. a. Write a story from the following press release:

> Universal Conglomerate Co. announced today that sales in the fiscal year just ended totaled $2.35 billion. In the previous fiscal year, the sales were $2.5 billion. Net income was $135.6 million, or $4.38 per share. In the previous fiscal year, net income was $167.8 million, or $4.97 per share.
>
> G.G. Jones, chairman of Universal Conglomerate, said the sales were lower because of strikes at the plants in Massachusetts and Alabama. He said net income was lower because of unfavorable tax rulings, the strikes, and because of changes in international currency valuations that adversely affected the performance of some of its international subsidiaries.
>
> Jones also announced that the company plans to merge with International Conglomerate Co. The merger would make the new company the largest in the United States.

b. Your instructor will play the role of Universal Conglomerate's public relations officer. Ask the questions necessary to make the story complete. Rewrite it with the new information.

c. Now prepare a webcast of this story, using sound and video as you think best.

2. Write a story from the following information. Make a note of the questions left unanswered by the example.

> J.B. Grebe, chairman of Universal Motors Corp., says the prices of cars have increased $1,000 over the last two years as a result of safety equipment the government requires. "Almost all of those changes were a result of pressure from consumer groups," Grebe says. "So the people who claim to be helping the consumer actually are contributing to the inflation that penalizes the consumer more than anyone else. Consumers aren't as dumb as the consumer groups would lead us to believe. If consumers want safety equipment on their cars, let them order it as an option, the way they do with air conditioning, alarm systems and sunroofs."
>
> William A. Sterling, chairman of Consumers Against Rip-offs (CAR), responds by saying Grebe is trying to divert attention from the "real issue," the protection of motorists' lives. "If there wasn't pressure on the auto companies to make their cars more safe, improvements would never be made. Grebe's statement indicates in effect that he is in favor of murdering motorists. He should be declared a public criminal."
>
> Ralph Starr, president of the National Safety Institute (NSI), says Grebe's figures on the amount of price increase caused by safety equipment closely resemble the figures NSI came up with in its own study. "We appreciate Mr. Grebe's frustration with

having business decisions dictated by the government, but we think the improvements in safety are worth the investment. We have calculated that 10,000 lives a year are saved by auto safety equipment. It would be good if consumers would have demanded these improvements, but since they have not, the government had to do it for them."

3. Find the names of the chief executive officers of Google, Yahoo!, General Motors Corp., Gulf & Western Co., AT&T Co., the Norfolk & Western Railway, Apple Computer and Prudential Insurance Co.

4. List the names, addresses, phone numbers and e-mail addresses of six good sources for the business beat in your town.

5. Select a local, publicly held company. Using the sources outlined in the section on where to find business news, perform the following:
   a. Develop an overview of the company using secondary sources.
   b. Develop a financial profile of the company.
   c. List the company's top officers.
   d. List the trade publications that most likely cover the company's activities.
   e. List the trade associations to which the company probably belongs.

6. Call the investor relations department of a local, publicly held company. Obtain a copy of the company's most recent annual report, 10-K and proxy statement.
   a. Start with the annual report. Look up the auditor's report. Is the company's report of the standard variety or is it more complex? If so, what problems do the auditors see? Explain.
   b. Read the footnotes. Get a feel for the jargon of the business and the form in which the information is presented.
      Turn to the chairman's or chairwoman's letter. What kind of picture does it paint? Rosy, drab, uncertain? Although most reports from the chair are positive, noteworthy nuggets frequently may be found.
   c. Look at the 10-K report. Read the report and learn in greater detail the types of business in which the parent firm and its subsidiaries are engaged. Are there

any surprises? Look for major lawsuits pending, for the extent of foreign sales and for information on the backgrounds of major officers and directors.

   d. Look at the proxy statement. Read the statement to learn what matters are to be voted on at the upcoming annual meeting. Are any of the issues controversial? If so, how has the local business press covered them? Look for the numbers. How much do the top officers earn in salary? In deferred compensation? In bonuses? Does this rank them among the higher-paid executives in the nation? Look up the annual Business Week Executive Pay survey for comparisons.

7. Locate five consumer stories in a major newspaper. Analyze the stories to determine if they pass the fairness test or if they are slanted toward the consumer or toward business. Be prepared to defend your conclusion.

8. Make a list of a dozen grocery items. Visit the three largest grocery stores in your town to compare the prices of the items. Write a story based on what you find.

9. Use an online service to "invest" $10,000 for the semester. Most services, usually under a heading such as "Personal Finance," allow you to build a hypothetical portfolio, which is then updated daily. Track movements in the stock.

   Keep a log of major fluctuations in your assets and follow business news to analyze why there has been movement in your stocks. Look for variations in market strategy, rumors, international relations, corporate management or economic indicators that would explain the changes. At the end of the semester, write a summary of your stocks' progress.

10. Go online and find corporate profiles of three companies in the same industry. Write a story that compares the companies' histories, current status and predicted futures.

11. The stereotype of journalists is that they are all terrified of numbers. To cover business, though, you must be able to handle basic math. Answer the following questions:

   a. The faculty members of a Midwestern university join a union and negotiate a raise. The raise will be given in three parts: 6 percent the first year, 4 percent the second year and 5 percent the third year. What is their total raise as a percentage?

   Given a base salary of $25,000, what is their total raise in dollars?

   What would the total raise be if the raises were given in the order of 4 percent, 5 percent and 6 percent?

   b. Education funding falls in the state, and faculty members are asked to take a pay cut of 9 percent—to $22,000 a year. What were they being paid?

   c. The city will face a ballot issue in April that would raise the sales tax from 4 percent to 6 percent. What percent increase is this?

d. The United Way of Arkansas has raised $127,300, or 67 percent of its goal. What is its goal?

e. The Ace Widget Co. is closing its Springfield plant and moving to Mexico, where it can take advantage of cheaper labor and evade Environmental Protection Agency regulations. The company employs 247 workers, and pays $14.75 an hour for an average of 37.5 hours per week. What is the company's payroll? Economists say that every dollar spent in a community is re-spent. They call this "multiplier effect." Given a multiplier effect of 3, what is the plant closing's impact on the local economy?

f. Stock in American Panda Manufacturing Inc. (APMI on Nasdaq) opens at $32 per share and drops three-eighths during the day. You own four round lots of APMI. How much did you gain or lose?

g. There are 275 teachers in You Learn School System. In contract negotiations, they are asking for a raise of 3.5 percent per year for three years on a base salary of $22,000 per year. The administration is willing to raise their pay 2.8 percent the first year, 3.1 percent the second and 3.2 percent the third. How far apart would the proposed salaries be each year? How much would the school system save each year under its proposal? How much would it save over the three years?

h. The Springfield Computer Company projects it will sell 125 million laptops within the next two years. This sets lights flashing and red flags waving in your head. Why?

CHALLENGE EXERCISE

12. Use the brief summary below to answer the following questions.

> Gannett's net income rose 10 percent to $86.2 million the first three months of 2003 from $78.7 million a year earlier. Earnings per share rose 15 percent to 62 cents; there were fewer shares outstanding. The company, publisher of *USA Today*, said newspaper, broadcasting and outdoor advertising divisions all showed improved results.

a. Define "net income."

b. Define "earnings per share."

c. What is the impact of having fewer shares outstanding on the earnings per share?

d. Rewrite this to make it more understandable to the average reader.

e. Find a local angle and rewrite.

16 Sports

1. Today's sports reporters are expected to do a lot more than write stories after games. They blog, often during the contests. They hold online chats with fans. They often appear on local radio and television. After surveying those media during one day and night, put together a job description of your favorite sports reporter.

2. Now put yourself in the place of the sports editor of your local newspaper. Write a planning memo detailing what you can give your readers that they haven't already received from television and the other media outlets. Explain your decisions.

3. Do the same from the perspective of the news director of a local television station. What opportunities and limitations are available to you in television that your newspaper competitor doesn't face?

4. Compare your judgment with that of the professionals. Examine the local sports section for the morning after your television survey. Refer to your notes on what the local television news provided to sports fans.

   — What differences and similarities do you find?
   — Write a memo to your boss, the editor or news director, explaining those findings.

5. One of the most important parts of sports reporting at the local level is the coverage of high school sports. Survey the high school coverage in your local paper and on a local television station.

   — Write a brief report in which you summarize your findings.
   — Your own high school days may not be far behind you. Analyze the coverage you've studied from the perspective of a high school student. What strengths and weaknesses do you find?

6. You've been assigned to cover high school sports for your local newspaper or television station.

   — Where will you begin your preparation?
   — What sources will be most useful?
   — How will you avoid the mistakes or build on the strengths your survey found in existing local coverage?
   — How will you use multimedia tools to improve your storytelling?

7. Define the following baseball statistics and, using the numbers provided, figure the statistics in each example:

   a. Earned-run average

   — 27 innings, 15 hits, eight runs, seven earned runs

   b. Batting average

   — 212 plate appearances, 57 hits, 16 walks, three sacrifices

   c. On-base percentage

   — same statistics as above

8. You have been assigned to cover your college's women's volleyball team. Prepare yourself and write a memo describing likely sources and listing three story ideas.

9. You have been assigned to cover your college's track and field program. Write a memo describing likely sources and outlining three story ideas.

10. Describe and list sources for five possible stories on participant sports in your community. The following example shows you what can be done with an event that seldom rates any coverage.

Break up Don Johnson.

So went the good-natured battle cry of mere competitors at the Senior Olympics yesterday.

"We're all in shape; we all run and exercise, but did you see the guy who beat me in the mile (run)?" said Jean Madden, who after 57 years still gets wide-eyed after seeing some things. "That guy Johnson is a machine. He's an animal. Did you see him? Unbelievable."

On first approach, Madden's friend, Don Johnson, looked every one of his 55 years. He is a lean 5-11. His head is having a special on pepper-gray hair these days, and the supply is quickly running out. A thicker forest of steel wool covers his chest. Yesterday, that chest was a heaving rain forest, thoroughly matted down by events.

In the last 12 years, it's been matted down often. It's been drenched by 24 marathons, soaked by three triathlons and rinsed by a sundry of other races. Human Races, Hospital Hill races, Pepsi runs, late-night runs, sunrise runs. Every week the chest is dampened by 50 to 70 miles of running, 40 miles of bicycling and 54 holes of golf. Some tennis, too.

"I guess I'm what some people would call a fitness freak," Johnson said.

Nah, animal's better. Yesterday morning saw the animal pedaling down Route B from his home in Centralia to Hickman High for the games' opening ceremonies and on to Cosmos Park. The 30-mile ride took him about 90 minutes, but he made it with time to spare before his first event of the day: a 1.6 mile bike race. He won it easily, hopped back on his

10-speed and headed back to Hickman, where he was entered in the mile run. He made the rest of the field look like a slow-motion replay, winning in 5 minutes, 31 seconds. He then finished second in the 100-meter run, behind Madden. He went to McDonald's for a quick lunch and then he was headed home on Route B.

Let us try to return Johnson to the planet Earth. Oh, here's something. Friday, he took the family station wagon instead of his bike from Centralia to the L.A. Nickell course at Cosmos, site of the games' golf competition. Animal? He was an old softie.

Old softie got out of that car at Nickell to shoot a 36 to win the golf competition. Animal.

11. Sports reporting should be more than a summary of who won. Like any other reporting, it needs the "why" and the "how" in order to be really satisfying. From the statistical summary that follows, write the best lead you can.

College men
NAIA Division I tournament
At Tulsa, Okla.
First round
Fresno Pacific 81,
Springfield College 56

SPRINGFIELD (29-6): Thoma 1-7 2-2 4, Muldrow 9-13 0-0 20, Beza 2-11 0-0 4, Combs 1-4 0-0 3, Peebles 2-9 2-2 6, Ross 1-6 0-0 2, Newbern 2-11 2-2 7, Chapple 1-2 0-0 2, Aubuchon, 0-0 0-0 0, Anthony, 0-0 0-0 0, Pearson 3-11 0-0 8. Totals 22-74 6-6 56.

FRESNO PACIFIC (24-7): Arline 3-4 2-2 8, Ty Amundson 7-15 0-0 18, Tim Amundson 2-5 2-2 6, Volenec 4-9 2-6 10, Moore 11-14 2-2 24, Tompkins 1-1 2-2 4, Jones 1-3 0-0 3, Piester 4-8 0-0 8, Nickerson 0-0 0-0 0. Totals 33-59 10-14 81.

Halftime — Fresno Pacific 40, Springfield 31. 3-point goals — Springfield 6-26 (Thoma 0-4, Muldrow 2-2, Beza 0-2, Combs 1-2, Peebles 0-1, Ross 0-2, Newbern 1-4, Pearson 2-9), Fresno Pacific 5-15 (Ty Amundson 4-10, Tim Amundson 0-3, Volenec 0-1, Jones 1-1). Fouled out — None. Rebounds — Springfield 35 (Muldrow 9), Fresno Pacific 44 (Moore 11). Assists — Springfield 10 (Ross 4), Fresno Pacific 22 (Volenec 7). Total fouls — Springfield 14, Fresno Pacific 9.

12. What further information should you have to put muscle on the bare bones of that lead? List the questions to which you, as a sports reporter, want answers before writing your game story.

13. The story reprinted here, written by a journalism student, probably answers most of your questions. Using the guidelines offered in the text, analyze this story's strengths and weaknesses.

Springfield College Done In by a Season-Low 29.7 Shooting Percentage in the NAIA National Tournament

By DANIEL FUSSNER
staff writer

TULSA, Okla.—The Springfield College basketball team had its worst shooting game this season in its biggest game.

Fresno (Calif.) Pacific held the Cougars, the No. 10 seed, to a season-low 29.7 percent en route to an 81-56 victory Wednesday in the first round of the 58th NAIA Division I men's basketball tournament.

The Cougars (29-6) were 22 of 74 from the field, including 6 of 26 (23.1 percent) on 3-pointers. The No. 23 seed Sunbirds (24-7) were 33 of 59 (55.9 percent) overall and 5 of 15 on 3-pointers.

The Sunbirds will play Arkansas Tech (27-5) today in the round of 16. Arkansas State defeated Midwestern State (Texas) 60-58 Tuesday.

Cougars coach Bob Burchard said the Sunbirds' physical play disrupted his team's offense.

"We couldn't handle those guys," Burchard said. "They were very big, very strong, and we did not do a good job of screening and getting ourselves open. I think a lot of that had to do with the physical nature of the game. Over the years, that type of game has caused us problems, and it held true tonight."

The size difference also played a role when the Cougars went on defense.

"I thought they were bigger and stronger at most positions, therefore they had good looks and consequently shot a better percentage than we did," Burchard said. "We had a difficult time. We tried to get the game going a little bit, tried to change defenses. We tried to neutralize some of that. We just never could get it done.

"The thing that concerned us the most was having them run the clock down on us and grind us out because we knew their size was really a problem. It always has been. And you've got to adjust to that game, and you've got to adjust to the flow of that game. I didn't think we did that very well. I thought we

allowed the physical nature of the game to neutralize us, and we tried to warn them about that."

The Cougars led 7-2. But the Sunbirds went on a 21-7 run, capped by forward Brian Volenec's dunk, and led 23-14 with 7:15 in the half. The Cougars cut the lead to 27-25 at 3:36, but the Sunbirds finished the half with a 13-6 run and led 40-31.

The Sunbirds put together a 20-6 run and led 60-39 with 12:40 to play and the Cougars never got closer.

Junior forward Thomas Muldrow was the only bright spot for the Cougars with 20 points on 9-of-13 shooting. Without his shooting effort, the Cougars were 13 of 61 for 21.3 percent.

Sunbirds center Don Moore scored 24 points with 11 rebounds. Senior Ty Amundsen added 18 points and Volenec had 10.

Steve Combs said the Sunbirds frustrated the Cougars on offense.

"It seemed like they knew every play we ran," the senior forward said. "I mean they scouted us really well and we couldn't get anything done."

Cougars forward Brandon Beza, who scored four points on 2-of-11 shooting, said several things contributed to the loss.

"We came out playing pretty strong, and then they started getting a little physical with us," he said. "We weren't taking the ball to the hole quite as strongly. We were altering shots. It just wasn't our day.

"I don't think we were forcing as much as we were doing little things here and there that were putting us in a hole, and we weren't recognizing that. It's just a little thing here, little thing here, little thing here, then you look up and we're down 13. Little thing here, little thing here and you look up and you're down 20. Basically, that's what happened. It just slowly crept away from us."

14. Your instructor will assign you to cover a sports event. Prepare yourself, do your reporting and write the story.

CHALLENGE EXERCISE
15. Your instructor will pick an idea from among those you compiled in response to exercises 8 and 9. Report and write the story.

17 Social Science Reporting

1. Go to the Web site of the National Institute for Computer-Assisted Reporting, nicar.org. Spend some time reading the tips and techniques you find there. Write a memo to yourself summarizing what you've learned.

2. Find an online news story reporting the results of a survey. Critique it, using the guidelines for reporting of survey results in Chapter 17.

   — How closely are the guidelines followed?
   — Consider the information the guidelines call for that may be missing from this example. How serious is the omission?

3. Now do the same with a television report of a survey.

   — Typically, broadcast reports leave out even more of the details than do printed reports. Is that true in this case?
   — How could the missing information be supplied?

4. If you can, contact the original source of the surveys reported in exercises 1 or 2. Try to get the results in the format in which they were supplied to the news organizations.

   — Compare the actual findings to the reports. What differences are noticeable?
   — Using the material in Chapter 17 or in one of the suggested readings, write a critique of the coverage in this case.

5. Now write your own story about the survey results you got for exercise 3. Make sure to follow the guidelines for accurate reporting on surveys.

6. Here is a shortened version of a story written by an advanced student based on a survey that was designed and conducted by a reporting class.

By MICHELLE LERNER
staff writer

Safety in the streets is what's on the minds of many Springfield residents these days.

A survey conducted by the *Springfield News* shows that crime, growth and street maintenance are top issues that concern residents as the April 4 election approaches.

Of the 400 randomly selected respondents interviewed last week, an overwhelming 82 percent ranked crime as either their first or second concern.

Growth ranked second overall among a list of five issues. Street maintenance ranked third, followed by the construction of a proposed recreation center and the status of the city's bus service.

"I'd love to see a recreation center," said Irene Smith, 65. "There are just other, more important issues to deal with."

Here's how the survey was conducted: First, reporters contacted 120 people throughout the city and asked what they thought were the major issues facing the City Council this election. Then the five issues that drew the most mentions were presented to a random sampling of 400 respondents. The survey was conducted by telephone. The survey has a margin of error of plus or minus 5 percent.

Despite crime's high ranking, statistics do not show an increase in either overall violent or nonviolent crime in 2003, according to the Springfield Police Department. In fact, crime overall was down compared to previous years. However, 2003 saw a record number of homicides in the city (10). Rape and burglary also increased.

"There is a common perception all across America that crime is on the rise," said Deputy Police Chief Dennis Veach. "Security and safety are the things people worry about most no matter where they are."

Many respondents pointed to the higher murder statistics as well as drug-related crimes as their specific worries. Though few said they felt unsafe, they expressed concerns about the future.

"A low crime rate is the reason I chose a town like Springfield to live in," said Brad Blake, a 31-year-old sales representative. "I just don't want to see that change."

Others pointed to a relationship between crime and development, citing trends in larger cities and around the country.

"The bigger a town gets, the more crime it's going to see," said Paul Stanfield, 49. "The city is failing to keep up in terms of manpower and crime prevention as Springfield continues to grow."

(Here is a graphic that accompanied the story.)

MAYORAL CANDIDATES:	Streets	Crime	Growth	Buses	Rec Cen.
Lester Reschly	2	1	3	5	4
Rhonda Carlson	2	1	4	3	5
Margie Meyer	3	2	1	5	4
Darwin Hindman	2	2	1	2	2
Keith Mandell	3	4	2	1	5
Pam Jordan	5	2	1	3	4
Residents' Average	2.8	1.7	2.5	4	3.7

3rd WARD CANDIDATES:	Streets	Crime	Growth	Buses	Rec Cen.
David Fox	3	4	1	2	5
Tim Nelson	1	4	3	5	2
Jim Sheridan	2	1	3	4	5
Donna Crockett	2	3	1	5	4
4th WARD CANDIDATE:					
Rex Campbell	2	1	3	5	4
Residents' Average	2.8	1.7	2.5	4	3.7

Analyze this story, using the guidelines in the chapter.

— What, if any, information is missing? How important is the omission?
— Overall, do you think this story is a useful piece of campaign coverage? Why or why not?

7. This story appeared near the beginning of the election campaign. Put yourself in the place of the newspaper's city editor.

— What follow-up stories would you plan? Why?

8. Surveys such as this one consume a great deal of resources—time, computer processing of results and money.

— In a memo to your boss, the managing editor, justify the expenditure of those resources instead of the traditional person-on-the-street interviews he suggests.

9. As news director of the local television station, you're not satisfied to let the newspaper set the agenda for the campaign.

   — What might your station do to follow, counter or get ahead of the print opposition? Explain.

10. Design a participant-observation project. Keep in mind these three problems:

    a. The problem of invasion of privacy. How will you handle it?
    b. The problem of involvement. What precautions will you take?
    c. The problem of generalizing. What else will you have to do in order to produce a complete story?

11. Design a systematic study of records. Define the reporting problem you're trying to solve. Identify the records you'll need and tell how you'll gain access. Specify the techniques you will use to collect and analyze your information.

12. Design a field experiment. State your hypothesis. Identify the dependent and independent variables. Describe the controls you will use.

13. Define the following terms:
    a. random sample

    b. chi square

    c. mean

    d. median

    e. mode

    f. stratified sample

    g. validity

    h. reliability

14. Associated Press reporter Evans Witt, in an article for the *Washington Journalism Review*, listed 10 rules for journalists writing about polls. They are:

1. Do not overinterpret poll results.
2. Include the results of other polls, even if they cast doubt on the latest results.
3. Always include and be aware of sampling errors.
4. Never forget the base.
5. Look at the exact wording of questions carefully.
6. Do not use nonscientific readings of public opinion for anything except entertainment value.
7. Be very, very careful when writing about polls conducted for candidates, special-interest groups or political parties.
8. Never forget that polls give little hint about the depth of people's emotions or commitment.
9. Do not disguise your own interpretations as poll results.
10. Use common sense and do not fall under the spell of the numbers.

Now find three news stories about polls. Analyze them by applying Witt's rules and the APME guidelines discussed in the text.

15. Design a poll of your own.
    a. Define the population.
    b. Draft the questions.
    c. Draw a random sample to be polled.
    d. Decide how to conduct your poll (in person, by phone, online).
    e. Describe the statistical tests, if any, that you will use. What computer program would be most useful?

CHALLENGE EXERCISE

16. The advocacy group Children Forever conducted a survey of 725 youths ages 10 to 16. The youths were contacted via e-mail June 5-7, 2004. The results:
    33 percent said they watch less than two hours of television per day.
    26 percent said they watch two to three hours of television per day.
    26 percent said they watch three to four hours of television per day.
    15 percent said they watch more than four hours of television per day.

    Also:
    76 percent said TV too often depicts sex before marriage.
    68 percent said sex on TV influences their peers to have sexual relations when they are too young.
    66 percent said TV shows that portray hostile families encourage young viewers to disrespect their parents.

    a. Create an information graphic based on the first four results.
    b. What questions do you need to ask Children Forever about the poll before you write a story?

c. Identify possible sources of bias in conducting the poll.

d. Write a lead based on all the results.

CHALLENGE EXERCISE

17. As a class project, select one of the survey designs class members have prepared and carry it out. Write a story, following the APME guidelines, about the results.

18 Investigative Reporting

1. Go to ire.org and read what you find about the winners of the most recent national investigative reporting competition. Make note of both the story topics and the techniques. What, if any, patterns do you find?

2. Using that same ire.org database, identify the reporting tools—interviewing, use of records, undercover work, surveys, etc.—these top reporters use most often. Explain why you think these are the favorites.

3. Go online. Look through 10 out-of-town newspapers. Identify any investigative stories you find.

   — How many investigative stories do you find?
   — Are they focused on individual problems or are they broader examinations of institutions or systems?

4. Now sample a week's worth of television. Again, you're looking for investigative reporting.

   — What do you see? How many network programs or stories appear to be investigative compared to the number on local newscasts?
   — Compare what you see to what you've read in exercise 1. Which medium provides more detail and documentation? Which stories are more interesting?

5. Look at your local newspaper and television newscasts.

   — How much investigative reporting do you find in either?
   — How does the local journalism compare in quality and interest to the national stories you've analyzed?

6. Many government agencies provide information online. Locate one of the following:
   a. 2000 census information for your state.

   b. The most recent federal budget.

    c. The most recent federal crime report.

    d. The number of computers exported from the United States in the most recent year for which figures are available.

7. You're a reporter for your campus newspaper. Based on what you know about the campus, choose a topic that might bear investigation. In a memo to your boss, the editor, explain:

    — Why you've chosen this topic.
    — How you'll conduct the "sniff" to determine your chances of getting a story.
    — Who you expect to be valuable human sources.
    — What documents you'll need and how you'll get them.
    — What computer applications you'll employ.

8. Out of school now, you're hired by the local paper or television, where the bosses have been impressed by your investigative skills. Determined to get off to a fast start in the new job, you walk in the first day with a memo to the boss. In it, you:

    — Suggest a topic for investigation.
    — Explain why you've chosen to begin with this story.
    — Outline the background information you've gathered from stories already written or broadcast on the subject.
    — Describe how you'll launch your reporting.
    — Estimate how long the project will take and what it will require in money, other resources and computer skills.

9. Here's a memo from a journalism grad, now a police reporter on a major newspaper, in which she explains why and how she and a colleague conducted a lengthy investigation.

    — How does the procedure described compare to standard procedures outlined in Chapter 18? If you spot any differences, what might account for them?
    — Put yourself in her place. Do you have the skills needed to do a project like this? What seem to be the most important skills she demonstrates?
    — This project required months of work and thousands of dollars. Was it a good investment by the newspaper? Why or why not?
    — After reading this memo, what questions would you like to ask Karen Dillon?

Editor's Note

    Karen Dillon and Bob Lynn of *The Kansas City Star* spent 10 months investigating the finances of the Kansas City Police Department and the operations of the Board of Police Commissioners, the department's governing body.

    The result was a three-day series that detailed a secret multimillion-dollar fund from which $16 million had been spent in two years. The unbudgeted fund, which dated back to 1939, was unknown to even city council members, who provide the department with millions of dollars a year in funding.

    Readers were told how the board violated state law and approved spending millions of dollars in illegal and secret meetings. The series revealed that the board was a rubber stamp for the department it was supposed to oversee, never turning down a request in eight years.

    It showed how the board spent hundreds of thousands of dollars in secret settlements of lawsuits and claims and how high-ranking officers double-billed taxpayers for meals and other expenses while traveling nationwide.

After the series was published, Missouri Gov. Mel Carnahan ordered an investigation into board operations, requiring the board to turn over voluminous records. The board and department have changed various policies and the way records are kept. In addition, bills have been introduced in the Missouri General Assembly and the Kansas City City Council that would allow the city to audit the department and would change the makeup of the board.

The *Star* is continuing to investigate the department, revealing even more problems. The most recent story showed that the department and Jackson County officials had violated state law by allowing the department to keep hundreds of thousands of dollars in unclaimed money that should have been turned over to the county.

How We Did It

The first thing reporters learn when assigned to the Kansas City, Mo., police beat is that it is a many-headed beast. Not only do they cover breaking crime news, they also are responsible for keeping up with problems in the department and monitoring the department's governing agency, the Kansas City Board of Police Commissioners.

The Kansas City and St. Louis police departments are unlike any other in the country. In both cities the departments are state agencies regulated by a board of police commissioners appointed by the governor. Both departments, however, receive their funding from the cities, which have no legal authority or control over how the money is spent.

When I began covering the Kansas City police beat in June 1993, the once-a-month board meetings were deadly dull. The board was different from any government agency I had ever covered because the commissioners always agreed. Dissent, or even healthy debate, was a foreign concept to a group that prided itself on unanimous decisions in support of the police department.

After votes were taken, commissioners often lauded the department, and by extension themselves, for its notable achievements and supposed national reputation.

But things just didn't seem right. For instance, when I asked for minutes of numerous meetings or records of expenditures the board had approved, I was often unable to get them. The board's attorney often promised to provide them but never did. After a day or so, I would be back to covering murders and handling the other daily pressures of the beat and the records would be forgotten.

Other strange things happened. In September 1993, I overheard the police chief talking to a commissioner about a lobbyist the board had recently hired. I couldn't remember the board ever discussing the lobbyist, much less voting to hire him. When I asked about it, I got vague responses.

There was a reason for that. I found out through later reporting that the board had approved hiring its lobbyist, who had extensive ties to the gambling industry, in a secret, illegal meeting. A simple telephone call to the Missouri Ethics Commission verified that he was a lobbyist for several casino groups.

Other examples of the secrecy of both the department and the board surfaced. In December the board approved a $91 million budget with no public discussion. When I asked the chief about it, he said there was nothing to discuss since salaries make up 80 percent of the budget.

The real genesis of the eventual series came nine months after I began covering the beat. A deputy chief, who many said was being groomed to be the next head of the 1,800 member department, was demoted to captain. A sergeant had accused him of coercing her to have sex.

Rumors of a six-figure secret settlement began to circulate. When I first asked about it, Police Chief Steven Bishop denied the department had paid a settlement. However, the woman's attorney acknowledged a settlement had been reached. Because the department insisted on a confidentiality agreement, however, she was barred from talking about the settlement.

Of course, the board never discussed the scandal in a public meeting.

After several sources told me payment of the settlement could possibly have come from a secret fund, I telephoned a former department employee who had been connected with top police officials.

The former employee told me about a secret multimillion-dollar fund, known to the few who were aware of it as the Treasurer's Account or "T-account." The employee said the fund was so well hidden that even city council members did not know about it.

Another former police employee directed me to other sources, some still on the police force, who said the T-account had been a secret fund for decades and was used for anything the city wouldn't budget. That included $25,000 retirement banquets complete with steak dinners and alcohol, new furniture for the chief's office and nationwide travel that would have the average tourist drooling.

Given that information, the newspaper detached me for two weeks from the daily beat to look into the fund further. Bob Lynn, an editor, was assigned to oversee the project.

We decided to file Freedom of Information requests for a cornucopia of department records dating back to 1980. In the requests, we asked for records concerning all settlements of claims and lawsuits, the accounting books and check register of the T-account and any board policies regulating the disbursement of the T-account funds. We also requested all minutes of board meetings for the past 15 years.

When I presented the chief and the department attorney with the request, they immediately said all records were open.

The department attorney introduced me to a sergeant in the financial unit and asked him to give me audits of police funding rather than the T-account financial reports. After a quick review of the audits with both men watching, I shrugged my shoulders and said everything appeared in order. I added that I wasn't a financial expert and asked for copies of the audits.

After the department attorney left the room, I persuaded the sergeant to show me records of the T-account that showed the receipts, disbursements and transfers that were made each day. It also showed that the monthly balance of the account ranged from $7 to $9 million. The money had never been budgeted. I asked the sergeant if I could make copies.

When I got permission, I began copying furiously. Sources said the command staff members were appalled and were meeting with the chief to try to stop what they believed would happen once I had the records and could analyze them.

Once I had made those copies, we asked through a Freedom of Information request for a computer disc of the records. But even though the Missouri Sunshine Law allows records to be copied onto a computer disc, the chief said no. Even though analyzing the records on computer would have been much easier, the newspaper decided not to complicate matters and did not sue.

After an initial review of the records, the newspaper decided to allow me to work indefinitely on the project. It was a difficult decision because reporters working other beats would have to fill in for me. Covering the Kansas City police is considered one of the top three beats at the *Star,* and newspapers these days often do not have the staff to commit for any long period of time.

The T-account monthly reports, which break the fund into several accounts, were a nightmare. The reports showed millions of dollars in revenue coming from fees such as report reproduction, unclaimed and seized money, criminal history record checks, communications and licenses for private officers.

The reports listed thousands of expenditures each month. Some of those expenditures caught our eye immediately because they didn't seem related to fighting crime. Those expenditures included coffee, fruit, flowers, picnics, banquets, furniture, retirement gifts such as cakes and batons, and souvenirs such as coffee mugs and police badge tie-tacs.

There also was an account for travel and education. We would later analyze it and learn the department in three years had spent almost a million dollars sending its officers to cities nationwide for seminars. In comparison, the St. Louis Police Department, which had 400 more employees than Kansas City, spent only $65,000 for the year.

Even though the records showed that spending from the T-account averaged $750,000 each month over two years, the account had maintained a monthly carryover balance that ranged from $7 million to almost $10 million.

With thousands of pages of T-account records to analyze line by line, Lynn took on the role of reporter and started working with me to create a database to better understand the financial goings-on with the T-account. We also examined eight years of the department's private audits of its money, which never mentioned the T-account by name. We were later told that only a financial expert would have found it.

At the same time, the department and board legal secretaries had provided thousands of pages of meeting minutes. While reading through those, we started finding a curious type of record, addenda.

The addenda were attached to minutes of certain meetings. Those minutes had never been made public. In fact, the board had never received copies of them or even approved them.

The addenda detailed, time after time, illegal telephone votes approving the expenditure of millions of dollars. And the minutes and addenda showed that the board in eight years had never turned down a request by the department.

We compared the dates of expenditures in the T-account to the minutes to see if the board's discussion or vote to spend that money had ever been recorded.

For example, the T-account revealed the salary of the lobbyist hired in August 1993. We found an addenda that had never been made public and that showed the board illegally hired the lobbyist at a luncheon with only two commissioners present. After a deputy chief got their votes, he telephoned the board president and got his vote.

We found numerous expenditures like that.

Even though the board and department knew we were investigating its finances, it continued to break the Sunshine Law. In April 1994, the board during a meeting discussed the acquisition of a helicopter for more than 20 minutes. It was the first I had heard about it. Inquiring further, I learned the commissioners had only learned about the helicopter two weeks before the meeting when each gave their approval in a seriatim telephone vote. Neither the vote nor the discussion in an open meeting were ever recorded in the minutes.

As the number of documents grew, they became unwieldy. We began categorizing them under various topics and alphabetizing them. Eventually they filled two large plastic tubs that were each about a foot and a half wide and three feet long.

In April we began preparing for what we believed would be difficult interviews over a variety of topics. We spent hours preparing questions and analyzing what the commissioners' answers might be based on the documents we had. The questions for each topic initially were open-ended and gradually became closed-ended and included questions based on the variety of responses we thought the commissioners might offer.

We also decided that for legal reasons, all interviews with commissioners would be taped.

In May, Lynn and I—armed with detailed questions and a tub of documents—attempted separate interviews with the board president and its attorney. Each interview lasted a little over an hour before being abruptly terminated.

Because of our questions, the board held an emergency meeting two days later. The commissioners lambasted us for "blindsiding" them and passed a resolution forbidding individual interviews. They agreed they would talk to the *Star* only if all commissioners were present with the chief and two attorneys.

Letters passed between the board president and Art Brisbane, the *Star*'s editor. It was decided that we would meet with two board members rather than all so the meetings law was not violated. The chief, assistant chief and the attorneys for the board and the department would also attend.

We had two three-hour taped interviews in July in which we questioned how money was spent and why. At the end of the second interview, the board president angrily announced all further questions would have to be submitted in advance in writing.

As any reporter knows, questions and answers in writing are difficult because it takes away the advantage of a confrontational interview. No matter how closed-ended we asked a question in writing, the board and department attorneys often were able to avoid answering the questions. That always meant more questions in writing.

But the written questions also had an advantage. Because it took so long, Lynn and I were able to continue investigating. We went to St. Louis where we met with police officials who acknowledged they have a "T-account," but on a much smaller scale. They also said that unlike the Kansas City department, which keeps T-account money for itself, the St. Louis T-account money goes to the city's general fund.

As the investigation progressed, the chief and most of the commissioners would barely acknowledge us, much less speak to us. As a precaution, we started noting and dating pleasant or unpleasant conversations with department officials. At the same time, the board wrote the editor questioning our reporting tactics.

While waiting on responses, we examined travel records and learned that the department had a policy that allowed officers to double-dip when they traveled. The department would pay officers up to $40 a day to eat even if they didn't eat or the meals were provided free.

In October, Bill Dalton, an editor who had been a projects reporter, was assigned as our editor. He began editing the stories, and coordinating graphics and photos for the series. Graphics were extremely important to help readers better understand the difficult financial issues.

At our request, the newspaper also hired an accounting firm. We were concerned because of a discrepancy between what we had figured was being spent from the T-account and what the department said was being spent. The accountants verified our findings: The department had spent $16 million in two years from the T-account.

Two weeks before the series was to run, Lynn and I started going through the stories line by line to verify each fact. We also re-added all the figures that we had spent months compiling. The stories then were sent to the *Star*'s attorney, who also went through the stories line by line and again with us.

The series that ran Jan. 22, 23 and 24 detailed the T-account, the board's illegal meetings and secretive spending of millions of dollars, the double-dipping and secret lawsuit settlements. Another story showed that at the same time that the department had more money than it revealed to the public, the department was able to pay some of the highest salaries in the Midwest. And it never hired police officers with T-account money.

The day the series ended, Gov. Mel Carnahan ordered an investigation into board operations. The board and department have changed questionable policies and the way they keep records.

Because we could not get many answers about questionable financial activities, we are continuing to investigate and write stories. The most recent story showed that in violation of state law, the department had kept hundreds of thousands of dollars that should have gone to the county.

"How I Got Here"

Karen Dillon became a journalist through unconventional means. After leaving high school in 1970, she moved to Iowa, where she married and had one daughter. When her daughter began grade school, she got a job as a typesetter at the *Boone News-Republican,* a small daily in a town about 40 miles north of Des Moines.

From there she moved into composing and became the assistant composing supervisor. After taking some photography classes, she began shooting for the paper as well. Eventually she was placed in charge of the darkroom and also was made a general assignment reporter.

While working at that paper, she got her two-year associates college degree and in 1985 went to the University of Missouri. She obtained an undergraduate degree in political science and a graduate degree in journalism. She interned at the *San Jose Mercury News* and the *Chicago Tribune.* While attending classes, she also wrote stories for the *Columbia Missourian,* the *Columbia Tribune* and the *Kansas City Times.*

While working on her journalism degree, she attended the journalism school's Washington program in Washington, D.C., and wrote for the *Mercury News* and the *Times.*

After she graduated in 1989, the *Sarasota (Fla.) Herald-Tribune* hired her to cover the police beat. In 1991, she received national recognition when she broke a story about Pee-Wee Herman, the children's comedian who was arrested at an adult theater.

The *Star* hired her in Nov. 1991. She has worked there as a police reporter, first in Kansas City, Kan., and now in Kansas City, Mo.

10. You suspect that T. A. Maxwell, president of the Teamsters union local in your city for nine years, secretly owns stock in the AAA Trucking Corp., some of whose officers have been convicted of felonies. Describe how you will investigate.
    a. The sniff.

b. Human sources. Who might talk? Where should you start? Who will you save for last?

c. What records might help? Where are they? What will you be looking for?

d. What is the most you can hope to prove? What is the least that will yield a story?

11. The first-day stories of a Pulitzer Prize-winning series by the *Akron Beacon Journal* are reprinted on pp. 138–44. Bob Paynter was the project editor who directed the yearlong project. Read the stories and answer these questions:

— How do these stories strike you? Are they what you think of when you see the phrase "investigative reporting"?
— The chapter sketches some of the reporting techniques used. In these stories, what techniques and tools do you detect?
— This is an attempt to understand one of the most complex issues facing American society. Discuss the opportunities and the obstacles in tackling a subject so big.
— What questions would you like to ask Bob Paynter?

A Separate, but Equal, Focus on Our Differences

Blacks: They Must Live Daily with the Irritating Reality of Subtle and Overt Racism in the Area

By CARL CHANCELLOR
Beacon Journal staff writer

The weather. Constant highway construction. No jobs.

Those were the first responses to the question: "What are the negatives of living in the Akron area?"

But the nervous laughter shared by the group of 11 blacks hunkered around the conference-room table suggested there was something left unspoken, something all were aware of but were reluctant to acknowledge.

"OK, I'll add number four. Racism."

Jacqueline Cason, 45, leaned back in her chair and scanned the faces of her fellow focus group members to see if she had accurately gauged the mood.

Vigorous nods of approval gave her the answer.

Unlike their white counterparts, for whom racism is barely a factor at all in their daily lives, a near-universal perception of African-Americans is that racism is alive and all too well in the Akron-Canton area.

That was among the clearest differences in attitudes detected between white and black focus groups commissioned by the *Beacon Journal* in January to help explore how skin color affects the way area residents view their community.

It's not that racism is some all-consuming affliction, according to the African-Americans gathered in the cramped conference room that evening. Instead, this group saw it as a dark force bubbling constantly just beneath society's surface, an evil thread woven into the American tapestry.

The famous African-American opera singer Marian Anderson once likened racism to a hair across one's cheek: "You can't see it, you can't find it with your fingers, but you keep brushing at it because the feel of it is irritating."

Group members said they had regularly felt this irritating hair across their cheek, in many situations, in places both expected and unexpected.

Some spoke of being stopped and interrogated by police for no apparent reason—other than skin color. That's a fact of life for young black males, group members said. They see it as harassment.

Others talked of being denied bank loans because they're black, of being steered to mostly black neighborhoods when shopping for a house, of being thwarted at work.

Still others recounted incidents—some years old, others painfully fresh—where they saw a double standard coming into play, a separate and distinct set of rules available for whites from that applied to African-Americans.

"If anyone doubts that racism exists, just listen what happened at my husband's job the other day," said a middle-aged mother of two, raising her hand as if to swear to the truthfulness of her story. She asked to remain anonymous because she feared reprisals against her husband.

A white man who works with her husband was upset at being passed over for a promotion in favor of a black co-worker, the woman said. He apparently thought the black man was less qualified than himself and attributed his own lack of advancement to reverse discrimination.

So, she said, "this guy came to work in a Ku Klux Klan outfit, hood, medals, everything," but only got a slap on the wrist from his white supervisors.

"All they did was give him two days off to cool down. If that had been a black man (and he did something similar) he would have been fired on the spot," she fumed.

Whites probably would not agree.

But, at least as reflected in the *Beacon Journal* focus groups, whites and blacks agree on very little where race is concerned.

King's Dream Is Fading

The point was brought home clearly when both groups were asked separately to listen to Dr. Martin Luther King Jr.'s *I Have a Dream* speech and gauge where we are as a society some 30 years later.

Whites generally felt that institutional racism had been eliminated, that the playing field had been leveled off and that pretty much everyone, regardless of race, now has an equal opportunity to succeed.

The consensus of the black group was that, while some progress has been made in the 30 years since King's speech, it's been not as much as many would have hoped.

"I think we have made some inroads, some progress, but it hasn't been significant. We certainly don't live in an equal society," said Cason, a West Akron homemaker who is active in Phillip's Chapel CME Church in Akron and sings in the church choir.

"In many ways, I think we have slipped back with Reagan taking everything away," she continued, speaking of what many blacks view as the watering-down and reinterpreting of civil rights law during the 1980s.

John Earnest, 40, who owns and operates a West Akron hair studio, vividly remembers the words of his father as they watched on television the thousands gathered before the Lincoln Memorial listening to King's speech.

"My father said Martin Luther King was an idealist. He never felt that the dream of equality and freedom in this country would ever be a reality. . . . Now, recalling what my father said and looking where this society is today, I think I would have to agree with him.

"Some progress has been made but not as much as I expected. I even get a sense that we are going backward from whatever advances were made," Earnest concluded.

An Older Man's Perspective

But, contrary to popular myth, not all blacks think alike and that's true on racial matters as well.

James Brown listened quietly to Earnest's appraisal, but the furrows deepening on his brow showed clearly that he didn't agree.

"I thought the speech was great. . . . But at the time I also didn't think it was realistic. . . . I didn't think it would happen in my lifetime," said Brown, at 60 the oldest member of the group.

"I grew up in Portsmouth, in southern Ohio. Spent my first 20 years there and I can tell you it was a different world then.

"I can remember if you were a black you couldn't even think about certain jobs. . . . You could work in the restaurants but you couldn't eat in them. You could be a housekeeper or a bell cap in the hotels but you couldn't sleep in one. I'm talking about segregation. . . . So I disagree. There has been a great deal of progress. A lot of what we have now we could never have had 30 years ago.

"And if we are going backwards it is only because we (blacks) have stopped."

Self-Determination

With those words, Brown introduced another main theme of the night and another area where blacks don't always agree with one another—the issue of black self-determination.

Interestingly, both groups—white and black—agreed that many of the problems facing blacks are self-inflicted, although they used far different words to articulate their views.

Some observations from the white group:

"The problems they (blacks) have are brought on by what they do themselves. They have a penchant for gambling, drinking, breaking the law. . . ."

"It's not society. They have to stop wanting somebody else to solve their problems. . . ."

"They (blacks) don't have a strong sense of family and that keeps them down. . . ."

"If you have the drive to do something you can do it. I mean blacks in Akron have an equal opportunity if they have the drive. It's their choice."

While the tone may seem harsh and self-serving to some, many blacks saw rays of truth in at least some of those observations.

"Life is tougher for blacks in Akron but we have a lot to do with it," said Paul Hardy, 39, a mechanical engineer for Goodyear. He said blacks have failed to take full advantage of the opportunities that have been afforded in part because blacks aren't preparing themselves educationally or professionally.

Group members also cited a lack of unity among blacks, lack of investment by blacks in the black community, and even inner-racial jealousy, as stumbling blocks to African-American advancement.

"I hate to say it but we don't like to see each other get ahead," said Phyllis Anderson, 29, a mortgage loan processor. "If a black person decides to move to someplace like Stow there will be other black people who will say that person is being uppity."

The Generation Factor

Several people in the group pointed to a disturbing tendency among blacks, particularly among African-American youth, to equate success, particularly academic achievement, with "acting white."

A 23-year-old recent college graduate, a baseball cap pulled down to the bridge of his nose, just shook his head acknowledging the uncomfortable truth of that observation.

"We have to start with our youth. We have to breed in every child a commitment to excellence," he said.

Brown, a union carpenter who teaches in the union's apprenticeship program, said he is very troubled by what he is experiencing.

"There was a time, not that long ago, that a lot of trade unions had no blacks," said Brown, adding that it took a lot of effort for the skilled trade unions to finally open their doors to minorities.

He said young African-Americans, right out of high school, now have opportunities to enter the skilled trades, but too many of them are squandering the chance.

"The apprenticeship is a four-year program where you learn on the job and attend classes. It's work and school. . . . Now these kids have no problem on the job sites and they have

the skills, but for some reason they don't go to the classes. You miss so many classes and you are put out of the program.

"You tell me why they won't attend classes? It doesn't make sense. They spend a year to two years in the program and are then put out because they don't go to class."

Hardy, taking up Brown's train of thought, added that the need to commit to excellence applies not only to youth, but to black adults as well.

"We as a people have to change our lives for the better. They (whites) aren't going to change their attitudes; that's something we can't control," said Hardy.

The white "attitude" toward blacks, as outlined by these 11 focus group members, consists of a mixture of fear, contempt, ambivalence and resentment.

"I think they feel threatened by blacks—particularly young black men. They are afraid of what they see on their TVs," said another group member.

Blacks generally agreed that the image of African-Americans transmitted by the media is overwhelmingly negative: nightly stories and photos of blacks on welfare; blacks being arrested for crimes; young black girls having babies out of wedlock. The list goes on.

But the group said the media only serve to reinforce negative stereotypes of African-Americans that many—if not most—whites already believe.

"It's just born in them," said Cason. "It's the way they are raised."

A female health worker who had remained silent for most of the evening finally spoke up.

"I think that most whites expect blacks to be inferior and expect blacks to fail. . . . Not only do they expect blacks to be inferior, they need to think they are. They have a psychological need to establish that position.

"These (types of) people are going to look for evidence, no matter how insignificant, to back up their beliefs," she said.

Friends of a Different Color

Not everyone at the table agreed. Nearly every member of the group said they have white friends who don't fit that description, friends with whom they share confidences and regularly socialize.

Anderson cautioned against lumping all whites together, saying that would be as bad as concluding that all blacks are the same.

But she did wonder aloud just how many whites really know black people. Blacks have to interact daily with whites, beginning at the earliest ages, she said. But the reverse is not necessarily true.

Earnest agreed that it is blatantly unfair to paint all whites with one brush.

"It was a white man who really helped me get my business started," said Earnest. He said this white friend, whom he termed "more like a brother," went out of his way to assist him in any way possible.

"He is a carpenter and for more than two months he

came to my studio and worked putting the place together. Whatever he could do he would do with no hesitation.

"I wanted to pay him for his time. But he would have nothing to do with my money. I knew what he did for me came from his heart," continued Earnest.

"You can't judge anyone by their color. Instead you have to judge them on the content of their character. You have to give people the opportunity to show what they are made of."

An End to Racism

Is it possible that Earnest's positive experience, along with the numerous healthy and warm interactions with whites experienced by several in the group, signal an eventual end to racism?

The group moderator asked: "Tell me what would it mean to you if you opened up your paper tomorrow and the headline read: 'Racism has vanished'?"

The question was greeted with snickers—a sound that spoke loudly to the African-American belief that this society will never be free from racism. Still, the group played along.

Anderson and Brown said the demise of racism would free them from the pressure of wearing a mask to fit into the norms set by white society.

"It would be weird not being made constantly aware that I'm black. . . . I would feel like I didn't have to conform" to white standards, said Anderson.

"I could live and express my own culture and not somehow feel ashamed," said Brown. "I could be free to totally appreciate my culture, which would also give me the freedom to appreciate other cultures."

Saundra Redding, 35, an attractive woman who works as an occupational therapist, said an end to racism would mean she would no longer have to "deal with other people's preconceptions, white and black. I could just be me."

But Cason summed up the skepticism of the whole group.

Reading a headline signaling an end to racism, she said, "would mean I had died and gone to heaven."

Whites: They See Racism as a Vital Issue, but Also as a Riddle That Leaves Them Groping for Solutions

By BOB DYER
Beacon Journal staff writer

See whether you can identify the person who said this a few weeks ago during a private meeting of 11 people in an Akron suburb:

"At the end of the week, I just wanted to go home and say it. . . . 'Nigger, nigger, nigger, nigger, nigger!'" A member of the Ku Klux Klan? Maybe the imperial wizard himself? Guess again: A 50-year-old African-American woman from West Akron. She was referring to the relentless politeness she had encountered in a predominantly white workplace.

The forum was a gathering of black area residents brought together by the *Beacon Journal* to talk about race. This was the second such meeting of the evening. The first was all-white. And during the first meeting—a two-hour session—the derogatory term was uttered only once, with apparent reluctance, by a woman quoting a friend who openly hates blacks.

What does that suggest? Mainly that whites are loath to use the dreaded "N-word"—at least in public. Whites have learned exactly what society expects in terms of racial attitudes. The real question is: Has that knowledge changed what's in their hearts?

The answer gets harder and harder to find. Why? Because many whites, if not most, seem to believe they no longer have the ability to candidly address the issue of race without automatically being branded as racist.

Call it political correctness, call it going with the flow, call it what you will. But the typical white American will go to great lengths simply to avoid the subject. And that skittishness may be getting in the way of solutions.

Pry below the surface, as the *Beacon Journal* did by arranging focus groups and conducting a series of lengthy follow-up interviews, and you will find little desire among whites to run around unleashing racial slurs.

Most whites apparently do not hate blacks. Most whites do not root for blacks to fail. Whites may expect blacks to fail, but that is quite different from loathing blacks, as was probably the case a half-century ago.

The white heart in 1993 seems to be a complex gnarl of mixed—even conflicting—emotions. To most whites, the question of race is not, if you'll pardon the expression, a matter of black and white.

Take affirmative action, for instance. "Half of me wants to say . . . it's in place to make sure the opportunities are there," says Joyce Burton, 37, a white longtime nurse at Children's Hospital Medical Center of Akron. "The other half of me wants to say that's unfair, that the best person should get the job.

"But working your way up and having the best education and the best opportunity sometimes is precluded if you are black. I see both sides of it."

Those whites with a more one-sided view usually bite their tongues. Although Akron resident Dick Reymann feels strongly that quota systems are patently unfair, he wrestled hard with the issue of allowing his name to be used in this story.

Why the reservations? Fear of violent reprisal from angry blacks.

"And also," he adds, "because it's a hopeless effort. If you perceive things to be unfair or slanted too far in one direction, there's nothing you can do about it. So why make trouble for yourself?"

But Reymann, 56, a former football player at Akron St. Mary's High School, a fireman in the Air Force and now a lieutenant in the Akron Fire Department, believes speaking out is the right thing to do. In 1976 he went to federal court to argue against the forced integration of the fire department, which at the time was all-white.

"I argued before and I'll argue today that it's not fair to have a system where your promotion or your hiring is determined by the color of your skin," Reymann says. "To me, that's racism.

"I don't dislike black people, and I don't blame them for what they've done as far as getting quotas. But they do think differently and act differently. . . .

"I'm accused of being the bigot in my family because I say blacks are different from white people. I've been in the service with blacks, gone to school with them, I work with them now in the fire department."

Classifying Blacks

Reymann insists that blacks are absent more often, in trouble more often and "have a penchant for drinking and gambling." He asserts his black colleagues take far more sick leaves than whites, and challenges a reporter to check the official records.

Computer printouts supplied by the city personnel department show that 47 of 86 black firefighters on the force more than six months called in sick at least once during 1992. That's 55 percent. For whites, 96 of 280 firefighters called in sick—or 34 percent.

For Reymann, at least, the conclusion is clear: "If a guy wasn't there, he wasn't there."

Other focus group members see such comparisons as counterproductive. Burton, the nurse at Children's Hospital, says: "Being a nurse and being dedicated to taking care of people, you learn to look at people as people, at their individual needs, rather than looking at them as black and white. You lose your objectivity if you start putting people into classifications."

Lack of Dialogue

Still, it seems to some whites that, in attempting to get to the heart of the differences between the races—differences that perpetually seem on the brink of ripping the nation asunder—they are asked to abandon all the observational faculties they would bring to any other issue.

Try to study inborn differences between the races and you are likely to be hooted down. Just ask NBC anchorman Tom Brokaw, who in 1989 had the misfortune of hosting a 90-minute network documentary that attempted to explain why blacks are disproportionately successful in professional sports.

Praised by press critics as thorough and fair, the program was roundly condemned by black leaders, who saw it simply as a way to discount the long hours of hard work logged by successful black athletes.

Brokaw says he took more heat about that documentary than any he has done in more than 30 years of broadcasting. "We are failing ourselves by not having a candid dialogue" about race, he said.

The type of reaction Brokaw got may be the reason so many whites see public discussions about race relations as one-sided. Fireman Reymann has a friend who canceled his subscription to this newspaper after reading an announcement about its yearlong race-relations project.

Owning Responsibility

"He said, 'I'm sick to death of hearing them say how bad all us white people are and how downtrodden the black people are,'" said Reymann, who is a bit weary of the topic himself. "I don't think the problem will ever be solved if that's the way it's approached.

"Why do their problems always have to be from the outside? Why is it always the community's fault or someone else's fault? It seems like they're always looking for the government or someone for solutions.

"There's still work to be done—white people are still prejudiced—but it's got to be two-sided, not one-sided."

Do not misunderstand the importance whites place on the topic, though. Most view race relations as a vital issue. When the focus group moderator first broached the subject, the conversation roared off for more than seven minutes before she was able to pose her next question.

One group member, to emphasize the magnitude of the problem, quoted white preacher Billy Graham, who, when asked in a recent television interview what he would do if he could wave a magic wand and eliminate one—but only one—of the world's problems, replied:

"Race. It divides the whole world."

He didn't say war. He didn't say famine. He said race. And that says a lot.

The *reason* whites worry about race, however, varies greatly.

At one end of the spectrum are the altruistic concerns of people like Graham who hold a belief that, as Dr. Martin Luther King, Jr. said three decades ago, "This nation (must) rise up and live out the true meaning of its creed—'We hold these truths to be self-evident, that all men are created equal.'"

At the other extreme: simple self-preservation.

Afraid of Blacks

For these last three decades, the issue of race has lurked ominously just below the surface of the American landscape, like a Nike missile ready to spring from its silo at a moment's notice.

To many whites in the *Beacon Journal* focus group, black skin equals fear.

"I went with a black friend to an all-black carnival," volunteered a 31-year-old auto painter. "It scared me to death."

As it turned out, he said, nothing bad happened. But the man's fear was very real.

Several participants said they were taught as children to stay away from blacks, to lock their car doors when blacks were around, to go out of their way to avoid black neighborhoods.

To soft-sell white fears of violence is to dodge a central issue in race relations. One would have difficulty overestimating the impact on the white psyche of the '60s riots—everywhere from the Los Angeles ghetto of Watts to the Cleveland communities of Glenville and Hough to Akron's own Wooster Avenue—as well as last year's mayhem in Los Angeles.

Most whites in the group were well aware that blacks remain at a serious educational and economic disadvantage. Moreover, the whites believe it is to their own advantage to help blacks catch up. But they don't seem to know what more to do.

Blacks Must Help Selves

The bulk of the effort, the local whites maintain, must come from blacks themselves.

Ernest Murphy, who works as a hairdresser in Cuyahoga Falls, says he is highly sympathetic to black problems but wishes their culture would enable them to follow the example of other minority groups in terms of family solidarity. He pointed to the situation in Miami, where, he says, Cuban immigrants have not only held their own but virtually taken over the city's political system.

"The key is they have a strong sense of family," he said of the Cubans. "In the black community, that is the weak spot. . . . The family unit has failed."

Even when the family remains together, others say, the lack of a strong work ethic keeps many poor blacks from even trying. "They see their parents on a (welfare) system and say, 'Why should I work?'" said a 35-year-old Akron mechanic.

However, most whites see at least one major reason for optimism: They believe their own attitude toward blacks has improved dramatically over that of previous white generations.

At the time King was first expressing his dreams for America, the typical white child was being taught that blacks should, at the very least, be avoided.

"Parents no longer teach their kids to hate blacks," says Lloyd Weimer, 61, a former mold-maker, template-maker and janitor at Firestone. Weimer recalls hearing a friend's mother say, "Don't put that penny in your mouth—a black person might have touched it!"

Says Weimer, a father of four: "I did not teach my children that black is bad or black is dirty." And his grandchildren, he says, are being raised in an environment where skin color is even less of an issue. Weimer credits part of that change in attitude to prime-time television, where he sees blacks being widely depicted in positions of responsibility.

Echoes the 38-year-old Murphy: "Our grandparents and parents had more prejudices than we do."

Evidence of Change

Perhaps nowhere is generational change more evident than in the case of Roberta Robertson, 40, who works in the law library at the University of Akron.

Robertson's grandmother, a native of Tennessee, was a member of the KKK.

She later moved to Akron. Robertson lived with her in the Firestone Park section of Akron until Robertson's family got its own house in 1963. Even then, Grandma was just around the corner, continuing to exert a heavy influence over the family's outlook.

But Robertson, unlike her grandmother, was growing up in a racially mixed area. Being in daily contact with blacks, she eventually made black friends. When Robertson got married in 1973, she chose one of those black friends as her maid of honor.

Grandma was horrified, and threatened to boycott the wedding. Eventually she showed up, but kept her distance.

Although somewhat embarrassed by that bit of family history, Robertson points out that her late grandma was a product of her time and region. "I understand how she was, living back in the sticks of Tennessee. It was all around her. That's the way it was. But I'm not proud of it."

Robertson adamantly denies that her close friendship with a black girl was merely a way to rebel against Grandma. The reason she rejected Grandma's philosophy, she says, is because of "the daily contact with people. Walking home. Being in school. Sharing recess and all those things. The dances in junior high after school. The basketball games. Being beat up by black people. Being beat up by white people and having the black people come to my side because I was a friend."

That type of progress within a family seems to fit in with a recent University of Akron survey commissioned by the *Beacon Journal:* if a black family moved next door, 70 percent of the Akron-area whites said they would either "give it no thought" or pay the newcomers a courtesy call.

Of course, whites know that is how they are *supposed* to answer.

An End to White Flight?

Although the nine whites in January's gathering generally acknowledged that black families sometimes are steered toward certain neighborhoods, they insist that seeing a black family behind a moving van no longer induces panic.

"I've had black people move into my neighborhood out in Ellet," says Reymann, the Akron firefighter. "It used to be all-white. And nobody's getting upset. You don't see panic selling. That's a vast change over what it was 15 years ago. So I thought to myself, 'We've finally achieved it. We've pretty well achieved equality here.'"

Whether that is true remains the subject of significant debate.

For one thing, despite Reymann's perception of progress, the Ellet area remains about 99 percent white, according to latest census figures.

And overall black dissatisfaction remains extremely high.

Most whites are aware of black dissatisfaction. But there is no consensus among whites as to where to go from here. In fact, requests for solutions generally are greeted with blank stares or deep sighs. Only a few are even willing to take a stab.

The Dilution Solution

According to retired Firestone worker Weimer, the solution is dilution.

"Interracial marriage is quite common now," he says while sitting next to his wife at their 113-year-old farmhouse in Springfield Township. "I just figure that's what society is heading for."

Statistics back him up. A recent Census Bureau report says interracial marriages have doubled in the past 12 years and now account for one of every 50 U.S. unions.

"Chinese, Japanese and Koreans—they're marrying who they want to," says Weimer. "(The problems of blacks will abate) as they become more fair (skinned) and less different than their white counterparts. I think that's the only solution to the problem."

Perhaps. But that thought provides little solace in the short run.

Another school of white thought says maybe everyone should just step back a bit from the whole question.

"Everybody spends so much time dwelling (on race)," says Murphy, the Falls hairdresser. "And you never get beyond it. It's like, move on!

"It's like a funeral service: You don't stay at a funeral service forever. You have to move beyond it."

12. Your state's election laws, like those of many states, prohibit political contributions by corporations. The leader of a consumer watchdog group tells you that she knows but cannot prove that several major insurance companies, using the State Insurers' Council as a front, are contributing illegally to at least a half-dozen legislators who are running for re-election. How can you investigate? Describe records and human sources that may be useful.

13. In a short paper, discuss ways in which you, as a reporter on a small newspaper, might work your way around the obstacles posed by shortages of money and manpower in conducting a major investigation.

CHALLENGE EXERCISE

14. **a.** Despite vigorous opposition from neighboring homeowners, a piece of land in your city is rezoned for construction of a nursing home. Soon afterward, you hear that the chairman of the zoning board, a college professor of modest means, has bought a home in the city's nicest neighborhood. Your suspicions are aroused. How will you begin to investigate?

b. Suddenly, you have an unexpected problem: Your publisher calls you in. She knows the professor to be an honest man, she says. "This appears to be a wild goose chase. Why don't you just drop it?" How do you respond? What arguments might you use and what approaches might you suggest to try to win permission to investigate? Suppose she won't budge? What would you do then?

19 Writing News for Radio and Television

1. Watch a local evening newscast and make a list of all the stories included. Compare these stories with the ones carried by your local newspaper (either that evening's or the next morning's). Then answer the following questions:
   a. Which television stories were selected primarily because of timeliness?
   b. Which television stories made you turn to the newspaper for more information?
   c. Which television stories do you think were chosen because of their visual impact?

2. Following are five stories written for broadcast. Read them and answer the following questions:
   a. Do the stories emphasize immediacy? If so, how?
   b. Are they written in a conversational style?
   c. Are they written tightly?
   d. Are they written clearly?

   A. State to choose contractor for major road project
      ST. LOUIS (AP)—State officials will choose between two contractors on Friday to design and build a 12-mile stretch of Interstate 64 in suburban St. Louis.
      The competing companies are based in Texas and California, but both are using Missouri-based companies as subcontractors. Missouri officials are using a new concept called "design build"—instead of the state designing the project and awarding a construction contract, the company chosen will be responsible for the entire job.
      Mo-DOT says that could cut construction time from a decade or more to less than four years.
      The project will reconstruct twelve miles on the west end of I-64, including a dozen interchanges and 32 bridges. Mo-DOT says the project could cost upwards of half a billion dollars.
      It is the first major construction on the road in 40 years.
      Construction is expected to begin this spring and conclude by Fall 2010.

   B. Some board members criticize new school superintendent
      ST. LOUIS (AP)—Three St. Louis school board members leveled complaints at a new school superintendent just before she presents data to the state board in Jefferson City tomorrow.
      St. Louis mayor Francis Slay is among those who have called for a state takeover of the St. Louis public schools after years of conflict.
      Board members told Superintendent Diana Bourisaw last night they did not feel the data she would present to the state was interpreted correctly. She was also criticized for not updating them sooner about what she would present at the state level. She also has defenders on the board who called her planned presentation an accurate snapshot.

Bourisaw was named interim superintendent in July after the resignation of Creg Williams, who was forced out after just 16 months on the job.

Bourisaw is the sixth St. Louis superintendent since 2003.

C. Prosecutors bust 27 people in online gambling investigation

NEW YORK (AP)—Prosecutors have brought charges against 27 people in connection with a billion-dollar-a-year Internet sports gambling ring.

Among those charged is a man identified by authorities as a professional baseball scout for the Washington Nationals and a high-stakes poker player.

The charges were brought in connection with a site called Playwithal-dot-com.

Search warrants executed in several locations have resulted in the seizure of gambling records, computers and hundreds of millions of dollars in property. That includes four Manhattan condominiums, cash, tens of thousands of dollars worth of casino chips and a football signed by the 1969 New York Jets following their Super Bowl victory.

Police say arrests have been made in New York, New Jersey, Florida and Nevada.

D. AP-Texas Floods

HOUSTON—A million dollars here, a million dollars there, and pretty soon you've got a clean waterway.

The Coast Guard figures it's already cost about three-and-a-half million dollars, but the cleanup of the San Jacinto (juh-SIN'-toh) River and Houston Ship Channel should be 95 percent complete by tomorrow.

Oil skimmers have been working the deep water, and vacuum trucks have been working the shallows near shore. They're cleaning up the sticky mass of diesel, crude oil and gasoline released by ruptured pipelines during last week's floods.

E. AP-Breast Implants

MINNEAPOLIS—Researchers say there's reason to doubt that silicone-gel breast implants cause connective-tissue diseases.

A government-funded study finds "no association" between the implants and the diseases.

The study was presented today to the American College of Rheumatology.

There was another study presented yesterday with similar conclusions.

In the study reviewed today, researchers looked at more than 120,000 registered nurses.

They found only five women with breast implants who also suffered from a connective-tissue disease—and all of them had rheumatoid arthritis. None had scleroderma (sklih-roh-DUR'-mah) or the other illnesses suspected of being linked to the implants.

3. Rewrite the following newspaper wire stories for broadcast. Assume that you are writing for a Springfield broadcast.

a. SPRINGFIELD—At 10 a.m. Tuesday, Springfield weather sirens will sound as part of the annual statewide tornado drill sponsored by the National Weather Service.

The exercise is part of Severe Weather Awareness Week, which runs tomorrow through Friday and aims to remind folks what to do when severe weather threatens.

If severe weather does threaten on Tuesday, the tornado drill will be postponed until Thursday to avoid confusion.

b. AP-Street Shooting

LOS ANGELES—Los Angeles police say a deadly gang attack was a battle over drug turf.

A half-dozen gunmen fired on a crowd of 10 men Sunday night as they drank beer and played cards. The attack killed three men and wounded six. Two of the injured are in critical condition.

Police Chief Willie Williams told a news conference yesterday that the victims were not gang members. But he said some had been selling rock cocaine in the South Central L-A neighborhood. And a day or two before the shooting, they were warned by purported gang members to stop dealing at that location.

Police have made no arrests in the case so far.

c. Ex-CFO for HealthSouth agrees to guilty plea

BIRMINGHAM, Ala. (AP)—A third former chief officer at HealthSouth Corp. agreed to plead guilty yesterday to charges arising from a widening accounting scandal.

Michael Martin, who worked as CFO from October 1997 to February 2000, was charged with conspiracy to commit wire fraud and securities fraud, and with falsifying financial information.

Martin, 42, of Birmingham struck a plea deal and is cooperating with authorities investigating the company, U.S. Attorney Alice Martin said in a news conference.

d. SPRINGFIELD—A 31-year-old woman was stabbed and robbed Friday morning in downtown Springfield, police said.

Shortly before 11 a.m. Friday, the victim was walking down an alley to the south of the 600 block of Park Avenue, said police Sgt. Andrew Wheeler.

Two teenagers accosted her and demanded money, Wheeler said. She told them she had no money, so one of them stabbed her twice in the leg, he said.

The teens then took an undisclosed amount of cash from the woman and fled west down the alley on foot, Wheeler said.

e. WASHINGTON (AP)—A partially devoured woman's body was found early Saturday in the outdoor lion enclosure at the National Zoo. A zoo official said two lions were in the enclosure at the time.

Police Department spokesman Sgt. Joe Gentile said the cause of death had not been established. The woman was not immediately identified.

A zookeeper discovered the body at about 7 a.m. He coaxed the animals back into the lion house and called police.

A spokesman for the zoo, Marc Bretzfelder, said the dead woman was not a zoo employee.

4. Assume that the following four stories will follow one another in a news broadcast in Chicago. Rewrite the leads, lead-ins and wrap-ups for these news items.

a. AP-Dollar's Demise

NEW YORK—The dollar is hitting record lows against the world's currencies. What does that mean for Americans?

The dollar's fall is already having effects on U.S. consumers. Saudi Arabia plans to raise the price of oil exported to the U.S., partly because of the dollar's weakness.

And travelers to Europe and Japan find their dollars buy less than just a week ago.

Prices of German cars, Japanese CD players, Swiss cheese and French wine inevitably will also rise to reflect the dollar's reduced purchasing power.

b. AP-Diet Failures

BOSTON—Why do so many dieters fail to keep off hard-lost weight? A new study suggests they're done in by their own efficiency.

Researchers at Rockefeller University found that losing weight makes a body more efficient at burning calories.

People gain back lost weight because their bodies need fewer calories, so extra ones get stored as fat. They add pounds even though they seem to be eating and exercising sensibly.

The work confirms the long-held suspicion that the body's own metabolism conspires against a successful diet.

Researchers say this doesn't mean it's impossible to keep off lost weight. It only suggests that it may require modest eating and sensible exercise for life.

c. AP-Skinhead Slayings

MIDLAND, Michigan—Two teenage skinhead brothers have waived extradition from Michigan to Pennsylvania.

They'll face charges they murdered their parents and younger brother.

Seventeen-year-old Bryan Freeman and 16-year-old David Freeman appeared briefly today in a court in Midland, Michigan. They gave subdued answers of "yes" and "no" to a judge's questions.

The brothers were arrested in Michigan two days after their family's bodies were found in their home near Allentown, Pennsylvania.

Their court-appointed lawyers say the teens are sorry about the deaths. But the lawyers won't say if the boys confessed.

d. AP-Armored Cars

LOS ANGELES—Some abortion clinic doctors want more than handguns for protection; they're buying armored cars.

A company that adds armored plating to cars says physicians throughout California and the country are buying bullet-proof vehicles.

Five people have been killed in abortion clinic shootings since 1993.

A spokesman for the O'Gara-Hess and Eisenhardt Armoring Company says after the Massachusetts abortion clinics shootings in December, they received 39 phone calls that produced three sales.

The cost of converting a conventional car to an armored one can run from a few thousand dollars to 150,000 dollars.

That top-end price turns a Cadillac Eldorado into a vehicle guaranteed to repel armor-piercing shells. Options include pistol ports, thick glass and tear gas jets in wheel wells.

5. Correct the following broadcast scripts for spelling and broadcast style errors.

A. WASHINGTON (UPI)—The Forest Service today proposed a policcy of planning fires in national forest wilderness areas to reduce risk of wildfires and to permmit fire too return to it's natural ecological role.

R. Max Peterson, cheif of the Agriculture Department agency, says the earlier policy of promptly suppressing all fires resulted in "unnatural accumulation of dead brush and trees in some wilderness areas."

He says permitting trained specialists to ignite and mannage fires would permit the use of fires "to reduce unnatural fuel accummulations and allow fire once again to play its natural role in the ecology of wikderness ecosystems."

Under the proposed policy change, all planneed fires in wildernesz would have to be approved by a regional forester.

Peterson says a team of experts . . . including botanists, wildlife biologists and fire and recreation managers . . . woulld study each situation and make recommendations. He says the public would be included in each decision, and the public will be asked to comment by Aug. 4th on the proposed policy change.

The Forest Service administers 25-½ million acres of the National Wilderness Preservation System, or about 85% of wilderness outside of Alaska. The rest is administered by the Interior Department.

B. WASHINGTON (UPI) — Scientists say people who travel or whose work schedule is changed drastically may be able to avoid "jet lag" and function nearly normally if they set enough sleep after the disruption.

A study shows loss of sleep is just as important a cause of "jet lag" — the urge to sleep at inappropriate times — as the disruption of a travelers' body clock during journeys through several time zones. Thomas Roth is head of the slee disorders center at the Henry Ford Hospital in Detroit and a co-author of the report in the journal Science. He says "a good part of jet lag is loss of sleep." He adds thjat is important because "historically the emphasis has been on the (time) shift. NOT on the loss of sleep."

After two normal days, the people in the study, conducted at Henry Ford and Stanford University, went to bed at noon for 3 days.

Those who coped most successfully with the change, in hours took a short-acting prescription sedative whhich stayed in there bodies 5 to 6 hours. They functioned normally or nearly so.

Another group of volunteers took a longer-acting sedative and got a good sleep, but reported feeling drowsy and sluggish when theyt got up. In some cases they were drowsier than those who took a placebo, a fake drug.

The placebo group lost sleep and also had a hard time staying allert during the following "day."

The report says behaviour of the placebo group confirmed sleep and subsequent alertness "are significantly impaired for at least three days after a sudden 12-hour shift in the sleep-awake schedule."

C. KANSAS CITY (UPl)—A former mobster turned FBI informer today sobbed uring in his ex-wife's $1-½ million lawsuit against the federal government . . . saying he had never taken his son with him to comit crimes.

Asked by government attorney Mary Sterling whether his son had ever accompanied him on a "score," Michael Ruffalo, Sr., cried, "I've done a lot of things in my life. I've never taken my son on something like that."

U.S. District Judge Howard Sachs, who is hearing the lawsuit of Donna Ruffalo without a jury, recessed court for about 10 minutes to allow Ruffalo to compose himself.

Mrs. Ruffalo, Ruffalo's ex-wife, is seeking damages from the federal government for hiding her son in the federal witness protection program with his father in 1986. The boy entered the program at age 9.

Ruffalo, who testified behind a screan under heavy guard by federal officials, said when he decided to enter the program he asked Mike, Jr., what he wanted to do.

Ruffalo said, "I asked my son if he wanted to go with me, and never see his mother again. He said he never hardly saw her anyway.

Ruffalo said he was the boys primary caretaker thoughou his 14 years.

He disputed testimony given earlier in the morning by Gayle Wiser, Mrs. Ruffalo's sister.

Mrs. Wiser said that her daughter, Evie, who is now 27, lived with Mrs. Ruffalo for aoubt 4 years beginning at the age of 11. Speaking of that time in their lives, Mrs. Wiser said . . . "She'd (Evie) rather live with her than with me." But Ruffalo said he did not think his former wife gave the girl very good care. He also said he often saw Mrs. Ruffalo drunk. But Mrs. Wiser had said her sister's separation from her son caused the alcohol problem.

At the time Ruffalo entered the program, Mrs. Ruffalo had legal custody of the boy threw the Jackson County Circuit Court. She subsequently filed a lawsuit in federal court seeking the return of the boy and asking for monetary damages. Sachs has ordered the government to permit her 3 visits a year with her son.

6. Visit the news departments of at least two local television stations. Ask for copies of scripts that have been aired. Examine and compare the formats and camera instructions that each station uses. Then write a brief report on how they differ from those suggested for use in the text. Then, using these same scripts, write a sentence or two evaluating the lead-ins for the filmed reports.

7. Watch an evening network newscast. For each filmed report, write 150 words evaluating how the commentary and film complement each other.

8. Get a copy of today's local newspaper. Write a five-minute radio news broadcast for your area. Devote one minute of the time to sports.

CHALLENGE EXERCISE

9. Too many specific numbers can confuse viewers or listeners. Unlike readers of newspapers, they can't return to the original statement to doublecheck the information. Read the following newspaper story; then rewrite it for broadcast, taking care to simplify the presentation of numbers:

CHARLOTTE, N.C.—First Union Corp. said it will buy First Fidelity Bancorp for $5.4 billion in the biggest U.S. bank buyout ever, creating the nation's sixth-largest banking company. The transaction will create a bank with $123.7 billion in assets, 10,543,000 customers and 1,970 branches in 13 states from Florida to Connecticut.

Charlotte, North Carolina-based First Union will be larger than New York's Chase Manhattan Corp., now the No. 6 bank.

First Union's acquisition of Lawrenceville, New Jersey–based First Fidelity is its first foray outside the South and could signal further consolidation in the Northeast when barriers to interstate banking fall in September.

First Union agreed to a stock-swap transaction valued at $64.29 a share, or 33 percent higher than First Fidelity's Friday close of 48¾. Each First Fidelity share will be exchanged for 1.35 shares of First Union common stock. First Union said it would issue about 105 million shares in the tax-free transaction.

20 Writing for the Web

1. Go to a newspaper Web site. Study it and critique it specifically. Give examples of how the writing measures up to the following criteria for writing online.
   a. Do the news items reflect immediacy?

   b. Does the site attempt to save readers time?

   c. Does it provide information that's quick and easy to get?

   d. Does it provide information both visually and verbally?

e. Were the stories too long? Were they cut sufficiently?

f. Does the writing contain lists and bullets?

g. Are the stories broken into chunks?

h. Do the stories provide sufficient hyperlinks?

i. Is there ample opportunity for readers to talk back?

j. Does the site include the "human touch"?

k. Does the site include information not included in the printed paper?

l. Does the site use multimedia (audio or video) to enhance understanding and add appeal?

2. Explain why online writers must present information in layers.

3. Why is it important to remember that "readers rule" online?

4. A teacher in a local elementary school found a gun in a student's backpack. List at least six different related stories you could write to go along with the primary story.

5. Write the following stories for a newspaper Web site.

    A. After a long day, you get home from work and finally put dinner on the table. You're about to sit down and enjoy your pork chops and mashed potatoes when . . .

    Brring. Brring.

    "Hello, I am so and so from such and such. Would you like to buy . . . ?"

    That scene no longer must be part of the nightly ritual under a Senate bill the House passed Wednesday creating a state no-call list for telemarketers.

    The proposal, which must still acquire final approval of the Senate before being sent to the governor, allows up to $5,000 civil penalty for any telemarketer who knowingly calls anyone on the no-call list. Anyone who receives more than one call from the same firm after being placed on the list can seek up to $5,000 for each violating call.

    The bill was passed unanimously, 118-0. The only critics were concerned that the bill would rob small businesses of important ways to make sales. But the bill's sponsor rejected that claim.

    "The question is, When does my telephone become an extension of your business?" said Rep. Don Wells, D-Springfield.

    Nonetheless, the critics succeeded in adding language exempting from the penalties businesses that make fewer than 100 such calls per week.

    The measure, if passed in its current form, would not take effect until July 2003. By January of that year, the attorney general must have established a no-cost method for citizens to join the list.

    Currently, citizens can avoid getting the calls by telling each telemarketer to place them on its no-call list. This bill seeks to fuse all the separate lists into one huge database.

    The proposal also bans telemarketers from using technology that blocks Caller ID components on phones. It also requires any e-mailed marketing messages to include either a return e-mail address or a toll-free 800 number citizens can use to tell the company to stop sending the messages.

    In an unrelated development with even greater public policy ramifications, the Senate tabled a proposal that would place a tobacco money spending plan before the voters after anti-abortion language was added to the measure.

    The language, part of the ongoing fight to ensure that no state money goes to abortions, brought a compromise attempt from the governor. He offered to sign an accompanying bill with softer anti-abortion language.

    The conflict threatens to derail any decision on what to do with the pending tobacco money before the next crucial elections. At the beginning of the session, Governor Ramirez, who is running for the U.S. Senate, made spending the money on health projects one of his major priorities. If the plan is derailed, he will be deprived of an issue to trumpet in the campaign.

In an afternoon news conference, Ramirez was visibly agitated over the development.

"If we want to be a state that continuously litigates over abortions, let's get with it, but if we want good policy, let's do that," he said.

He was referring to the ongoing court battle between anti-abortion lawmakers and Planned Parenthood over whether state funds given to that group indirectly pay for abortions.

B. School board candidates are still on the campaign trail. Tuesday night they met at the Lenoir Retirement Community Center to address the concerns of senior citizens.

Unlike previous debates, where much of the discussion focused on the $35 million bond issue appearing on the April ballot, the bond was barely mentioned at all.

Instead, the senior citizens wanted to know about year-round schooling, what changes the candidates would enact and teacher unionization.

School board candidate Henry Lane said he believes there is "a changing tide" when it comes to using trailers as classrooms.

However, if year-round schooling were implemented, it would decrease the need for trailers, he said. Lane said a multitracking schedule would help overcrowding by reducing the number of students in daily attendance at the school by 25 percent.

Board President Elton Fay, also in the running, said year-round schooling isn't a practical idea.

"What Mr. Lane fails to tell you is that if we are to avoid erecting additional buildings, to save on construction costs, the cost of educating our children would go up substantially," Fay said.

Fay added that year-round schooling would mean different schedules for students of different ages.

"This community does not want schools on totally different schedules," he said.

Candidate Larry Dorman said that as a board member, he would focus on eliminating overcrowding in the schools and increasing teacher pay.

"If money weren't an issue, I'd build all the schools necessary," Dorman said.

Incumbent Kerry Corino said the increasing population makes it difficult to counteract large class sizes.

She said it is unfair to make comparisons between public and private schools because public schools cannot turn away students.

"Private schools can pick who they want; public schools cannot pick who they want," Corino said.

One senior citizen inquired as to whether teachers in the district can unionize.

Fay said teachers in this state cannot, by law, bargain collectively. He also said he doesn't support collective bargaining for teachers.

"The teachers are anti-union," Corino said. "That tells you a lot of things about how this city operates."

6. Online reporting can include sound, video and animation. Study a newspaper online, and identify several stories that might have been complemented with sound, film or animation. Explain what this would have added to the story.

7. Jacob Nielsen stresses the importance of credibility in online writing. He says it is often unclear where the information came from and whether it can be trusted. Then he says, "Links to other sites show that the authors have done their homework and are not afraid to let readers visit other sites." Some online editors argue that you should not send readers away from the newspaper they are reading. Discuss the issue.

8. Choose a major breaking story in today's news. Visit five online newspapers and compare the coverage. Choose the one you think provided the best online coverage. Specifically, why did you choose the one you did?

9. Most city and regional magazines have Web sites. Visit at least five city sites. Describe the one that has the most useful information and is the easiest to use.

10. Choose the major story in today's local newspaper. Study how the story was handled on the paper's Web site. What did you find? Was it an example of "shovelware"? Was the online version merely shorter than the newspaper version?

CHALLENGE EXERCISE
11. Fred Mann of Philadelphia Online warns about the lack of separation of editorial and advertising online. He says, "They slither together like snakes. It's hard to tell where one stops and another begins." Study two newspaper sites, and comment about how well they succeed in keeping editorial and advertising separate.

21 Writing for Public Relations

1. What are the major differences between writing news for the news media and writing for public relations?

2. Contact the person in charge of public relations at a corporation, university, hospital or other institution. Interview that person about the scope of his or her duties, and then outline them here.

3. A 10-year-old child is in serious need of an expensive operation. A sorority has decided to raise funds to make the operation possible. The sorority asks you to publicize its project.
   a. What would your target audiences be?

b. What media would you choose for which part of the story? Why?

c. What print materials would you develop?

4. Read the following news releases. Correct any deviations from Associated Press style and any other errors. After each release, comment on the newsworthiness and effectiveness of the release. Also circle facts in the story you would need to check.

A. As Grant Elementary School's Partner in Education (PIE), Boone County National Bank is not only giving books to every classroom to celebrate National Children's Book Week, it's also backing up that gift with over fifteen hours of volunteer time. Over 25 bankers will show Grant students they know a lot more than numbers November 15-19 by reading those books to students.

"Our goal is to demonstrate how important reading is to their future success," says Kim Hudson, Boone County National Bank's PIE Coordinator. "What better way to show our support than to give of ourselves."

The Bank on Books program began as a way for the bank to become involved in Grant's effort to reach its goal of one million reading minutes in one year. This year's goal has stretched to 2.5 million minutes of reading by the school year's end. Rather than just include volunteers in the reading program, the PIE Steering Committee decided it would be great to see professionals taking the time to support the importance of reading.

In addition, the Bank on Books program has become part of Boone County National Bank's commitment to America's Promise. The America's Promise program, initiated by American Bankers Association, serves as a nationwide catalyst, urging public, private and nonprofit organizations to focus their combined talents and resources to improve the lives of our nation's youth. The goal is to increase participation by 10 percent in programs directed toward children, a goal easily refaced by Boone County National Bank employees.

"As usual, Boone County National Bank people have come through. As busy as the work-day is, people were willing to make time for the kids. It's such an important message for them to hear," Hudson added.

For more information about Bank on Books, contact Kim Hudson at 573–816–8542.

B. Parents suffering with finding ways to pay for their childrens' college educations can finally get solutions to their college funding problems.

"Most families who earn $40,000 or more and own a home assume they are not eligible for financial aid. However, many families with incomes of over $100,000 are actually eligible for some types of "need-based" financial aid. They simply need to know how to get their fair share. Over 70% of college students are receiving some type of financial aid" says Jim Burt, a college funding specialist.

According to Burt, there are several easy things parents can do to substantially increase the amount of money they get from colleges. . . . For example there are several schools that historically give better financial aid packages than others. "If families do proper income and asset planning before filling out the forms, they can increase eligibility by thousands of dollars."

Burt offers a few simple tips to parents with college funding problems. "If a parents has only half an hour to end their college funding problems, I would suggest the following: 1) make sure they do not over-value their home on the financial aid forms 2) try not to save money in the child's name as it weighs more heavily than parents savings and 3) don't be afraid to negotiate with a college for a better financial aid package.

Jim Burt is very outspoken and can easily explain the complex rules of paying for college. To interview him, call (904) 679-3481.

C. On the surface of things, it might appear that the reason a medicine chest is thus called is that it's a good place to store medicines. Not so, according to the Food and Drug Administration. Potential danger lurks when there's medicine in the medicine chest. One reason that bathroom medicine chests are usually right over the sink, and accessible enough to tempt the curiosity of children who live in or visit your house.

To help you know not only how to child-proof your medicine chest but to keep it safe and up-to-date for adults too, the Food and Drug Administration a free reprint from its magazine the *FDA Consumer*. For your copy of *What's in Your Medicine Chest*, write to Consumer Information Center, Dept. 645K Pueblo, Colorado 81009.

Even if there aren't any children in your household, the medicine chest is not a good place for drugs, since the warm moist atmosphere of the bathroom can cause some drugs to deteriorate. Ideally, both prescription and non-prescription drugs should be kept in a cool, dry place.

What else should be kept in that cool, dry place will depend on the makeup of the family. If there are young children in the family, you're likely to need baby aspirin, anti-bacterial topical ointments, and medicine to treat the symptoms of diarrhea. Almost every family will want to keep aspirin or a non-aspirin pain reliever on hand.

No matter what the age of your family, avoid overstocking drugs. Some drug products lose potency on the shelf over time, especially after they are opened. Other drugs change in consistency. Ideally, supplies in the medicine chest should be bought to last over a period of no more than 6 to 12 months.

Be sure to review the contents of your medicine chest every 6 months and discard old supplies. Also be sure that any new prescriptions you get are clearly dated.

Tablets that have become crumbly, medicines that have changed color, odor, or consistency, or are outdated should be destroyed. Empty the bottle of medicine into the toilet, flush it down and rise out the bottle. Don't put leftover drugs in the trash basket where they can be dug out by inquisitive youngsters. Newly purchased drugs that don't look right should be returned to the pharmacy. Drug products that have lost their labels also should be destroyed.

And, as a final safety precaution, always keep the telephone number of the local poison control center, doctor, hospital, rescue squad, fire and police departments near every phone in the house. And tape the emergency phone list wherever you keep medicines and emergency supplies, as well as inside the bathroom medicine chest door.

When you order *What's in Your Medicine Chest* (free) you'll also receive a free copy of the *Consumer Information Catalog*. Published quarterly by the Consumer Information Center of the General Services Administration, the free *Catalog* lists 200 selected free and moderately priced federal consumer booklets.

5. For each of the news releases in exercise 4, suggest other approaches you might take to present this information more effectively and efficiently.
   a.

b.

c.

6. Interview a public relations professional. Ask how a media campaign either averted a disaster or helped cope with one. Write a brief report.

CHALLENGE EXERCISE
7. Look at the calendar of upcoming events at the university you are attending. Select an event and write a news release about it for your local newspaper. Then rewrite the release for a radio station.

22 Media Law

1. a. Which part of the U.S. Constitution protects the press and you as a journalist? What does it say?

b. Why should there be protection for the press?

c. What laws are intended to provide access to public records and meetings?

2. a. Define "libel."

b. What four areas of a person's life should you as a reporter write about with particular care?

c. What are three traditional defenses for the press in a libel action?

d. What kind of protection from libel suits do the courts allow members of the three branches of government?

3. What factors limit your privilege or right to report on the three branches of government?

4. What is the most important element in fair comment and criticism?

5. a. What is the test applied by the Supreme Court in *The New York Times* vs. Sullivan that assists the press in reporting on public officials?

   b. What are the differences between the Butts case and the Walker case?

   c. Define "public official."

   d. Define "public figure."

6. You go into a rooming house near campus to get information about conditions in student housing that is privately owned. Do you have the legal right to be there? Why or why not?

7. You take a picture of a woman with her skirt blown over her head as she comes out of a fun house at the county fair. Are you likely to lose a privacy suit if you print the picture?

8. On three occasions you observe the mayor of your community in a local nightclub when it appears he has been drinking too much. Two council members tell you they believe the mayor is an alcoholic, but they won't let you use their names. What additional information, if any, would you try to gather before deciding whether to print the story?

9. Read the following story and determine if any passages in it are potentially libelous. If you believe you have found a libelous passage, describe how you would go about checking the material for accuracy or avoid the libelous statement.

> A man was crushed to death today when a co-worker was unloading bricks for the construction of a church and a power lifter failed.
>
> When electricity to the hydraulic lifter was severed, the lifter failed and the load of bricks fell on Henry Donovan, 44, of 209 N. Delaware St. He died instantly, Coroner Richard Smith said.
>
> The accident occurred when Arthur Payne, 42, of 303 N. Richard St., pulled the electrical cord on the power lifter. Co-workers said he thought the device was not being used.
>
> John Randolph III, 22, of 208 Whispering Pines Road, was operating the lifter at the time. He tried to warn Donovan, but the victim could not move out of the way in time, the workers said.
>
> "Some people just aren't careful on construction sites," Randolph said. "This is a tragedy that could have been avoided."
>
> Donovan is survived by his wife, Helen, and five children, Henry Jr., 15; Helena, 14; Anna, 12; Richard, 11; and Regina, 9. Funeral arrangements are incomplete.

10. Read the following and determine if any passages in it are libelous. If you believe you have found a libelous passage, describe what you would need to do to print it or whether you need to omit it.

A sophomore at Springfield University claims a chemistry professor has sexually harassed her.

Cindy Watring, 146 Columbus Hall, says the professor, David Moore, has touched her during tutoring sessions in his office and has invited her to his apartment several times. She said she declined his invitations.

"I am having trouble in the class, and I have to go see him to get help with my papers and projects," she said. "But I am scared to go in his office now."

Moore denied having any improper contact with the student and threatened this newspaper with a libel suit if it published the story.

Watring said she is thinking of filing a formal complaint with the university. "I don't know how to do that," she said. "I just don't know what to do."

11. Determine if any of the passages in the following story are potentially libelous. If any are, explain what you would do to print the information or whether you would leave it out.

Provost Ronald Kemper has been asked to resign, sources have told the *Campus Voice*.

Kemper declined to talk to the *Voice* about the situation, but sources close to him say that he will announce his resignation in two days.

An administrative source told the *Voice* that Chancellor Bernadette Anderson has asked Kemper to resign because of widespread faculty dissatisfaction with the job he has been doing.

"He has lost the confidence of the faculty," the administrator said. "He can't get any administrative proposals through the faculty because they don't trust him."

Through a spokesperson, Chancellor Anderson denied that she has asked for Kemper's resignation.

A member of the Faculty Senate, Mary Barnridge, an assistant professor of English, said several faculty members think Kemper should leave. "He tried to cram a proposal to eliminate several programs down our throats. He didn't want our reaction; he just wanted approval," she said. "The faculty got turned off by the way he handled the situation."

Two other faculty members who declined to be identified agreed with Barnridge. "He's a lost cause," a professor of Spanish said. "We just don't believe anything he says."

Kemper became provost 11 years ago.

12. What legal problems, if any, occur to you upon reading the following story?

The Springfield University Board of Curators voted in closed session to fire Chancellor Bernadette Anderson.

The *Campus Voice* has learned that the board will announce its decision in a press conference tomorrow.

13. Are any passages in the following story potentially libelous? If so, cite them and support your evaluation.

The Planning and Zoning Commission haggled over the proposed energy ordinance Wednesday and decided it was unresearched, unenforceable and unfair.

In a 6-2 vote, the commission recommended that the City Council defeat the bill when the commission votes on it next month. Marjorie Cox and Chester Edwards cast the dissenting votes.

Larry Niedergerke, acting chairman, instructed Edwards and Cox to draw up a dissenting resolution for the council to balance the commission's recommendation.

The proposed ordinance would require weather-stripping, new insulation for water heaters and air ducts, and new minimal levels for roofs. The council sent the ordinance to six advisory panels earlier this year for recommendations. So far only the Community Development Commission has approved the ordinance.

P&Z Commissioner Keith Schrader said the proposed ordinance does not demonstrate cost effectiveness, and he questioned whether its requirements would be a sound investment for homeowners.

"I would really like to know how much money would be spent on insulation as opposed to how much saved," Schrader said.

Schrader said he is not completely opposed to an energy ordinance, but he needs to see hard figures before he supports the ordinance.

Edwards agreed that the ordinance should be researched more carefully but said that some sort of ordinance is necessary.

"I think we all need to be good stewards of our natural resources," he said. "There are some things in this ordinance that I don't like, but I just didn't want to vote it down."

Cox said higher standards are necessary to make homeowners and landlords save on energy costs.

Nonetheless, enforcement is what caused many commissioners to voice their opposition to the proposal.

"I'm very much in favor of letting people make their own decisions, and their own mistakes at times, rather than (resorting to) legislation," Rex Campbell said.

Clayton Johnson agreed. "We can't tell people to put on an extra sweater or long underwear, but we might as well if we are going to legislate one of these items," he said.

"It just seems to me that we are waiting for God and government to take care of us, and I don't think that should be."

"Bill Rodgers wrote this thing, and it's pretty clear to me that Bill Rodgers is a fool," said Commissioner Robert Cummings.

Rodgers is a city staff member who works in the Planning Department.

14. What passages in the following story are potentially libelous and why?

KENNETT SQUARE, Pa. (UPI)—The doctor heading the team investigating the death of Kentucky Derby winner Swale said Wednesday the cause of death may never be known. However, Dr. Helen Acland would not rule out the possibility of foul play.

Acland, chief of the Laboratory of Large Animal Pathology at the University of Pennsylvania's New Bolton Center, said tests on tissues taken from the three-year-old colt did not reveal the cause of death.

She said examination of the tissues, taken during an autopsy performed hours after Swale collapsed and died Sunday at Belmont Park near New York, supported preliminary findings that ruled out a heart attack as the cause of death.

"We found an enlargement of the heart that is usually found in athletes," Acland said during a news conference at the rural facility, 40 miles outside of Philadelphia. "We also found microscopic lesions of the liver and kidneys but not severe enough to contribute to the demise of the animal.

"It's possible we may never know the cause of death. There are some things that can cause death in horses that don't leave a trace."

Acland said her "gut feeling" was that the horse died of a "cardiac dysfunction, but we may never be able to confirm that. There are other things that can make the heart stop besides a heart attack."

Acland did not rule out foul play in the death of Swale. She said extensive toxicological tests would have to be done to determine if poisoning was involved, and those tests still could prove inconclusive.

"I'd be able to answer that better in a few weeks after we've gone through a range of chemical tests," she said. "Judging the history of the animal, he seemed to be well taken care of. The possibility (of foul play) is small, but I have trouble defining small. I'd like to defer that question until we've performed some testing."

15. Write a story based on the following information. Be sure to eliminate potentially libelous information.
   a. Mark Dillow, 43, of 209 Perch Lane, has been charged with violating the city's rental-housing license ordinance. The offense carries a possible sentence of a fine of up to $1,000 and six months in jail. The ordinance calls for inspection and subsequent licensing of rental housing to ensure that minimal standards are met.
   b. City inspectors, acting on a complaint from tenant John Bowers, 21, of 303A Court Drive, found that the apartment was not licensed and had not been previously inspected. An inspection revealed 17 fire and safety hazards in Bowers' apartment alone. The city has informed Dillow it will inspect three remaining apartments at 303 Court Drive next week.
   c. City Prosecutor Mel Cross said the case will be heard in Municipal Court Monday. Dillow would not comment, but he will be defended by Joan Anderson, a local attorney who handles all of Dillow's legal work.
   d. This is the first time the city has taken a landlord to court since the inspection law went into effect in January.
   e. City Housing Inspector Richard Laventhol said, "I've never seen so many violations in one spot. There were frayed electrical wires, leaky toilets, you name it. The place was disgusting. A guy who allows his property to get run down like that should be sent up the river. It's not fair to the tenants."
   f. The city prosecutor would give no further comment.

16. Browsing through the newspaper from another campus, you see an article that you would like to publish. You don't see any copyright notice on the newspaper. Do you need permission? Do you need permission if you credit the source? Why or why not?

17. You are the editor of a newspaper in a town of 65,000 people. One of your reporters has just given you a story about the public administrator, the elected official who is appointed by courts to administer the affairs of people who die without wills or people judged mentally incompetent to manage their own affairs. The administrator manages thousands of dollars' worth of assets from the estates of the deceased and similar amounts in holdings of the mentally incompetent. Your reporter has learned that once the administrator was elected, she transferred all of these accounts to one of the five local banks. Further, the bank in question lists the public administrator as a minor stockholder (less than 1 percent). The state's conflict-of-interest law is weak and does not clearly extend to public administrators. Discuss the legal implications of publishing the story. Then discuss the issues of fairness. Even if there is no problem with libel if you publish the story, is it fair to the administrator to do so? Consider that earnings on the accounts in question would not be nearly enough to cause an increase in the earnings of a minority stockholder of the bank.

CHALLENGE EXERCISE

18. Write a short essay explaining how the concepts of libel and fair use have been affected, if at all, by the popularity of the Internet, the development of blogs and even the use of cell phones to capture and transmit scenes in real time.

23 Ethics

1. There are three broad philosophical approaches that can provide answers to ethical questions: deontological, teleological and situation ethics. Use them to work through the following:

   a. A terrorist snatches a youth in a ticket line at the local airport and demands to be given passage to a foreign country. Police officers are negotiating with him at a distance in the airport. From your position, you could get videotape for the evening news. Describe how the deontologist, the teleologist and the situationist would react to the situation and what reasons each would use to justify the decision.

   b. As a police reporter, you learn that a merchant has been robbed of $6,000 in receipts. She was walking to the bank when the robbery occurred. The police ask you to withhold the information because many of the downtown merchants, who also walk to the banks with their deposits, are afraid that they, too, will be robbed. Would you withhold the information or any part of it? Identify the philosophical category that best describes your response.

2. Use the Potter Box to reach a decision about the following ethical dilemmas. In step three of the box, show how at least four ethical principles apply. Do not use the same principles for each of the cases.

a. SITUATION

Four sources, all of whom demand anonymity, tell you that a candidate for governor in your state has accepted secret campaign contributions from special interests in exchange for favors once the candidate becomes chief executive. The candidate denies the charge vehemently and objects to answering anonymous sources. There are no records to substantiate the charge. Should you run the story? Should you include the names of the informants?

VALUES

PRINCIPLES

1.

2.

3.

4.

LOYALTIES

JUDGMENT

b. SITUATION

You are interviewing a high government official about her possible involvement in a bribery scheme, when she is called out of the office. While alone, you notice documents on her desk that may shed some light on your investigation. Would you read the documents? Steal them? Ask her about them when she returns?

VALUES

PRINCIPLES

1.

2.

3.

4.

LOYALTIES

JUDGMENT

c. SITUATION

You are a reporter for a television station. A man calls to tell you that he is going to set himself on fire in protest over the administration's failure to do anything for the unemployed. Would you tell him you would not come? Try to talk him out of it? Ask him not to call anyone else?

VALUES

PRINCIPLES

1.

2.

3.

4.

LOYALTIES

d. SITUATION

You are a television camera operator. You get to the river at about the same time as a police car. The two officers are trying to save a child from drowning. You can swim, and they could use your help. Would you shoot the scene? Set down the camera and help?

VALUES

PRINCIPLES

1.

2.

3.

4.

LOYALTIES

JUDGMENT

e. SITUATION

An elderly woman calls the city desk and asks the newspaper not to publish her name or address in the story about the burglary at her home. She is afraid because she lives alone. Would you carry out your paper's policy of carrying her full name, age and address? Use only her name but no address? Comply with her request?

VALUES

PRINCIPLES

1.

2.

3.

4.

LOYALTIES

JUDGMENT

f. SITUATION
A group of professional burglars has moved into your city. They are known to be reading your paper, particularly the obits, society columns and wedding announcements, to choose their victims from among those who will not be at home. The local police ask you to eliminate those articles for several weeks. Would you ignore the police? Eliminate street addresses?

VALUES

PRINCIPLES

1.

2.

3.

4.

LOYALTIES

JUDGMENT

g. SITUATION

You are a copy editor for the local newspaper in a city of 50,000. Your neighbor, who is a candidate for city council, asks you to write news releases for him. Would you do it?

VALUES

PRINCIPLES

1.

2.

3.

4.

LOYALTIES

JUDGMENT

3. You are writing a feature story and find some excellent quotes about your subject from another written source. May you use those quotes as if you obtained them yourself, or must you credit the other written source? What if you obtained the quotes from a Web site?

4. Do you think the news organization for which you will work should have a code of ethics? Why or why not?

How should a news organization enforce a code of ethics?

CHALLENGE EXERCISE

5. Do an online search for codes of ethics for journalists. After studying them, compose the major points of your own code of ethics.

Appendix 1
Twenty Common Errors of Grammar and Punctuation

Punctuation Exercises (I)

1. The account executive, who was wearing a blue suit, was a Harvard graduate.

2. His wife Denise was in her 40s but she acted like a 10 year old.

3. Her secretary Helen and her executive assistant, Bob, accompanied her.

4. The third office which has green drapes is Tom's.

5. The short stocky muscular young man was no member of the middle class.

6. The broken old man drank all alone in the smelly pink bar.

7. If employees care enough they will give an all out effort.

8. Nodding to him to come she smiled congenially.

9. The tall newly-constructed building is unsafe.

10. Because she knew the company well she trusted its products.

11. The age old truism took a strange new twist.

12. The friendly looking dog did not bother anyone.

13. The weak unsteady desk was poorly-constructed.

14. The computer which had just been repaired was destroyed in a fire.

15. The limousine had turned left and he could no longer see it.

16. He was old fashioned but he was not closed minded.

17. The tall brick house stood in a neatly-kept lot.

18. He never liked being interviewed, and often refused to see reporters.

19. Playing the game well, was important to her.

20. At the time of the murder she was out of town.

Punctuation Exercises (II)

1. Although he worked hard he pleased few people.

2. The children in the room, and their parents who stood by them, were completely silent.

3. The association was growing, the staff was not.

4. She tried using the copier, but was unsuccessful.

5. Working through the night she finished the job.

6. After she completed the exam she left town.

7. Instead of going to the library she took a nap.

8. Bill studied hard, nevertheless, he failed the test.

9. Generally students who miss class regularly are unhappy with the professor.

10. The time was up so the points did not count.

11. The facilities, equipment, and personnel were excellent.

12. Unless you feel qualified you should not apply.

13. You did not come, because you felt you were not wanted.

14. The rains came and they did not stop for three days.

15. The woman who is wearing the mink coat is his wife.

16. Playing with a broken thumb Tom failed to score.

17. The heavy equipment dealer also had a small farm income.

18. The weary old man walked slowly along the long dusty road.

19. Tom, Bill and I are not going.

20. Walking in the rain without an umbrella, can be therapeutic.

Punctuation Exercises (III)

1. The tall square building will be torn down.

2. The woman, who was eating the cherry pie, is a surgeon.

3. The thin balding middle-aged man is the president.

4. Because she was economy-minded she bought the small one.

5. His father was old fashioned but he loved MTV.

6. He left his middle class neighborhood but he lost none of his middle class values.

7. The properly-trained secretary knew about non-restrictive clauses.

8. The company which had the better benefit package was her obvious choice.

9. The expensive blue tie appealed to the dapper young executive.

10. The canary yellow hat did not go with the heavy blue coat.

11. Before she worked here she worked there.

12. He tried hard yet he seldom succeeded.

13. She knew he would go, it was just a matter of time.

14. If I come I will not wear a tie.

15. What I need, is a long vacation.

16. Work proceeded nicely; and no one seemed to notice.

17. I was in charge and I accept full responsibility.

18. She succeeded, because she was immensely capable.

19. William did little work but he always seemed busy.

20. No one on the magazine staff agreed, therefore, the plan failed.

Pronoun Exercises

1. He took Tim and I to the movie.

2. Between you and I, pronouns can be difficult to use correctly.

3. He was the young man that caught the foul ball.

4. He did not know who to ask.

5. A writer must always check their sources.

6. The professor spoke to Jill and I just last week.

7. Whom do you think cheated on the exam?

8. More people that work at home are happier than those who don't.

9. Instead of he and I, he chose she and Sheri.

10. The corporation guaranteed all their products.

11. Everybody wishes they could write well.

12. It is me who should take the blame.

13. It was not whom you think it was.

14. Each student brought their own lunch.

15. The group is having their meeting this morning.

16. An architect should never publicize his fees.

17. She walked right behind Bill and I.

18. Who are you talking about?

19. A criminal must pay for his crime.

20. Is that her coming down the hall?

Exercises with Verbs and Verbals

1. If I was you, I wouldn't go.

2. The motion on the floor if passed will stop debate.

3. If more information is desired by you, please call.

4. He suddenly left the room, saying he was tired of questions.

5. Playing baseball in the park, his left leg was injured.

6. He only did that one time to thoroughly confuse the judges.

7. I will go there next week if the weather permits.

8. Maurice and all his friends likes hot dogs.

9. If that was the case, he would still be in office.

10. Working through the night, his back began to ache.

11. He only will have worked at the magazine for six months in February.

12. To be successful, good work habits are necessary.

13. If I was there, I surely would remember.

14. Bill, along with all of his buddies, love to dance.

15. The proposed constitutional amendment will ban gay marriage.

16. You will not ever do that again if I have anything to say about it.

17. Mary and those who think like her is often wrong.

18. He hurried down the hall, saying he was late.

19. If he was really drunk, he would not be speaking so clearly.

20. He only did these exercises because he was asked to do them.

NOTE: For new exercises on AP style, go to the Exercise Central for AP Style Web site at www.bedfordstmartins.com/APExercisecentral.

Appendix 2
Wire Service Style Summary

1. Correct the following sentences for capitalization, where necessary.

   a. Marcia Clark was the Prosecuting Attorney in the O.J. Simpson case, and Johnnie Cochrane was the primary defense attorney.

   b. His Jeep was the last one the Army had.

   c. The California and Oregon Legislatures blamed each other for the stream's condition.

   d. In the Vietnam war, the United States feared intervention by the Chinese.

   e. The all-stars included Outfielder Brian Jordan of the St. Louis Cardinals.

   f. The justice department said it would not appeal the decision.

   g. The Rocky mountains are the dominant geological feature of the West.

   h. The latin population is the fastest-growing in the region.

   i. She prefers roquefort cheese on her crackers.

   j. The fm band is now the most popular on radio.

2. Correct the following sentences for capitalization, where necessary.

   a. She bought a jeep so she would have no trouble in the desert.

   b. Ramon sought a realtor for help in locating a house.

   c. The store was at Kon Tiki and Ridgelea streets.

   d. The tv was tuned in to the Royals-Yankees game.

   e. Martinez said, "it will be a while before you see that again."

   f. "Give me a kleenex," said the teenager.

g. James Watt, former Secretary of the Interior under Ronald Reagan, was a controversial figure.

h. "I'd walk a mile for a camel," the cigarette commercial actor said.

i. Christians believe that Jesus Christ is the son of god.

j. For Muslims, Allah is the name of the deity.

3. Correct the following sentences for capitalization, where necessary.

a. She placed the bowl of jello in the frigidaire.

b. The army jeep collided with a car at Fifth and Elm streets.

c. "Let's have a coke," the realtor said.

d. The Tennessee and Mississippi Legislatures voted for repeal.

e. The Arkansas Legislature will convene today.

f. "It was a tough decision," the President said.

g. Lloyd Bentsen was the Secretary of the Treasury during part of Bill Clinton's Administration.

h. "They were the best passing team we've seen all year," said cornerback Eric Wright.

i. He was described as a Greek God.

j. God is merciful because he forgives.

4. Following the guidelines for abbreviation, correct these sentences, where necessary.

a. Memphis, Tenn., and Kansas City, Kan., are a day's drive apart.

b. He lives at 1042 South Demaret Drive in Milwaukee, Wisc.

c. Ortega moved to 322 Orange St. SE in Pittsburgh, Penn.

d. Ms. Santana is a rich woman, according to Business Week.

e. Southern Cal is in Los Angeles, Cal.

f. The C.I.A. is supposed to avoid domestic activities, which the FBI handles.

g. He was going 65 m.p.h. in a 30 m.p.h. zone.

h. Antigua, WI, is a cold place in the winter, she said.

    i. Let's watch TV when we get to Cheyenne, WY, tonight.

    j. The U.S. ambassador to the United Nations told him to forget it.

5. Following the guidelines for abbreviation, correct these sentences, where necessary.

    a. All who attended were from Honolulu, Hawaii, and Dallas, Tex.

    b. Jackson, Ms., was the scene of the confrontation.

    c. He is a native of Lawrence, Kans.

    d. The deadline is March 19, but may be extended to Apr. 1.

    e. John lives at 302 South Trenton Blvd.

    f. He was driving at 90 m.p.h.

    g. It was the worst winter storm since January 12, 1957.

    h. Mr. and Mrs. Aurelio Rodriguez were the guests of Ms. Maude Clinton.

    i. He was to appear on K.S.D.-T.V.

    j. The fire destroyed the home at 396 Bluff Drive S.W.

6. Correct all improper punctuation in the following sentences.

    a. "Tell him I said 'Forget it,' when you see him," Jones said.

    b. The Grapes of Wrath is one of the most popular books of all time.

    c. "TV Guide" is the best-selling magazine in the United States.

    d. "Tell him there are no more grapes", Dreiling said.

    e. It is the best thing to do, and I think it will work.

    f. She said it couldn't be done but we did it.

    g. Survivors include his wife, Helen; three sons, John, Devin and Richard, and two grandsons.

    h. He spent three more years in prison after serving a 10 year term for burglary.

    i. The best movies were made in the 1960's, he said.

7. Correct all improper punctuation in the following sentences.

    a. James Michener wrote the novel "Hawaii".

    b. All the boys attended (except John.).

    c. Dr. Ralph Simpson, Jr. started practice in May 1978.

    d. President Kennedy was killed Nov. 22, 1963 in Dallas.

    e. She has lived in Omaha, Neb., and Kansas City, Mo.

    f. The 8 and 9 year old girls will practice baseball today.

    g. He threw a 90 yard touchdown pass for a last second victory.

    h. The heavily-damaged car was towed away.

    i. "Where is the grocery store?," he asked.

    j. It was the worst three-year period since the 1920's.

8. Correct the use of numerals in the following sentences.

    a. He is the Number One quarterback in Tennessee this year.

    b. Oregonians cast 34,546 votes for Rodgers and only 3156 for Contrell.

    c. There were six people in the party of fourteen who had been there before.

    d. There is a chain of convenience stores known as 7-Eleven, and the name is spelled that way.

    e. The temperature was 89 degrees in the shade.

    f. I'd walk a thousand miles for a drink of water right now.

    g. The survey results changed only .04 percent from one month to the next.

    h. The prime minister lives at No. 10 Downing Street.

    i. There are only three sergeants left in the platoon.

    j. 1492 was the year Columbus arrived with 3 ships.

9. Correct the use of numerals in the following sentences.

    a. The Yankees won the game 10 to three.

    b. He is the No. 1 astronaut in the space shuttle program.

    c. The temperature dropped 6 degrees in four hours for an overnight low of 27.

    d. There were four Missourians, three Kansans and 14 Oklahomans at the meeting.

    e. John Dillon, 26, of 206 Willow Way, won three percent of the vote.

    f. He had five dollars in his pocket and $6 in his hand.

    g. U.S. Highway One parallels the East Coast.

h. He said he would be there at six p.m. but he did not arrive until 8.

i. The unemployment rate dropped .04 percent to 6.2 percent.

j. He lives on 10th Street near the 5th Avenue intersection.

10. Correct the errors in spelling, punctuation, capitalization and other areas of style in the following sentences.

a. The New York and New Jersey Legislators could not agree on a solution.

b. Eau Claire, Wis. and Rapid City, S.Dak. both are college towns.

c. The San Diego Padres and the Los Angeles Dodgers are tied for the lead in the West and the St. Louis Cardinals lead the Central.

d. Pete Sampras and Martina Hingis dominated the world of tennis this year.

e. Brigadier General Paul Ramos and Financier Hougala Mugaba met secretly in the Caribbean.

f. San Francisco was well-equipped to treat victims of Aids because of its large gay community and the expertise of doctors there.

g. Wilmington, Delaware, is the home of many corporations because of Delaware's lenient incorporation laws.

h. The Miami Herald is one of the nation's best at covering the situation in Latin America; the Herald's large Hispanic readership is interested in news of that area.

i. A tornado tore through Jonesboro, Ark., today and caused damage estimated in the millions of dollars.

j. South Africa's policy of apartheid was repugnant to most Americans.

k. The Abilene (Tex.) Reporter-News was aggressive in covering the activities of financier T. Boone Pickens.

l. The New Mexico Lobos scored a last-minute touchdown Saturday to upset the Arizona Wildcats 24 to 21.

m. "The Grapes of Wrath" was one of John Steinbeck's great novels.

n. Athens, Ga., is the home of the Number One Georgia Bulldogs.

o. "Hockey Night in Canada" is one of the top rated shows in that country.

p. The Denver Broncos captured the imagination of the Mountain States with their last-minute heroics.

q. America's Cup is the most coveted trophy in yachting.

r. The Beatles were a hit in their hometown of Liverpool, England, before vaulting to stardom in the U.S. and elsewhere around the World.

s. Juventus, a team in the Italian soccer league, won that country's championship.

t. The North Carolina Tarheels are consistently one of the best teams in college basketball.

u. Halley's Comet captured the country's imagination with its appearance in 1986.

v. Kansas State University in Manhattan, Kan., has been a Big Eight power in basketball for many years.

w. Killer whales are misnamed; they really are mild-mannered creatures.

x. Al Roker of NBC's Today show probably is the nation's best known weatherman.

y. When its time to sell the house, I'm going to call a realtor.

11. Correct the spelling and style errors in the following sentences where necessary, using the appropriate copy editing symbols.

a. The best place to eat in Rattatan, Wisc. was a place called The Brat, he said, but it went out of business last year.

b. Fort Hays, Kansas was a calvary outpost in the 1800's.

c. Brewing companies spend millions of dollars on TV advertising each year, according to advertising industry experts.

d. Sergeants earn more than corporals in the US army, and they earn more than lieutenatns in the Russian army.

e. Ricardo gutierrez rode the quarterhourse to victory in the local county fair race.

f. 1984 was an election year, she told the delegates, so no texes were raised.

g. He became a first class scout in the first year he was eligible.

h. More than 4,900,000 people live in that state, according to the latest figures from the United States Bureau of the census.

i. The first full year of the war—1942—was a devastating one for American morale.

j. John Wayne was an American institution for years, but he won an oscar only in the last year of his life.

k. "When you go out, be sure to take the garbage", he said.

l. Its ridiculous that no boy from that school has ever been a starting quarterback at a major collefge, considering the success of the program.

m. The outfieldder hit .268 in his last full seson in the magors before the leg injury halted his careeer.

12. Correct the style errors in the following stories using the appropriate copy editing symbols.

> **A.** WASHINGTON (AP)—The Treasury Department is considering restricting each American to three Federally-insured bank, savings institution or credit union accounts—no matter how little money is in each.
>
> The department asked the Federal Deposit Insurance Corp. to estimate how much the proposal would save and to describe potential problems in administering it, FDIC Acting Chairman Andrew C. Hove Jr. said Wednesday.
>
> The Independent Bankers Assn. of America is vigorously opposed.
>
> **B.** WASHINGTON (AP)—The Government said home building plunged six percent in October, extending the longest construction slide on record and sinking housing starts to their lowest level since the 1981–82 recession.
>
> Industry observers pointed to shrinking consumer confidence and the growing inability of builders to obtain credit as causes of the 9-month decline reported yesterday by the Commerce Department. Many believe the slide will continue into next year.

13. Correct the style errors in the following story using the appropriate copy editing symbols.

At least one person is dead and six injured after a two-car wreck Wednesday evening on U.S. Highway 40 west of Midway that brought out state troopers, four paramedic units and 35 Lincoln County firefighters.

Three injured were transported to Springfield Hospital, where one was listed in critical condition late Wednesday, and 2 were listed in serious condition.

Three others were taken to Lincoln Hospital Center. Hospital officials refused to discuss their conditions.

One of the injured also suffered a heart attack, said Rob Brown, a Lincoln County Fire Protection District spokesperson. That person was in cardiac arrest at the scene, with no pulse or vital signs, Brown said.

Brown described the seven victims' injuries as ranging from mild back and neck problems to internal injuries. "I'm sure there were broken bones," he said.

A red Chevrolet Nova ran a stop sign at the corner of Ballard Road and Highway 40 and hit a red Ford Escort, which was moving west on Highway 40, said state trooper Charles Schaffer. Police said the intersection has a history of bad accidents.

Both cars landed in a wide ditch on the north side of the highway.

The Escort landed on its roof. Some of the passengers in both cars were thrown from the vehicles.

Police would not identify the drivers or the injured, pending notification of relatives. Witnesses said those involved in the wreck were as young as 10 years of age.

Danny Allenbaugh and Marco Arrendondo, two Fayette High School students, were among the first to arrive at the scene following the accident.

They parked their vehicle so its headlights would face both wrecked cars. The lights shone on one of the victims, a girl, who was lying in front of their car.

While they waited for ambulances to arrive, the students helped two women who were trapped in the upended Escort get out of the car.

The women, both students at Central Methodist College, did not seem to be seriously injured, Allenbaugh said.

14. Correct the style errors in the following story using the appropriate copy editing symbols.

Gusty winds fanned the flames of a fire Thursday afternoon that caused $30,000 dollars' damage to a boardinghouse on Paris Road.

Firefighters rescued one resident from the second floor by ladder and another from the basement, said Lieutenant James Daugherty of the Springfield Fire Dept.

No one in the house at 1308 Paris Road was injured, Daugherty said, but a fireman broke a toe while working on the ladder.

At one point, all the city's major fire-fighting vehicles were present for the three-alarm fire, said a firefighter on the scene.

The first alarm came in at 3:32 p.m. The blaze was brought under control in fifty minutes.

Daugherty said damage to the house was mostly on the second and third floors. Careless smoking on a couch was listed as the probable cause of the fire by fire department officials.

"We've got our work cut out for us now," said R. J. Newell, owner of the house, as he stood out front surveying the damaged green and yellow building. "A lot of money there, that's what this looks like to me."

He had just finished repairing an ice machine when one of his tenants found him at work and told him the house was burning, he said. "They told me that was more important than what I was doing."

Newell, who runs a general maintenance company in Springfield, said the tenants would help him repair the damage. "They don't have anyplace else to go," he said. "That's why they're here.

"Everybody will probably pitch in," Newell said. "Cooking, cleaning, building, something."

The three-story building contains 11 apartments, Newell said. 16 people were living there at the time of the fire, he said.

Several residents of the house stood across the street and watched the fire-fighters working. Most were worried about their possessions.

"I've got a guitar down there," said John Kendrick, who has lived in the basement for eight months.

15. Correct the style errors in the following story using the appropriate copy editing symbols.

A 39-year-old Springfield man was robbed early Thursday at gunpoint while making a deposit at Century State Bank, 2114 Paris Rd., according to police reports.

The victim, an employee of Pizza Hut, was making a night deposit at about 1:30 A.M. when a pickup truck with two men drove into the bank parking lot.

The passenger in the pickup was wearing a mask made of a see-thru fabric similar to panty hose, said Capt. Dennis Veach of the Springfield Police Dept. The passenger got out of the truck, pulled out a hand-gun and then demanded the victim's money.

The victim handed over the cash and the suspects drove away on Whitegate Dr.

The robbers are both white males. The driver was heavy-set and had short, dark blonde hair. The passenger was wearing blue jeans and an unknown color jacket.

Veach said Thursday's robbery doesn't appear to be linked to two other robberies of pizza store employees in the past week. A Domino's Pizza delivery person was robbed Tuesday night at gunpoint at Ashwood Apts., 1201 Ashland Road. The victim, a 19-year-old woman, was walking back to her car at 9:30 p.m. after delivering a pizza when she was robbed.

On Dec. 27, a Domino's Pizza employee was robbed by a man with a single-barreled shotgun. That robber entered the Domino's at 3102 Green Meadows Way just before midnight.

CrimeStoppers is seeking information leading to the arrest of the suspects in the robberies. They are offering a reward and guarantee anonymity. CrimeStoppers is at 555-8477.

16. Correct the various types of errors in the following story using the appropriate copy editing symbols.

The spell of hot, dry weather that has hedl the area in it's grasp for the last few few weeks is taking its tole on grasslands and fire fighters.

Saturday, in the wake of 15- and 25-mph winds and a high temperature of 99 degrees, fire protection agencies from across the area responded to sixteen calls.

At the largest of those, a 25-acre grass fire on Peabody Road north of Prathersville and west of Route 19, paramedics treated on sight at least five of 35 fire fighters for heat exhaustion, county fire chief Debra Schuster said.

Three more of the heavily-clad firefighters were hospitalized for heat exhaustion, and two of those were flown to Springfield Hospital by helicopter. All were treated for about 1 hour and released.

Dennis Sapp, fire captain of Station No. 1, said the blaze at Peabody Roady, which burned out of control for an hour before it was contained, probably was started by a trassh fire. The blaze endangered some nearby farmland and the barn on it, but was extinguished before anything but grass was burned.

Schuster said fires like the one on Peabody Road had been starting all day, especially in the northern part of the city and coutny. Schuster said some of the fires could have been the work of a arsonist, but careless burning was a more likely cause.

"We don't have any evidence there is an arsonist," Schuster said. "We surehope we don't have someone running around starting fires on purpose, but there is that possibility."

Copy Editing and Proofreading Symbols

1. Edit the following story using the correct copy editing symbols:

Cole County officials will exhume the body of an eldelry man to determine

whether there is any connection between his death and a Springfield man arrested

here on charges of first-degree robbery and of kidnapping an 85-year-old Lincoln

County woman.

Authorities said Sprngfield resident Eric Barnhouse, 28, an insurance sales-

man, may be connected to the death death of the Cole County man, the disappear-

ance of a Troy woman, the assault of a Warrenton woman and the death of a Fulton

woman. He also was charged with stealing money from an elderly Boonville woman.

Barnhouse contacted the Cole County man just before the man's death, said

Richard Lee, an investigator with the Cole County prosecuting attorney's office.

Cole County officials are looking for anything that may lead to a suspicious cause of

death, Lee said.

"There was no autopsy performed at the time of death, so we're not sure what

the cause of death was," Lee said.

No charges have been filed in the Cole County case.

Earlier this week Springfield police played host to a meeting of area law en-

forcement officials interested in sharing information about Barnhouse.

Since then, more charges have been filed, and Barnhouse is suspected of being

involved in several other cases.

Barnhouse was already being held in the Lincoln County Jail when Springfield police served him a Warren County warrant Jan. 9 for 1st-degree burglary. Officers also charged him with resisting arrest and with probation violation from a previous Lincoln county burglary conviction.

Police served Barnhouse with another warrant Wednesday charging him with kidnapping and burglary of a Lincoln County woman. Barnhouse was invited into the local woman's home on December 31 after he identified himself as an insurance agent, police said.

According to police, Barnhouse returned to the woman's home later that day and asked her for a check for 3 insurance premiums. The woman refused, and he held her at gunpoint and demanded she go to the bank and cash a check.

After driving around Springfield for several hours with the victim, the woman gave Barnhouse $60, and he returned her to her home unharmed.

When Springfield police arrested Barnhouse on Jan. 9, they discovered the purse of a woman who disappeared the same day from her home in Troy, which is 50 miles northwest of St. Louis.

Springfield police also believe Barnhouse posed as an insurance agent Jan. 7 to an 84-year-old woman in Warrenton.

According to the victim's statement, she was beaten unconscious. He had placed a rag with some type of liquid over her mouth before she passed out, she said.

Fulton police are waiting for a toxicologist's report on the death of an elderly woman they believe Barnhouse called on before she died. Barnhouse attempted to cash a check from the woman's account, said Mick Herbert, Fulton police chief. Results of her autopsy were inconclusive.

2. Edit the following story using the correct copy editing symbols.

Springfield police have arrested a local woman three times in the last 9 months, most recently on Thursday in connection with the December attempted robbery of a taxi driver.

Willa Walter, 34, of 3601 W. Ash Street was arrested by Springfield police at

2:52 a.m. Thursday. Police "had not even considered her as a suspect" before receiving a Crimestoppers tip Wednesday, Capt. Dennis Veach said. Walter remained in the Lincoln County Jail on Thursday afternoon in lieu of $25,000 bail.

Police arrested Walter for the Dec. 14 attempted robbery of a Bob's Checker Cab. The taxi driver had delivered a woman to the intersection of Garth Ave. and Sexton Rd., Veach said, when she pulled out a revolver and demanded money. After a brief struggle, the woman fled without the cash. At the time of the incident, Walter was free on bond from another armed robbery arrest, this one involving the April 9 holdup of a Texaco gas station at 2102 W. Ash St. Springfield police arrested her a few hours after the robbery, thanks to a witness at the gas station who wrote down her car's license plate number. She pleaded guilty Nov. 30.

But Walter and the police met again fairly soon. Less than a month later, Walter was arrested again, this time on misdemeanor theft, assault and marijuana possession charges. She awaits sentencing for those charges Feb. 25.

3. Correct the following story using proper proofreading symbols.

A Crime Stopper call helped police find a suspect in the Tuesday shooting of a 28-year-old Springfield man.

Police arrested Aaron Brewster, 24, of St. Balentine on Firday at about 10 a.m.

Police received a call about a shooting on Allen Walkway about 9:55 P.m. Tuesday. They arrived and found a man on the ground with a single gunshot wound just above the heart, said Cpt. Chris Egbert of the Springfield Police Department.

Following surgery, the victim was in stable condition at Linocon County Hospital on Friday. Police did not know his condition Saturrday.

Brewster had been staying in Springfield for a few months but calls St. Balentine his home, said Sgt. Bill Haws.

The shooting, which occurred near the victims house, was the result of an argument about a female friend of the two men. Several people were present, including the woman over whom they were arguing, Haws said.

Police arrested Brewster without incident at 908 North Garth Ave.

Brewster remained in the Lincoln County Jail on Saturday on charges of probation and parole violation, armed criminal action and first-degree assault. Bond has not been set.

4. Correct the following story using proper proofreading symbols.

Springfield police arrested a local woman on suspicion of forging and cashing bogus payrroll checks at area supermarkets.

Shirley M. Hannah of 1301 Ridge Road was released from Lincoln County Jail after posting $45,000 bond, a sheriff's department spokesman said.

Hayes, 21 was arrested Saturday after an employee of Food Barn, 705 Business Loop 70 West, recognized her because she'd previously bounced a check at the store, Sgt. Dean France said.

France said investigators believe Hannah was working with at least one other person for about a week. Capt. Mick Covington said they opened a fake business account at a Springfield bank to obtain bogus payroll checks.

"It appears someone opened a fraudulent account in the same name as a legitimate company, France said. He said Hannah is suspected of cashing at least twelve checks.

Springfield City Map

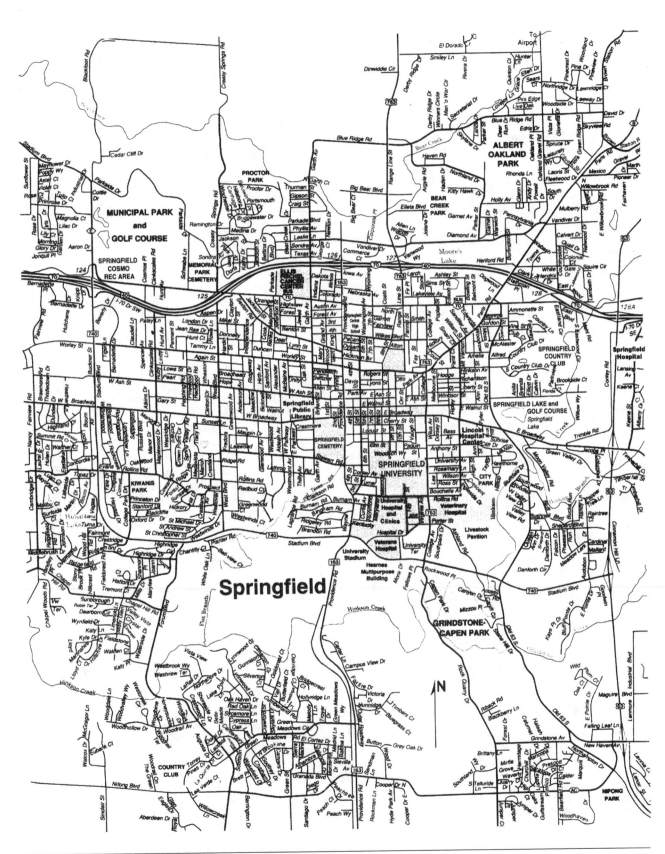

Springfield Directory of Institutions

Springfield City Government

Mayor: Juanita Williams
Police Chief: Paul Blakemore
City Clerk: Mary Cutts
Director Water and Light: Megan Dinwiddie
First Ward: Hong Xiang
Second Ward: Juan Guttierez
Third Ward: Elizabeth R. Levine
Fourth Ward: Sherwin Imlay
Fifth Ward: Jun Ping Yang
Sixth Ward: Afua Noyes

Director of Community Services: Diane Acton
City Prosecutor: Louanne Barnes
City Treasurer: Loren Jungermann
City Auditor: Joseph Knight
Director of Public Works Dept.: Margaret Longfellow
City Manager: Diane Lusby
Director of City Finance Dept.: Thomas Nowell
Fire Chief: Bernard Perry
Director of Health Department: Ken Yasuda

Springfield Public School System

Superintendent: Max Schmidt
School Board President: Jerry Crawford

School Board Members: Janet Biss, James K. Lattimer, Rachel
    Pullman, Brian Schmidt, Anna Theiss

Springfield University

Chancellor: Bernadette Anderson
Director, University Library: Earl Burchfield
Vice Chancellor for Student Affairs: Brenda Daye
Dean, School of Medicine: Donald Faust
Dean, College of Business and Public Administration:
    Sherri Fitts
Dean, School of Law: Wu-Feng Fun
Dean, Graduate School: Harvey Gorjanc
Dean, College of Agriculture, Food and Natural Resources:
    George Huisman Jr.
Dean, Arts and Science: Luce Iragaray
Dean, College of Education: Kelle Juzkiw
Provost: Ronald Kemper
Assistant to the Chancellor for University Affairs:
    Jen-Lu Liao

Registrar and Admissions Director: Paul R. Meadows
Vice Chancellor for Development: Amanda Netdem
President: Michael R. Quinn
Dean, College of Engineering: Haroon Qureshi
Dean, School of Accountancy: LeRoy N. Rice
Dean, School of Journalism: John Seina
Vice Chancellor for Administrative Services:
    Jacob Singleton
Dean, School of Library and Informational Science:
    Dolores Von Flatern
Academic Affairs Vice President: Washington Wade
Dean, School of Human Environmental Sciences:
    Wen Wui Xu
Dean, College of Business and Public Administration:
    Min Hui Zhang

Lincoln County Government

Sheriff: Sue Fuller
Circuit Court Division I: Judge Robert Wagner
Circuit Court Division II: Judge Todd B. Schwartz
Circuit Court Division III: Judge Linda Garrett
Recorder of Deeds: Pauline Heinbaugh
County Assessor: Maria L. Kincaid

County Commission Members: Andrew Kramer, Joseph Reed,
    Nicole Ziden
County Clerk: Emily Parks
County Collector: Betty L. Ramsey
County Fire Protection District Chief: Debra A. Schuster
County Prosecuting Attorney: James Taylor

Springfield Hospital

Administrator: Rochelle Crowell
Chief of Staff: Kelly G. Maddox

Director of Public Information: Jose Tray

Springfield City Directory

A

Abbot, James (clerk, J.C. Penney Department Store), 2011 Garnett Drive

Abbott, Quentin (manager, Airport Administration), 1612 Limerick Lane, Apt. 4G

Abraham, Jesse (pilot, Springfield Regional Airport), 106 Highland Drive

Action, Larry D. (Spanish teacher), 15 E. Leslie Lane

Acton, Diane (director, Community Services), 407 Pecan St.

Adamms, Williams (secretary, Shelter Insurance), 1410 Forum Blvd.

Adams, Bill (director, Springfield Truck Inspections), 101 Sondra Ave.

Adams, Craig and Susan, 304 Texas Ave.

Adams, Jackson and Mary (accountant), 356 Pear Tree Circle; sons, Mike and James

Alger, Donn, 1607 Stonybrook Place

American Red Cross, 1805 W. Worley St.

Andersen, John (retired) and Ruth, 88 Jefferson Drive

Anderson, Bernadette (chancellor, Springfield University), 1532 Amelia St.

Applegate, Therese, 800 Sycamore Lane

B

Baker, David (safety specialist, Springfield University Extension Service), 206 Oaklawn Drive

Ballard, Bruce D., Route 2, Box 18227

Bangle, Mike (heating technician), 1402 Rollins Road

Barnes, Harvey (architect), 1814 Oakcliff Drive

Barnes, Louanne (Springfield city prosecutor), 2000 Deerborne Circle.

Barnridge, Mary (professor, Springfield University), 1456 Rosemary St.

Bartles, May (head librarian of Springfield), 3805 Barrington Drive

Baumer, Brad (owner, Brad's Books), 56 Hyde Park Drive

Betz, James (director, Parks & Recreation Dept.), 1804 Quarry Park Drive

Bietz, Jacob, 2600 Hikel St.

Biss, Janet (school board member), 4387 W. Broadway Ave.

Black Funeral Home, 2222 E. Broadway Ave.

Blackmore, Paul (retired), 1416 Shannon Place

Blackwater, Samuel (Parks and Recreation Dept.), 205 University Ave.

Blake, Bradford (sales rep., ABC Laboratories), 2304B Keane Drive

Blakemore, Paul (chief of police), 1705 Rebel Drive

Bliss, Janet (Columbia police officer), 2300 Hollyhock Drive

Bombauer, Maxine (social worker), 2009 Bridgewater Drive

Bowen, Lawrence K. (insurance salesman), 208 Maple Lane

Brock, K.L., 400 S. Sixth St.

Brock, Sharon, 700 Park de Ville Place

Brown, Rob (Lincoln County Fire Protection District), 240 Paris Road

Bucci, Dan (assist. gen. mgr., Lincoln Downs Race Track), 4675 Worley St.

Burchard, Robert (basketball coach, Springfield College), 601 N. Ninth St.

Burchfield, Earl (director, Springfield University Library), 106 Business Loop 70 W.

Butler, Alfredo (laborer) and Lilah (sales clerk), 206 Elm St.

C

Chaney, May, 1600 Sylvan Lane

Channey, Bob (professor, Chemical Engineering), 3605 Madera Drive

Channey, Margaret, 812 Maplewood Drive

Chinn, Kahi, 303 Stewart St.

Chinn, Tom, 4201 Creasey Springs Road

Cipola, Christine, 1130 Ashland Road

Clark, Eric, 2500 Ridefield Road

Clark, Ethel, 200 Unity Drive

Clay, Wayne, Route 1

Cohen, Floyd, 507 Bourn Road

Cohen, Randy (student), 1516 Rosemary St.

Cohn, Randell (store manager, Express Lane), 204 Sexton Road E.

Conners, John (professor, Engineering), 1300 University Ave.

Cornell, Pearl (volunteer, Springfield Hospital), Route 4

Cottey, Kim (sales associate, Wal-Mart), 1603 Smiley Place

Craig, Duane (cook, Candle Light Lodge), 6206 Ridge Road

Craig, Vera (custodian), 3704 Danvers Drive

Crawford, Jerry (president, School Board), 2802 Butterfield Court

Crews, Roger, 2206 High Oak Court

Crookstein, Don and Jane (independent farmers), 1719 Highridge Circle; daughter, Jeanelle (student); son, Thom (student)

Crowell, Rochelle (administrator, Springfield Hospital), 212 Calvin Drive

Cruise, Roger (executive director, State Press Association), 2921 Oakland Road

Cunning, James W. (assist. mgr., Hardee's), 505 W. Stewart Road

Cutts, Mary (city clerk), 1608 Princeton Drive

D

Daugherty, James (Springfield Fire Dept.), 1005 E. Broadway Ave.

Davis, Chris (self-employed oenologist), 1601 Smiley Place

Day, David (receptionist), 700 Hilltop Drive

Daye, Brenda (vice chancellor for Student Affairs, Springfield University), 5414 Boxwood Court

Dinwiddie, Megan (director, Water and Light Dept.), 1432 Garth Ave.

Douglas, Harold, 122 McBaine Ave.

Douglass, Thomas, 1521 Windsor St.

Drummond, Monica, 4527 W. Fourth St.

Du Bois, David, 1500 Forum Blvd.

Dubovick, John, 300 Providence Road

Dudley, Dennis, 320 Bridgewater Drive

Dunbar, Ralph, 706 Demaret Drive

E

Eifler, Jay, 200 Waugh St.

Eimer, William, 120 Paquin St.

Einfeld, Wendell, 111 S. Barr St.

Ennis, Tammy (student), 603 Juniper Ridge

Esposito, Nancy (staff nurse), 206 Ridgeway Ave.

Evenson, Gary (attorney, Evenson Ltd.), 3698 Chapel Hill Road

Evenson, Mary (computer operator, Dept. of Natural Resources), 511 High St.

Everson, Alan R. (janitor), 1704 Countryside Lane

F

Faith Baptist Church, 3711 Summit Road

Faust, Donald (dean, School of Medicine), 2909 Falling Leaf Lane

Fernandez, Carlos (media coordinator, Lincoln County), 3675 Sycamore Lane

Finney, Michael (priest, Newman Center), 3703 Lumpine Drive

First Baptist Church, 900 W. Broadway Ave.

Fitts, Sherri (dean, College of Business and Public Administration), 1318 St. Andrew St.

Fletcher, George, 321 Hickam Drive

Flint, Ernest, 500 Woodridge Drive

Flohra, Lee, 456 Oak Lawn Drive

Fuller, Sue (sheriff, Lincoln County), 709 Fairview Ave.

Fun, Wu-Feng (dean, School of Law), 1027 E. Broadway Ave.

G

Garrett, Linda (Lincoln County Circuit Court judge, Div. III), 2216 Concordia Drive

Glen, John (construction worker, Pike Construction), 508 Hunt Ave.

Glenn, George (fire marshal, City of Springfield), 4645 Lynnwood Drive

Gorjanc, Harvey (dean, Graduate School, Springfield University), 811 Southhampton Drive

Gorman, Steven (lieutenant, Fire Dept.), 2039 E. Walnut St.

Graham, Thomas C. (archaeologist), 1204 Manor Drive

Green, Ralph (pastor, Newman Center), 100 W. Worley St.

Gross Co. Engineers, 260 W. Broadway Ave.

Guttierez, Juan (Second Ward, City Council member) 3724 Southridge Drive

Guyton, John, 645 Haven Road

Guzy, Tina, 907 Kathy Drive

H

Harm, Erin, 20 Hourigan Circle

Harm, Sally (dietician, Springfield Hospital), 2106 Chapel Hill Road

Harvey, A.G., 1400 Rosemary Lane

Harvey, Leta, 404 West Blvd. N.

Hassinger, Edward, 324 Mayflower Drive

Heaster, Shirley (beautician, Feminique Hair Salon), 1804 Grindley Ave.

Heinbaugh, Pauline (recorder of deeds), 16 Hitt St.

Henri, Margaret (telephone operator, AT&T), 3107a Hyde Park Drive

Henry, Thomas (physician), 222 South Jefferson St.

Higgins, Henry and Cloris (realtor, West & Haver), 209 Fourth St.

Higins, Henry (waiter, Murry's), 3107 Green Meadows Way #41

Hill-Young, Jennifer (botanist), 1995 Luna Lane

Hinckley, Thomas M. (program coordinator), 6 Edgewood St.

Hockman, Carl (operations analyst), 901 E. Cooper Drive

Hope, Raymond Lee (salesman, Springfield Auto Supply) and Mary, 1707 N. Ann St.

Huisman, George, Jr. (dean, College of Agriculture, Food and Natural Resources), 2009 Rose Drive

I

Iddings, Garrett, 444 Lenoir St.

Ide, Tony, 890 Bourne Ave.

Idel, Renee, 90 Keene St.

Imlay, Sherwin (Fourth Ward, City Council member) 2304 Mission Court

Iragaray, Luce (dean, School of Arts and Science), 1416 University Ave.

Ivy, Patrick, 566 S. Ponderosa St.

Izmerian, Eleece, 764 Kittyhawk Drive

J

Jarvis, Angie, 906 E. Pointe Drive

Jashnani, Wendy, 324 Anthony St.

Jasperse, David, 9689 Blueridge Road

Johnsen, John (field service engineer), 406 Keene St.

Johnson, Lindell B. (unemployed), 3033 Jellison St.

Johnson, William R. (owner, Oakland Car Wash), 2120 Smiley Lane

Johnson, William S., 2505 Kyle Court

Jones, John (Springfield Department of Publc Works), 2505 Kyle Court

Jones, Ruth (marketing associate), 1501 Whitburn St.

Jungermann, Loren (city treasurer), 2236 Country Lane

Juzkiw, Kelle (dean, College of Education), 1607 Park de Ville Place

K

Kahle, Ronald (publisher), 810 Again St.

Kane, Angela (student), 263 Blue Ridge Road

Kemper, Ronald (provost, Springfield University), 425 Forum Blvd.

Keystone, Charles (unemployed), 311 E. Ash St.

Kincaid, Maria L. (Lincoln County assessor), 2425 Colorado Ave.

Knight, Joseph (city auditor), 1314 Hinkson Ave.

Kramer, Andrew (Lincoln County Commission member), 143 Glen Drive

Kramer, Andrew A. (day care provider), 203 S. Ann St.

Kronk, John (employee, Restwell Funeral Service), 2500 Waterside Drive

Kruger, Brent, 666 Lynnwood Drive

Kruse, Steve, 945 W. Broadway Ave.

KTGG-TV, 190 Business Loop 70 E.

Kueffer, Christine, 544 W. Wilbert Lane

L

La Chance, Duane (Gross Engineers), 206 E. Woodrail Ave.

Lache, Ronald H. (retired lt. col.), 105 Alhambra Ave.

Lache, Ronald and Thelma (retired), 105 Alhambra Drive

Lattimer, James K. (school board member), 3622 Pimlico Drive

Lea, Wendy (teaching assistant, Springfield University), 1315 University Ave.

Lee, Rusty E. (extension associate, Springfield University Extension Service), 2180 Redbud Lane

Lehr, Angie (student), 6605 Hillstop Lane

Levine, Elizabeth R. (Third Ward, City Council member), 270 Fallwood Court

Liao, Jen-Lu (assistant to the chancellor for university affairs), 13 Arapaho Circle

Longfellow, Margaret (director, Public Works Dept.), 606 Mikel St.

Lopez, Fernando (watchman, T&L Electronics), 348 Elm St.

Lusby, Diane (city manager), 67 Gipson St.

Lynch, Merlyn, 3220 Holly Ave.

M

Maddox, Kelly B. (dentist), 909 Ashland Road

Maddox, Kelly G. (chief of staff, Springfield Hospital), 1632 Granada Drive

Madsen, Orrin, 13 Ninth St.

Madson, Jamelle (Springfield University registrar and admissions director), 789 Hominey Branch

Matten, Jeanne (lawyer), 306 Overhill Road

Manning, Greg (clerk, Brad's Books), 6 Spring Valley Road

Markison, Louis M. (computer analyst), 1605 Telluride Lane

Maxwel, Thomas A. (president, Teamsters Local 1248), 300 Westwood Ave.

Maxwell, Thomas R. (public housing manager), 4410 Alan Lane

McClure, Pam (secretary), 1014 Southpark St.

McCubbins, Eugene (pastor, Faith Baptist Church), 15 Pendleton St.

Meadows, Paul R. (registrar and admissions director), 34 Middlebush Drive, Apt. 56

Memorial Park Cemetery, 909 Baldwin Place

Merchants National Bank, 600 E. Broadway Ave.

Miller, Rahsetnu (associate public defender, Lincoln County), 2085 E. Walnut St.

Miller, William H. (plant manager), 1716 Bettina Drive

Moore, David (professor, Springfield University), 345 College Ave.

Moore, Mary, 808 Again St.

Mose, Betsey (owner, Hideaway Bar and Grill), 200 Route K

N

Neal, Donna L. (student), 34 Waysite Drive

Neil, Madsen (retired), 119 Bicknell St.

Netdem, Amanda (vice chancellor for development, Springfield University), 2465 Sunset Lane S.

Newell, R.J. (manager, ACME Cleaning), 1308 Paris Road

Newman Center, 317 Brenda Lane

Ngo, Hier, 4067 Sylvan Lane

Nguyen, Trong, 998 Vandiver Drive

Nichols, Barbara, 9887 Clark Lane

Nichols, Virginia (architect), 115 Lake St.

Nishada, Milo (student), 438 College Ave., Apt. B

Nowell, Thomas (director, City Finance Dept.), 980 Rhonda Lane

Noyes, Afua (Sixth Ward, City Council member), 765 Unity Drive

O

Oats, Donald (receptionist), 1808 Bear Creek Drive

Oats, Tanya (hygienist), 207 N. Providence Road

Oglesby, James R. (stress lab coordinator), 1908 Iris Drive

Oglesby, Richard J. (staff nurse, Springfield Hospital), 4201 Rock Quarry Rd.

Omokaye, Gan, 231 Holly Ave.

Oncken, Christian, 4550 Otto Court

O'Neal, Harold, 544 Rangeline Road

Oney, Patricia, 880 Paquin St.

Osgood, Heather, 338 N. Garth Ave.

Oswalk, Carol, 7988 W. Rollins Road

P

Parker, David, 110 Ripley St.

Parker Funeral Service, 606 Washington Ave.

Parks, Emily (Lincoln County clerk), 521 Yuma Drive

Perkins, John (salesman, Springfield Lumber), 2931 Parkway Lane

Perrin, Daniel (student), 333 Stadium Blvd.

Perry, Bernard (fire chief, Springfield Fire Dept.), 8325 Worley St.

Pitts, Chris (janitor, Springfield University), 312 Anderson Drive

Pitts, Robert (carpenter), 210 Anderson Drive

Pliske, Gena (relief worker, Red Cross), 214 S. Ninth St.

Popandreau, George (owner, T&L Electronics), 3785 E. Terrace Road

Poplar, James, 5642 N. 11th St.

Pourot, Antoinette (student), 208A August Terrace

Prado, Dominic (insurance agent), 311 E. Worley St.

Property and Casualty Co., 303 First Ave.

Pullman, Rachel (school board member), 956 Ash St.

Q

Qian, Li, 344 University Ave.

Quade, Jennifer (student), 444 Jesse Lane

Quinlan, Steve, 700 W. Broadway Ave.

Quinn, Michael C., 306 Rockingham Drive

Quinn, Michael R. (president, Springfield University), 1416 College Ave.

Quisenberry, Nadine, (account mgr., Shelter Insurance), 222 Hinkson Ave.

Qureshi, Haroon (dean, College of Engineering), 1001 University Ave.

R

Rachel, Jerome, 700 English Drive

Rackley, Daniel, 98 W. Phyllis Ave.

Rains, Henry (house painter), 106 W. Ridgely Road

Ramsey, Betty L. (Lincoln County collector), 543 Falling Leaf Lane

Reed, Joseph (Lincoln County Commission member), 2155 Honeysuckle Drive

Restwell Funeral Service, 2560 Walnut St.

Rice, LeRoy N. (dean, School of Accountancy), 45 Mission Court

Rice, Nancy (electrician), 1741 Riveria Drive

Rock Haven High School, 2025 S. Providence Road

Rodriguez, Henry (clerk, Target Department Store), 364 Peabody Lane; son, Ryan (student)

Rodriguez, Jose (assistant city manager, City of Springfield), 3114 Orchard Lane

Roets, Gary (owner, Gary's Jumbo Shrimp), 6204 Ridge Road

Roets, Rebecca, 602 Rollins Court

Rosen, Henry (Gross Engineers), 411 S. Williams St.

Rudloff, Travis (mechanic), 1000 Prestwick Drive

S

Sapp, Dennis (Lincoln County Fire Protection District), 6651 Nifong Blvd.

Scanlon, Brennan (teacher, Driver's Ed), 304 Oakridge Court

Scanlon, Jim (Springfield Central High basketball coach), 1810 Creasy Springs Road

Schelpp, Melvin (retired), 209 Route K

Scherr, Randall J. (chef), 301 Shepard Court

Schmidt, Amy (teller, Commerce Bank), 201 W. Phyllis Ave.

Schmidt, Brian (school board member), 2567 Ridgeway Ave.

Schmidt, Darin (telephone operator), 214 St. Joseph St.

Schmidt, Max (superintendent, Springfield School District), 5789 El Cortez St.

Schmitt, Brian (word processing operator), 2103 Riney Lane

Schuster, Debra A. (Lincoln County Fire Protection District chief), 946 Arbor Drive

Schwartz, Todd B. (Lincoln County Circuit Court judge, Div. II), 856 Colonial Court

Sears, Doris (office manager, Sears Construction), 1805 Lovejoy Lane

Seina, John (dean, School of Journalism), 1111 Fairway Drive

Shaver, Scott (director, Lincoln County Planning Department), 2067 Skylark Drive

Singleton, Jacob (vice chancellor for administrative services), 573 Hunt Court

Smith, Irene (day care director, Green Meadows Preschool), 4560 Nifong Blvd.

Smith, Irene (retired), 1401 Business Loop 70 W.

Smyth, Mary (teacher, Green Meadows Day Care), 3567 Green Meadows Road

Sosinski, Marcelle, 2990 W. Hanover St.

Spencer Metal Processing Co., 211 E. Grindstone Ave.

Spillman, Roger (driver, Central Dairy), 2010 Rhonda Lane

Springfield Auto Supply, 6400 S.W. I-70 Drive

Springfield Central High School, 1000 Business Loop 70 E.

Springfield City Hall, 406 E. Broadway Ave.

Springfield Feed Co., 38 W. Elm St.

Springfield Hospital, 1600 E. Broadway Ave.

Springfield Memorial Cemetery, 104 Woodrail Ave.

Springfield Municipal Power Plant, 1004 Business Loop 70 E.

Stanfield, Paul (teacher), 4025 Grace Ellen Drive

Stark, Colleen M. (student), 534 Grand Ave.

Stephenson, Enid (realty manager), 316 Rock Road

Stone, Albert (retired), 2935 Parkway Drive

Stone, Mary, 1900 Rose Drive

Stookey, Timothy (student), 309 Lake Lane

T

T&L Electronics, 4404 U.S. Highway 90

Taylor, James (Lincoln County prosecuting attorney), 644 Misty Glen

Theiss, Anna (school board member), 323 Ridgemont Court

Thurmond, Stan (Springfield police officer), 19 Lemmon Drive

Townsend, Marshall, 88 Broadway Village Drive

Toyoshima, Satoshi, 988 Bernadette Drive

Tracy, Tammy, 800 Ashland Road

Tray, Jose (director of public information, Springfield Hospital), 799 Tracy Drive

Truman Sports Complex, 8301 Stadium Blvd.

Turner, Linda (dentist), 106 W. Burnam Road

Turner, Ralph, 803 W. Rollins Road

Tyler, Richard, 877 Edgewood Ave.
Tyrolder, 9993 Sylvan Lane

U

U-Haul Moving Center, 788 Sexton Road
U.S. Army Adviser, 700 W. Ash St.
Ubl, Gerald, 9000 Oak Cliff Drive
Ukoha, Oruada, 700 Demaret Drive
United Medical, 888 E. Ash St.
United Pentacostal Church, 888 Benton St.
Upham, Bonnie, 300 Alexander Ave.
Uplinger, Andrew, 800 Strawn Road
Upson, Carl, 55 Woodrail Ave.
Uthlaut, Adam, 4300 W. Broadway Ave.

V

VFW Post 290, 1999 Ashley St.
Vaca, Carlos (Columbia firefighter), 24 Pinewood Drive
Vago, Tony, 479 Kentucky Blvd.
Vair, Terry, 4088 S. Bethel Road
Varjack, Paul (freelance writer), 356 Argyle Road
Veach, Dennis (deputy chief, Springfield Police Dept.), 213 Texas Ave.
Von Flatern, Dolores (dean, School of Library and Informational Science), 887 Conley Ave.
Voss, Dan, 4889 Mimosa Court
Vought, John, 2209 Hulen Drive
Vroegindewey, Linda, 47 E. Stewart Ave.
Vucheitch, Ginny, 4007 Woodrail Ave.

W

Wade, Washington (academic affairs vice president, Springfield University), 333 Fairmont St.
Wagner, Robert (Lincoln County Circuit Court judge, Div. I), 634 Evans Road
Wapniarski, Christy (student), 567 S. Williams St.
Watring, Cindy (student), 123 Columbus Hall
Welch, Emmy (manager, Dillards Department Store), 327 Glenwood Ave. S.
West, James (Parks and Recreation Dept.), 205 Nifong Blvd.

Westenhaver, James and Martha (president, Merchants National Bank), 300 E. Clark Lane
White, Clarence B. (intern), 1909 Dartmouth St.
Williams, Juanita (city mayor), 8479 Miller Drive
Woolkamp, Lynn (detective, Lincoln County Sheriff's Dept.), 765 Lakeshore Lane

X

Xenakis, Paul, 955 Woodrail Ave.
Xiang, Hong (First Ward, City Council member), 2801 W. Rollins Road
Xu, Feng, 4888 Amelia St.
Xu, Wen Wui (dean, School of Human Environmental Sciences), 104 E. Stewart Road

Y

Yang, Jun Ping (Fifth Ward, City Council member), 3107 Green Meadows Road
Yasuda, Ken (Health Dept. director), 897 Sycamore Lane
York, Dale, 488 W. Brookside Lane
York, Kim, 59 E. Hoedown Drive
Yost, Takuya, 4400 Hominy Branch
Youngquist, Luke, 344 Maryland Ave.
Youngwirth, Joseph, 25 N. Ninth St.
Younis, Amani, 408 Hitt St.
Yund, Glenn, 499 Waugh St.

Z

Zablow, John, 855 Lyon St.
Zafft, Jeff, 488 E. Phyllis Ave.
Zhang, Min Hui (dean, College of Business and Public Administration), 9760 Dripping Springs Road
Zhong, William, 455 Rock Quarry Road
Zhu, Jingcai, 488 S. College Ave.
Ziden, Nicole (Lincoln County Commission member), 4222 Brewer Drive
Zwonitzer, Gary, 555 Laurel St.
Zyk, Harvey, 8222 Stadium Blvd.
Zyk, Pam (City Council member), 8947 Stadium Blvd.
Zylstra, Alexandria, 455 Hitt St.

Acknowledgments

AP wire stories. Assorted lead paragraphs from The Associated Press. Reprinted with permission of The Associated Press.

American Bar Association. "But the Public Wants to Know . . . New Booklet Focuses on Fair Trade and Free Press Issues." Copyright © American Bar Association. Reprinted by permission.

Carl Chancellor. "Blacks: They Must Live Daily with the Irritating Reality of Subtle and Overt Racism in the Area." Copyright © Akron Beacon Journal. Reprinted by permission.

Consumer Reports. "Teens Hooked on Cigarettes." Copyright ©1992 Consumer Reports. Reprinted by permission.

Bob Dyer. "Whites: They See Racism as a Vital Issue, but Also as a Riddle That Leaves Them Groping for Solutions." Copyright © Akron Beacon Journal. Reprinted by permission.

John C. Merrill. "Journalistic Ethics, Machiavellian Style." Speech delivered at the National Conference on Ethics and the Professions, University of Florida. Reprinted by permission of the author.

Helen O'Neill. "Kidnapping Grandma Braun." From The Associated Press, four-part series, March 21, 22, 23 and 24, 2005. Copyright © 2005 The Associated Press. Reprinted with permission of The Associated Press.

Outstanding Young Americans News Release. "Board of Advisors for the Outstanding Young Men of America Awards Program . . ." Copyright © 2005 Outstanding Young Americans. Reprinted by permission.

Martha D. Saunders. "Learn to Listen with Your Heart." Reprinted by permission of the author.

Fraser P. Seitel. "The Ten Commandments of Corporate Communications." Speech delivered at the Cincinnati Chapter of The Public Relations Society of America. Reprinted by permission.

Amy Rabideau Silvers. "Keller Was Proud to Be Driving the Big Rigs . . . ." From the *Milwaukee Journal Sentinel*, Wednesday, November 28, 2006. Reprinted by permission of Copyright Clearance Center.

William Walstad. Speech to the American Economic Association on High School Economics Education. Reprinted by permission of the author.

G. Evans Witt. "Ten Rules for Journalists Writing About Polls." From The *Washington Journalism Review*. Copyright © G. Evans Witt. Reprinted by permission of The Associated Press.